Comrade or Brother?

Comrade or Brother?

A History of the British Labour Movement

Second Edition

MARY DAVIS

PLUTO PRESS
www.plutobooks.com

First published 1993
Second edition published 2009 by Pluto Press
345 Archway Road, London N6 5AA and
175 Fifth Avenue, New York, NY 10010

www.plutobooks.com

Distributed in the United States of America exclusively by
Palgrave Macmillan, a division of St. Martin's Press LLC,
175 Fifth Avenue, New York, NY 10010

British Library Cataloguing in Publication Data
A catalogue record for this book is available from the British Library

ISBN   978 0 7453 2577 4   hardback
ISBN   978 0 7453 2576 7   paperback

This book is printed on paper suitable for recycling and made from fully
managed and sustained forest sources. Logging, pulping and manufacturing
processes are expected to conform to the environmental standards of the
country of origin. The paper may contain up to 70% post consumer waste.

10   9   8   7   6   5   4   3   2   1

Designed and produced for Pluto Press by
Chase Publishing Services Ltd, Sidmouth, EX10 9QG, England
Typeset from disk by Stanford DTP Services, Northampton
Printed and bound in the European Union by
CPI Antony Rowe, Chippenham and Eastbourne

To my mother, Celia Davis (*née* Yampolsky), for the past and the present, and for the rich heritage bequeathed to me by the once large Yampolsky family – Jewish immigrants to Bethnal Green from Tsarist Russia.

To my children, Joseph and Esther, and my grandchildren, Callum, Leah, Luis, Charlie, Ella and Hannah, for the joy of the present and the hope of the future.

CONTENTS

INTRODUCTION

This is the second edition of a book that has been a long time in the making, although the practical possibility of actually writing it is comparatively recent. Why a second edition? Partly because the first one sold out and there have been many requests for it, but also because I wanted to add material and emphases that I thought lacking in the first edition. In addition, the publisher was keen for me to go beyond 1951. I am not a fan of 'contemporary history' (surely a contradiction in terms) because, as all trained historians know, state papers, and especially Home Office papers, are very useful primary sources and the 30-year rule is still extant. Of course, these are not the only sources and I don't rely on them in a work of this kind. However, it is already clear that recently published reputable secondary sources dealing with, for example, post-Second World War governments up to the mid 1970s have benefited greatly from a close inspection of cabinet and other state papers such as to encourage a revision of the traditionally accepted consensus view of British politics which was assumed to exist until Margaret Thatcher disrupted it.

Anyway, I still feel that the kind of study of the labour movement attempted within these pages is long overdue – a strange statement perhaps given the huge growth of labour history as an academic discipline over the last 30 or so years. The literature on this subject is, by now, immense, so can another general history, especially in light of the trend towards increasing specialisation, be sustained? The reader will obviously be the final judge, but it would seem appropriate here to explain my aim in making this attempt and in so doing perhaps substantiate the claim for yet another book. However, before explaining my original purpose as outlined in the first edition, from which I have not departed, there is another pressing reason of a more ideological nature in wanting to reissue this book. It concerns the nature of labour history itself, which like all other branches of history has undergone immense changes reflecting the fundamental issue underlying all working-class history; that is, as Savage and Miles[1] put it, the question of 'agency', or why and how workers become politically active. The historiography they outline relates such agency to the fortunes of the British labour movement, which is in itself linked to an understanding of class and class relations. Unsurprisingly, they chart the steady decline of interest in the subject of class from the supposedly influential 'golden age' of the labour movement in the 1940s and 1950s to its alleged decline in the 1980s and beyond – a decline that has led to an historicist questioning of the role of working-class agency in general. Such a turning away from the concept of class has had an inevitable impact on the interest in writing its history and organisation. However, because I don't share this negative view of class, I am more determined than ever to ensure that labour history remains alive and accessible to its inheritors.

So, my purpose in writing this book is threefold.

The vast majority of the work on the history of the British labour movement has been written by and for academics. This is certainly not a criticism – much pioneering work has been accomplished and our knowledge of the subject has deepened beyond 'the great events' and the 'great leaders'. Nonetheless, the more painstaking the search to reconstruct historical reality, the less accessible the fruit of that research has often proved to be. Maybe this should not matter too much. After all, does good history writing need to be accessible to an audience beyond the dreaming spires of academia? Serious scholarship is one thing, popular historical chronicling quite another. However, this somewhat artificial distinction is much less easy to make when dealing with the subject of labour history. There are two main reasons for this. First, the inheritors of that history are very much alive and well in the active labour movement in Britain today. Second, as anyone who, like me, has been involved in trade union

1   M. Savage and A. Miles, *The Remaking of the British Working Class 1840–1940* (1994).

education will know, the history of the movement is altogether lacking in the otherwise excellent courses provided by the TUC and affiliated unions. The main focus in these 'student-centred' courses is the workplace and the building of effective trade union organisation. The courses are concerned with current realities and acquiring the skills to deal with them. Learning about, let alone reflecting on, the origins and historical development of the movement is not part of the scheme of things. And yet shop stewards and activists at all levels frequently express a desire to acquire this kind of knowledge, the evidence for which is shown in the popularity of the relatively few courses run for trade unionists (usually in the evening) on this subject.

Having taught one such course for the past 30 years and witnessed the tremendous and unflagging enthusiasm of the students, I can give personal testimony to this observation. It is hardly surprising that labour history should be such a popular subject for labour movement activists. All oppressed and exploited groups have the right to reclaim their past – none more so than the working class itself. The inheritors of the struggle for working-class rights and trade union freedoms are predisposed to want to know something of their past – if the labour movement itself fails to impart such information, then it will either filter through in a distorted form or remain unknown. Indeed, it remains a criticism of the British labour movement that it neglects its own history save for the occasional celebratory or commemorative foray. Hence my first purpose: an accessible history for today's activists.

Having perceived the necessity for workers to know something of their own history and organisation, the problem raised earlier about accessible secondary source material is at once apparent. However, accessibility is not the only criterion. A general historical account of the labour movement written as a narrative, sympathetic or otherwise, would not fit the bill. What is required is something which would, within the framework of an account of the development of the labour movement, provide a stimulus for assessing certain key themes and issues, many of which have relevance for the activists of today. In other words, what is needed is something analytical, which stimulates thought and discussion, but is at the same time partisan from a working-class standpoint. Why partisan? Because most people are, historians included. We all have opinions and outlooks which shape our view of the world, and in the case of historians this influences their view of the past no matter how objective their work appears to be. Such a process is overt or covert depending on whether the 'outlook' of the writer conforms to the predominant norm of his or her own society – the further away from the norm the more overtly biased or partisan the writer is said to be. To the extent that the prevailing outlook in our society is one that values individualism and market forces, then the present writer is overtly partisan in that her outlook is founded on values that are entirely contrary to the norm. It is perhaps as well to be open about one's standpoint from the outset.

As a labour movement activist myself of many years' standing whose theoretical (and hence practical) perspectives are still, unfashionably(?) informed by marxism, I see the labour movement as a vehicle which not only expresses working-class aspirations, but also struggles to achieve them. This entails winning reforms in this society, but also recognising the extent to which the power of capital, through its control of the means of production and the state, has and continues to prevent the ultimate goal of the working class – namely, the ending of exploitation. Such a goal is not always consciously expressed – whenever it has been, class struggle is at its sharpest and consensus politics most seriously threatened, often with devastating results, as this history shows. Rival ideologies lie at the very heart of such a struggle and are as contentious today, both within the labour movement and outside it, as they were at any time during this history. To declare my partisanship within this battle of ideas in the writing of this book is not, therefore, simply a matter of nailing my colours to the mast in the interpretation of long-forgotten battles. It is part of the process of encouraging debate and discussion around the key ideological questions about which there has been much debate in the past and which still have relevance in determining the future of the labour movement of today.

Hence a second purpose in the writing of this book is revealed: to revive the spirit of debate, using the vehicle of labour history, among the activists of today. In so doing it is to be hoped that much of my interpretation will be questioned and criticised – the past does not belong to me, it belongs to us all – my intention is to allow a wider audience to reclaim it in an active way.

There is also a third purpose in writing this history. Like many other feminists and anti-racists I have long been concerned about the historical and prevalent image of the working class as all-white and all-male. If we define the working class as those who neither own nor control the means of production and hence have to sell their labour power to those who do for a wage, then clearly women and black people are integral elements. It also follows that they should, therefore, be integral elements within the labour movement, as indeed they are and always have been. However, a persistent gender- and colour-blind approach has obscured this fact. It is further obscured because of the understandable tendency to write the history of the movement in terms of those who rose to prominence within it, and of course, women and black people rarely did (and still don't). A general work of this kind cannot pretend to properly redress this imbalance since far more research needs to be done, especially in the field of black workers' participation. Much more has been done on the history of women workers and trade unions. But herein lies a problem. Redressing the balance in relation to women is not simply a matter of disproving the myths by discovering hitherto forgotten women leaders, because this in itself takes the focus away from the fact that in the main the movement was and is led by men. On the other hand, most of the evidence we have indicates that women were not only present and active, but also encountered insuperable obstacles, male attitudes being chief among them. The tendency recently to write accounts of women's organisation separate from the 'main movement' does not force us to understand these obstacles and the frequent battles against them within their proper context. Hence my aim is to integrate what we know about women workers historically (and the even smaller amount we know about black workers) into a general labour movement history. This is not merely an antiquarian nicety but essential for understanding the development of the movement, including one of its chief weaknesses. Connecting the hitherto separate spheres of class, race and gender in a manner which comprehends both their distinctiveness and interrelationships is long overdue. However, it is only through an understanding of the primacy of class as an economic relationship in the dominant mode of production that the connections between class, race and gender can be correctly understood. Thus I argue for an explicit link between history and theory (and not just any theory!). The renegotiation of the gender division of labour was central to the process of industrialisation in Britain – the first industrial nation – and to the formation of a working class. Since women were among the first factory workers, they led early industrial action, whether on an informal or formal basis, and were among the first trade unionists. Gender remains central to the continual restructuring and renegotiation of capitalist relations over the past two centuries. This is also true of the history of black people. The fact that such an obvious point has had so little repercussion for the study of mainstream working-class and labour history requires a remedy.

Finally, a word about method and organisation. The book is divided into three parts, all of which correspond to a new stage in the development of capitalism and hence to some extent a new stage within the labour movement too. The first chapter in each of these parts has the same title: 'Economic and Political Background'. The aim of this is to enable the general reader who may have no knowledge of the period under discussion to place the labour movement within an economic and political context. The history of the movement abstracted from society is, to me, incomprehensible. It is also important to understand changes in the occupational structure since this had (and still has) a significant bearing on trade union organisation. The place that women occupied within the labour market will also be looked at in this context. The following chapters within each part then trace the main development of the labour movement with key themes for discussion and further reading suggested in a bibliography at the end of each.

Because this is a general work covering such a vast period, no pretence is made to original research, although some primary sources, particularly memoirs, speeches and autobiographies, have been used where appropriate. It is a work of interpretation, which draws heavily on the mass of secondary sources, good, bad and indifferent. I have not attempted to acknowledge this, other than where I have quoted directly, in the customary academic fashion via footnotes (except in Chapter 16). Instead, I have indicated the sources used at the end of each chapter, and where possible these include contemporary novels. General works which have been consulted throughout are listed at the end of this Introduction. I have not wished to interrupt the flow of the text and have done so only to attribute direct quotations. The specialist scholar, therefore, will find this book less useful than the inquiring shop steward or labour movement activist for whom it is intended and whose possible lack of knowledge of the subject has not, I hope, been confused with lack of intelligence.

Most of the preparation of this book has been assisted throughout by a novel process of 'active writing' in which a microcosm of the target readership in the form of a monthly meeting of Labour History Study Circle/evening class, funded by the TUC at the Centre for Trade Union Studies, formerly at South Bank University, to discuss and criticise these chapters hot off the word processor. It would thus be tempting to blame the students for inadequacies in the finished product and reserve the praise for my own efforts. Books cannot be written by committees, so I must take full responsibility, but in doing so hope that the class has learned as much as I have from the exercise and I thank them for indulging me with the privilege of foisting my work and ideas on them. The Centre for Trade Union Studies is now based at London Metropolitan University, where we continue the tradition of labour movement education through our BA, MA and MRes courses in Labour and Trade Union Studies in which labour history still forms an essential component in all of them.

Mary Davis
October 2008

Bibliography

Bellamy, J. and Saville, J. (eds.). *Dictionary of Labour Biography*, 7 vols. (Macmillan, 1994)

Boston, S. *Women Workers and the Trade Unions* (Davis-Poynter, 1980)

Cole, G. D. H. and Postgate, R. *The Common People* (University Paperbacks, 1971; first published 1938)

Fryer, P. *Staying Power – The History of Black People in Britain* (Pluto Press, 1985)

Harrison, J. F. C. *The Common People* (Croom Helm, 1984)

Hobsbawm, E. J. *Labouring Men* (Weidenfeld & Nicolson, 1968)

Hobsbawm, E. J. *Industry and Empire* (Penguin Books, 1969)

Hunt, E. J. H. *British Labour History 1815–1914* (Weidenfeld & Nicolson, 1981)

Lane, T. *The Union Makes Us Strong* (Arrow Books, 1974)

Lawton, R. (ed.) *The Census and Social Structure* (Cass, 1978)

Lewenhak, S. *Women and Trade Unions* (Benn, 1977)

Mitchell, B. R. *Abstract of British Historical Statistics* (Cambridge University Press, 1962)

Mitchell, J. and Oakley, A. *The Rights and Wrongs of Women* (Penguin Books, 1977)

Morton, A. L. and Tate, G. *The British Labour Movement* (Lawrence & Wishart, 1956)

Neff, W. *Victorian Working Women* (Cass, 1929)

Pelling, H. *A History of British Trade Unionism* (Penguin Books, 1963)

Price, R. *Labour in British Society* (Routledge, 1990)

Ramdin, R. *The Making of the Black Working Class in Britain* (Gower, 1987)

Rendall, J (ed.). *Equal or Different – Women's Politics 1800–1914* (Blackwell, 1987)

Roberts, E. *Women's Work 1840–1940* (Macmillan, 1988)

Rothstein, A. *British Foreign Policy and its Critics 1830–1950* (Lawrence & Wishart, 1969)

Savage, M. and Miles, A. *The Remaking of the British Working Class 1840–1940* (Routledge, 1994).

Webb, B. and Webb, S. *The History of Trade Unionism* (Chiswick Press, 1898)

Williams, G. and Ramsden, R. *Ruling Britannia: A Political History of Britain 1688–1988* (Longman, 1990)

Part 1

The Industrial Revolution

1

ECONOMIC AND POLITICAL BACKGROUND, 1780–1850

Britain in 1850 would have been unrecognisable in every way to an adult who had fallen into a deep sleep in 1780 and awoken 70 years later. Of course, great changes occur in every society even within a shorter historical time span, but the changes in this period were so far-reaching that the commonly used term 'industrial revolution' to describe them hardly does justice to their magnitude. The changes were not sudden, nor were they confined to industry. During this 70-year period Britain was transformed from a predominantly agrarian and rural society into one whose wealth was based on industrial production and whose population was increasingly located in fast-expanding towns, some of which had been mere villages 70 years previously.

The visible changes were less significant than their underlying causes. Beneath the surface the balance of wealth creation and distribution was undergoing a radical change, the obvious (though not immediately perceptible) sign of which was a change in the class structure of Britain. This was not a matter of tinkering at the edges, but as hindsight shows turned out to be the most fundamental change in Britain's class structure and class relations since the decline of serfdom. Bourgeois and proletarian came to replace peasant and lord as the dominant classes in society. This in its turn was reflected in political changes which finally enabled the new industrial capitalists, the new wealth creators, to emerge triumphant over the aristocracy. But in a peculiarly British compromise, the values of both sections of the old and new ruling class managed to find a consensus which ensured a degree of political stability not found in other European countries.

The Development of Capitalism

The term 'industrial revolution' also masks the true character of this era – it was one in which the capitalist mode of production assumed absolute dominance, a feat which could not have been possible without industrialisation, but was nonetheless not *caused* by it. Likewise, the industrial revolution did not bring about the use of machinery. Its significance lies in the fact that its discoveries enabled a new source of motive power (first water, then steam) to be harnessed to the already existing and new machinery. This in turn meant that full-scale *mass* commodity production became possible. The era of modern capitalist industry had begun.

The First Phase – Merchant Capital

Capitalism was not a sudden creation of the late eighteenth century. There were two distinct but linked phases in the history of capitalist production. The first phase, merchant capital, together with capitalist agriculture, emerged triumphant in the seventeenth century following its long battle with feudalism. Its success was represented politically by the victory of the Parliamentary side (represented by Oliver Cromwell and the Roundheads) over the old guard feudal aristocrats (represented by Charles I and the Cavaliers) in the English Civil War. This first phase of 'immature' commodity production was characterised by the fact that the instruments of production themselves were sufficiently 'simple' to permit their ownership by individual producers. Domestic production was controlled at first by the guilds, but later by richer craftsmen or by merchants who had accumulated capital through overseas trade. The establishment of the great livery companies in the sixteenth and seventeenth centuries is a reflection of this. These companies acquired a legal monopoly of their respective trades, whilst the huge trading companies, such as the East India Company, had a legal monopoly of overseas trade within their area of operation. Such monopoly privileges were protected by the state, which during much of the seventeenth and eighteenth centuries operated on the basis of mercantilist economic theory.

'Mercantilism' held that the source of a nation's wealth lay not in its productive capacity but in its trading strength. Hence the acquisition of favourable trade balances was the goal of the economy. Such a goal could only be achieved through economic regulation by the state. Consequently, a panoply of legislation, known collectively as the Navigation Laws, and the Old Colonial System, in addition to the granting of monopoly rights, was obligingly enacted and policed by the state. This might seem paradoxical given that English society including the state was dominated by the landowners, who were preoccupied with protecting their own interests. However, from the seventeenth century onwards there was an interdependent harmony between the merchants and the landowners – the former had the means and the money, the latter had the political power. The potential conflict between them was mitigated by the fact that the decay of feudalism enabled the wealthier merchants to invest their vast wealth in the land itself and hence to renew the 'vitality' of an otherwise decaying and parasitic landowning clique. It was this fresh injection of wealth into agriculture and the establishment of capitalist relations of production which enabled it, by the early eighteenth century, to become highly productive – in short, to undergo what is commonly termed an 'agrarian revolution', enabling England to become not only self-sufficient in food, but an exporter of grain. This in turn had an important impact in stimulating and sustaining an expansion in population, the significance of which became apparent only later. Much of this was accomplished with a great deal of political upheaval to which the battles of the seventeenth century bear testimony. Nonetheless, the harmony could only last while the means of production itself remained at its 'immature' phase and hence required no great amount of new capital investment to maintain a high profit. All that was required during this phase was state protection and monopoly rights for the few to ensure that there was no competition from 'interlopers'. So, although merchant capital was linked to commodity production, such production could and did remain at a very basic level in the home country, supplemented as it was by exploitation of Britain's colonies (the oldest of which was Ireland). Initially, these colonies were simply plundered, but later in the seventeenth century they also became important markets for English goods. This meant that they were themselves allowed to develop some production provided that this was strictly in accordance with the needs of the English and that any trade in the goods so produced was expropriated and controlled by England. This included, of course, the lucrative slave trade, which in itself permitted the development of the even more lucrative sugar, tobacco and cotton trades in the West Indies and later in the southern states of America (these latter also being English colonies). The trade in human beings initially was not confined to black people, but because the west coast of Africa provided such an abundance of human commodities (quite literally), the triangular trade (in which slaves were taken from Africa and transported in vile conditions to America or the West Indies) assumed great importance. It was hugely profitable in itself, but its significance was greater than providing greedy merchants with super-profits. Slavery provided, without knowing it, the bridge between merchant and industrial capital in Britain. It satisfied the former, while providing the latter with the raw material of their future wealth – raw cotton.

The Second Phase – Industrial Capital

The possibility of developing the means of production to enable capitalism to proceed to its fully industrial phase was in a sense linked to the very success of mercantilism. Vast stores of accumulated capital lay in readiness for productive investment in no matter what, but on the other hand, the lucrative opportunities for industrial investment developed in opposition to mercantilism. A new class of producers slowly developed outside the protected circles of the landowning/mercantile oligarchy. Such a development was not to be wondered at; its realisation was dependent on a number of factors, among which the technical inventions of the late eighteenth century acted as a spur. Most schoolchildren learn about Kay's Flying Shuttle, Hargreave's Spinning Jenny, Crompton's Mule and other inventions (the most important of which was the steam engine), which revolutionised the means of production.

The practical utilisation of such technology only became possible when the conditions were ripe. These conditions were bequeathed by the success of merchant capital. For example, for industrial production to develop it is necessary to have a growing proportion of the population engaged solely in manufacture. This is only possible if society can produce enough surplus food first to stimulate and sustain a growth in population, and second to feed its non-agricultural workforce. Herein lies the significance of the agrarian revolution mentioned earlier, and the enclosure movement to which it was linked. It is quite wrong to suppose that enclosures drove people off the land and forced them into the towns – the so-called enforced proletarianisation thesis. Whilst it is true that enclosures did alter the system of landownership in favour of ever-larger estates, it had the effect, certainly in the short term, of *increasing* the demand for agricultural labour. The fact that the population continued to grow throughout the eighteenth century also enabled the growth of the domestic market for manufactured goods. In addition, favourable conditions were in being through the existence of developed markets overseas, a reasonable system of transport and a sophisticated commercial infrastructure, including a banking system through which the capital accumulated from this first phase of trade and production could be redirected to any more profitable enterprise when the opportunity arose.

The Cotton Industry

The first industry to be fully prepared for such a challenge was the cotton industry. First spinning (using the labour of women and children) and then weaving were fully mechanised and gradually relocated in large factories near a source of motive power to drive the new machines. It was, however, slavery which made the whole development possible in the first place. Raw cotton cannot be grown in Britain; it is a wholly imported raw material from the plantations of the West Indies and North America, and such plantations were worked entirely by the labour of slaves.

At first water power was used to drive the machines which processed the raw cotton. Thus the early factories were located near fast-flowing streams (hence the use of the term cotton 'mill'), but later, after the invention of the steam engine, the mills were moved to be within easy reach of coal – the new energy source. South Lancashire provided an ideal site for the cotton industry, not only because of its coalfields, but also because of its canal link with Liverpool where the imported raw cotton entered the country, and from which the manufactured product could be exported. The technology of steam power allied to other inventions was applied later to other branches of the textile industry (woollen cloth and linen), and later still to such industries as iron and steel production. Cotton it was that paved the way.

The preconditions for industrial development were laid in previous centuries of capitalist development. It was mass production, not capitalism, which was the new discovery. The question remains why it was not simply a smooth transition from its first to its later stage rather than, as it proved to be, an almighty upheaval, socially, politically and ideologically. This second phase of capitalist development required not only an improvement in the means of production, but also a major change in the relations of production – such change could not be 'accommodated' within the existing system, for it presented a direct challenge to it. In short, it challenged the landed and merchant oligarchy which had ruled Britain in the preceding centuries. The confrontation might have been a revolutionary one, as it was in other European countries, but for the fact that the landed aristocracy in Britain displayed an infinite capacity to adapt and compromise. It had already displayed such a capacity in the post-feudal era by the transformation of agrarian class relations and its compromise with merchant capital for the mutual benefit of both. Rich merchants had bought their way into political power by themselves becoming landowners. In this sense the compromise was not as painful for the aristocracy, which by this time had thrown off all its feudal relics and was fully capitalised. The term aristocracy is thus slightly misleading, but is used to distinguish ennobled landowning capitalists from their merchant, commercial or industrial counterparts. Furthermore, the use of this term implies, as it should, a continuity with a very old landed class, which in Britain, more than in any other European country, retained its estates almost intact for centuries. The reason for this was the strict enforcement of property laws, in particular primogeniture and strict settlement and entail. These were the rules whereby property (in the form of land) had to be passed intact to the eldest son. Three very important consequences flowed, unwittingly, from this. First, the land was preserved in large estates and hence was amenable to techniques which would increase its yield and change its production relations; second, it meant that a peasantry (a peasant being someone who owns his land, albeit a small plot) hardly existed in Britain; and third, it meant that those who had money could not buy land but formed instead dynastic or commercial alliances with those who owned it. The fact that Britain by the mid eighteenth century still remained a country whose main source of wealth was the land masks the reality of the penetration of capital into agricultural production and the interrelationship between agrarian, commercial and merchant capital.

Industrial capital, however, posed a much more far-reaching challenge to the old system. The new factory owners were not interested in the slightest in buying their way into the landed aristocracy. They were busy transforming Britain into a country whose predominant source of wealth was industrial rather than agricultural production. They were ready to challenge the old order root and branch if it stood in the way of their relentless pursuit of surplus value.

Politics and Ideology

The entrepreneurs who pioneered the process of industrialisation did not emerge from the charmed circles of the existing ruling class. Rather, they were more likely to have been small masters or richer artisans keen to exploit a good thing when they saw it. The new technology did not require a vast capital outlay in the early stages and anyway most enterprises were fairly small scale, at least at the start. The main obstacles in the path of this phase of capital development lay in the fact that the entire economic and political system was geared to preserving monopoly privileges for the old order. The right to vote and to be elected was restricted in the main to those who owned land and were card-carrying members of the Church of England. The right to overseas trade was strictly controlled by the great trading companies and was encumbered by a bewildering array of import and export duties. The House of Commons and the two main parties within it, Whig and Tory, existed to preserve such privileges against not only the 'swinish multitude' (Edmund Burke's phrase) but also against the new threat of these industrial parvenu interlopers. Small wonder then that, in their opposition to the Great Corruption of church and state, the new class of entrepreneurs appeared so radical at the end of the eighteenth century.

The new industrialists had their own (nonconformist) denomination of Christianity and their own economic and political theories to guide them. Adam Smith, David Ricardo, James Mill and Jeremy Bentham were their ideological mentors. The new 'science' of classical political economy, founded by Smith, was developed in opposition to mercantilism. The notions of laissez-faire, free trade and freedom for the operation of the market mechanism were in sharp contrast to the established traditions of protectionism and state intervention. Smith and his school even opposed Britain's existing colonial policy, supporting American independence on the grounds that if America remained a British colony, its economy would continue to stagnate and hence it would be a less useful market for British manufactured goods.

Although the British government was forced to recognise the fact of American independence by 1783, the needs of the growing new business community were hardly noticed, let alone catered for. Contemporary observers of whatever political persuasion were not sure how to assess the as yet small-scale changes in the economy. In any case, the long war with France from 1793 to 1815 and the attempts to defeat British radicalism (itself inspired by the French Revolution) were the sole concern of public policy.

During these years, however, textile and armaments manufacturers flourished. By 1815, with most of Europe in a state of economic collapse and the American market ready to buy as much as Britain could produce now that the French wartime economic blockade was lifted, great new opportunities existed for the take-off of mass production techniques using the new technology.

The postwar government appeared impervious to such developments. Under Lord Liverpool the Tories continued to act in the interests of their class. The symbol of protectionist policies was the Corn Laws of 1815 – a piece of legislation based more on dogma than on reason. A set-piece battle loomed between the unenfranchised owners of the 'new money' and the ruling-class representatives of 'old wealth'. By 1822, however, it was clear that the moment of crisis had passed – the ruling class had seen the danger and were prepared to compromise. Surprisingly enough, it was the Tories who took the initiative. They were the party most responsible for changing Britain's economic policy to accommodate the needs of the industrialists, while the Whigs, when in power, initiated the corresponding political reforms. Together, both were enough to buy off the 'captains of industry' and hence to ensure a fusion of the old and the new money, so avoiding the political and social upheavals that rocked the thrones of most other European countries in 1830 and 1848. The secret unlocked by the British ruling class in the first half of the nineteenth century was to detach any opposition from the force the rulers feared most – the working people. A victory for the masses would entail a lasting defeat for the existing order; far better then to head off such a threat by a voluntary change of attitude from above.

The old Toryism was incapable of perceiving the need for such concession. Toryism in general was rescued by such men as William Huskisson (President of the Board of Trade), Robert Peel (Home Secretary) and George Canning (Foreign Secretary) and others, all of whom came to prominence in the cabinet reshuffle of 1822. They, in an attempt to forestall political reform, appeased the manufacturing interest, at least temporarily, by initiating moves in the direction of freeing trade. The Navigation Laws were modified to permit foreign countries to trade directly with British colonies, many import duties were reduced and even the Corn Laws (introduced to protect the landed interest) were modified. None of this went far enough. It merely whetted the appetite of an increasingly prosperous and confident bourgeoisie for more reform which, at the very minimum, included the right to vote.

The Reform Act of 1832 was the culmination of years of political struggle during which the bourgeoisie were quite happy to make common cause with the working class. When, eventually, a reluctant Whig government, led by Lord Grey, was forced to give way, the resulting political settlement was just sufficient to break the dangerous unity of the third estate. The Act fulfilled Grey's stated aim of providing a measure which would 'afford sure grounds of resistance to further innovation'. It would appear on first reflection, therefore, that the Reform Act changed little: it added only 217,000 voters to the electoral roll and had very minimal effect on the composition of the House of Commons. Prime ministers and their cabinets continued to be drawn in the main from the ranks of the aristocracy throughout the nineteenth century.

On the surface, therefore, everything remained the same. Britain was still ruled by aristocrats. But as always there is a big difference between appearance and reality. From 1832 onwards the old order could only maintain its tenuous existence provided it reflected the interests of the class which really owned Britain's wealth – the owners of the new means of production, the bourgeoisie. The political history of Britain until 1867 reflects the gradual adaptation of policy in the light of the new compromise. A certain degree of governmental instability ensued as the main political parties struggled to find new identities which conserved their old interests while at the same time acknowledging that which was new. This led ultimately to a split in the Tory Party in 1846 when its leader, Peel, finally accepted the logic of his gradual conversion to free trade (as witnessed in his budgets of 1842 and 1845), by repealing the Corn Laws – the last symbol of the old protectionist system.

The change in government policy on this and many other matters was not simply the product of the intellectual wisdom of Whig and

Tory leaders. Rather, it was a response to the unrelenting pressure of the business community which no government after 1832 could afford to ignore. The Whigs under Lord Melbourne went a long way to satisfying the political demands of the bourgeoisie with such measures as the Poor Law Amendment Act, the Municipal Corporations Act and a host of others. The Tories, under pressure from such middle-class organisations as the Anti-Corn Law League, went a long way to satisfying the economic demands of the business interest. Both parties, however, did not need to be pressurised into fulfilling the objective that all men of property, old and new, shared in common, namely the protection of their property rights against the force of the common enemy, the real creators of their wealth – the working people.

Thus it was that by the middle of the nineteenth century, Britain's foreign and domestic policy was subordinated to the needs of the bourgeoisie. Free trade and laissez-faire were triumphant, leaving the way clear for Britain as the first industrial nation to exercise an unrivalled dominance over world trade. Britain had become the workshop of the world, her wealth solidly based on the pre-eminence of the textile, engineering and shipbuilding industries. The only threat to such prosperous stability resided in the increasingly better organised and class-conscious labour movement which, during these years, posed a continual problem for the ruling class. Such a threat was fuelled by appalling hardship which industrial capital in its early years (characterised by repeated booms and slumps) inflicted on its workforce. Where possible, resistance was met with repression, but sometimes concession was the only way to prevent the ultimate of all horrors – social revolution.

By 1850 the language of class was commonplace – it was clear that the stark relations of production based on the ownership of capital on the one hand, and the sale of labour power on the other, were the dominant feature of the economy to which all else was reduced. There had been some doubt about this at the end of the eighteenth century when many had regarded the industrial changes as a mere blip on the economic landscape and the myth of the golden age of the English rural idyll was invoked as the alternative to the 'dark satanic mills' (William Blake). Even if the mass of the population didn't work in such hell-holes, the fact was that capitalist relations of production undermined the independent artisan of whatever trade. Hence, although it was possible to perceive distinctions within 'the working people' relating to trade, skill and degree of control over the work process, there was a growing perception that the relationship between capital and labour, whatever form it took, was based on exploitation.

The Workforce and Women

The occupational structure of the workforce, linked with its geographical location, had changed beyond recognition by 1850. Precision is difficult since reliable evidence is hard to come by. The first of what came to be a regular census every ten years was taken in 1801. Before that, useful though fragmentary information has been compiled using a variety of chiefly local sources from parish registers and some tax returns. Until 1837, when civil registration of births, deaths and marriages became a legal requirement, census evidence was unreliable and this unreliability was compounded by the lack of skill of the unsupervised census enumerators. Methods improved after 1841 and it is only from then on that, despite many other limitations, the census becomes the chief primary source of information on population trends.

The three censuses taken between 1801 and 1831 (inclusive) provide valuable information on the size of the male and female population and give crude information on broad occupational categories (agriculture, trade, manufacture and handicraft), but tell us little about women's work. The enumerators kept a simple tally, which apart from the deficiency of the kind of information sought, was prone to inevitable recording inaccuracies. In 1841 the tally method was replaced by a system more akin to today's methods by which each head of household was required to complete a questionnaire from which the enumerators compiled their statistics, but again there was hardly any classification of occupation. Demographic historians have thus had to make their own estimates of the structure of the labour force in the first half of the nineteenth century using a variety of primary sources, chief among them being returns by factory inspectors. These show that from 1835 onwards, in the textile industry (especially in cotton and woollen factories), Britain's largest industry, women employees outnumbered men and continued to do so throughout the century and beyond. Out of a population of roughly 16 million in 1841, the textile industry employed around half a million people, making it second only to agriculture as an employer of labour. Women accounted for some 56 per cent of this total. But despite their predominance in this first factory-based industry, women were not to be found in the new up-and-coming industries like engineering, iron and steel production, or railway construction. But given that such industries occupied only a minority of the workforce anyway even as late as 1861, it would clearly be erroneous to assume that women's exclusion has any bearing on the total number of women employed. Despite the lack of reliable and detailed information, it would be safe to assume that women continued to work, as they always had in their traditionally accepted spheres. We know that domestic service was the biggest single employer of female labour. But we know far less about the numbers of women engaged in dressmaking, millinery and the like – all workshop or even home-working occupations, which escaped notice because they were so taken for granted. The small numbers of women who worked in less traditional areas, like chain-making in the West Midlands or as 'pit brow lassies' (at the surface of coal mines), have attracted more attention precisely because they were atypical. The same can be said of the much larger number of women who worked in textile factories. They excited a great deal of controversy even at the time because their presence brought women's labour into the open in a way that the more traditional and 'unseen' occupations did not.

Bibliography

Ashton, T. S. *An Economic History of England – the 18th Century* (Methuen, 1966)

Burnette, J. *Gender, Work and Wages in Industrial Revolution Britain* (Cambridge Studies in Economic History, 2008)

Chambers, J. D. and Mingay, G. E. *The Agricultural Revolution 1750–1880* (Batsford, 1966)

Deane, P. *The First Industrial Revolution* (Cambridge University Press, 1965)

Dobb, M. *Studies in the Development of Capitalism* (Routledge, 1947)

Flinn, M. W. *Origins of the Industrial Revolution* (Longman, 1966)

Hill, C. *Reformation to Industrial Revolution* (Pelican, 1969)

Honeyman, K. *Women, Gender and Industrialisation in England, 1700–1870* (Macmillan, 2000)

Pinchbeck, I. *Women Workers and the Industrial Revolution* (Cass, 1969; first published 1930)

Pollard, S. *Essays on the Industrial Revolution in Britain*, ed. C. Holmes (Ashgate, 2000)

Wrigley, E. A. (ed.) *An Introduction to English Historical Demography* (Weidenfeld & Nicolson, 1966)

2

THE IMPACT OF THE FRENCH
REVOLUTION, 1789–1815

The magnitude of the huge changes wrought by industrialisation was hardly understood at the beginning of the process. A factory proletariat had barely come into existence at the turn of the eighteenth century and the modern language of class and class struggle was almost unknown. Nevertheless, the economic effects of industrialisation and the political effects of the American War of Independence and the French Revolution inspired new thinking and the formation of new, independent and radical forms of organisation of working people. With a frightened eye on France the government met British radicalism with harsh repression. All forms of protest, however mild, were deemed to constitute a serious threat to the existing order.

The French Revolution

The French Revolution of 1789 can only be compared in its impact worldwide to that of the Russian Revolution of 1917. Not only did it shatter the old order in France but its ideology (encapsulated in its slogan 'Liberty, Equality, Fraternity') also inspired the downtrodden of many other countries inside and outside Europe to follow suit.

In England ruling-class reaction to events in France was less predictable than elsewhere. England was the only European country to have undergone a revolution to free itself from the yoke of feudalism and absolute monarchy (the revolution of 1640). If the French were about to do likewise whilst preserving property rights, albeit in an altered form, then even William Pitt (Tory prime minister 1783–1801, 1804–06) was prepared to give it a cautious welcome at the outset, especially since a section of the aristocracy in France had fired the opening shots in the opposition to Louis XVI. The newly rich entrepreneurs in Britain who had money but no political rights gave the revolution a more enthusiastic welcome, identifying with the well-to-do section of the third estate. However, both groups in England revised their views when it became apparent that the masses in France had demands of their own and for a short time, until 1794, under the leadership of Robespierre, occupied centre stage. This left only the working people of Britain to continue to support and identify with the more far-reaching aims of the real revolutionaries in France. Coming as it did at the beginning of a major process of economic transition in Britain, the French Revolution had a more widespread political effect here than did the American War of Independence of the previous decade, even though the latter had prepared much of the ideological ground for the subsequent eruptions in Europe.

There was a long radical tradition in Britain which had reached its zenith at the time of the English revolution of 1640 and subsequent Civil War. There are many parallels to be drawn between this revolution and that in France more than a century later, not the least being a popular democratic strain representing the interests of the propertyless. This was expressed in England by the Levellers and the Diggers and in France by the Jacobins. In both countries popular radicalism was ultimately defeated, resulting in the triumph of a new oligarchy, which in both cases represented a compromise between landed and commercial property. This compromise in England, misleadingly named the Glorious Revolution, was achieved in 1688. However, it was not until 1789 that once again a truly independent and democratic popular radical movement came to the fore on a scale far greater than the movement generated to support the American struggle against British colonial domination 13 years previously.

Thomas Paine and Mary Wollstonecraft

The essence of the popular democratic ideal in Britain was to be found in the writings of Thomas Paine, and in practical terms in the work of the Corresponding Societies. Paine's most famous book, *The Rights of Man*, was published in 1791 in reply to Edmund Burke's *Reflections on the Revolution in France*. This latter was a diatribe against the revolution, condemning the masses who participated in it as the 'swinish multitude'. Burke's argument was based on the traditionally accepted premise that political rights were founded on the ownership of property – those who had none were 'blessed' only with duties. This was the natural order of things – to tamper with the natural order would lead only to anarchy. Paine's book not only defended the cause of the revolution against its most outspoken conservative critic, but also argued that the French principles of equality could and should be applied in England. Based on them, in Part Two of the book, he drew up a practical social and political programme for far-reaching reform, radical even by today's standards, let alone by those of the eighteenth century.

Paine's radicalism, however, must not be confused with socialism, the latter being a much later development in the history of political thought. Paine did not attack property rights as such; his main target was the landed aristocracy and the hereditary principle. In this his appeal was as much to the unenfranchised traders and manufacturers as to the propertyless masses. Nonetheless, *The Rights of Man* showed that political democracy was not an abstraction, but was based on a revolutionary notion that all men are born naturally equal and that the purpose of government is to make natural rights effective. Governments which fail to do this must be opposed. 'Government', he asserted, 'is nothing more than a natural association' to be based on equal representation, not on privilege, monarchical or otherwise. Such views, combined with the social programme, captured the essence of the democratic ideal and ensured that his writing became a universal textbook for the working-class movement for many decades. Within three years it had sold over 200,000 copies.

Although Paine's programme included the almost unheard-of demand for maternity benefits, it did not have much else to say specifically about women, despite the fact that women played an important role in the French Revolution. However, in the heightened ferment of radical ideas and class understanding that ensued in the coming decades, there was, for the first time, the glimmerings of an awareness of the appalling injustices suffered by the 'unseen' half of the human race. One of the main arguments running throughout this book will be that the question of women's rights only becomes a public issue for the working-class movement as a whole at moments of great social and political upheaval generated by mass movements inspired by ideologies which challenge the existing order root and branch. This was one such moment. Inspired by the revolution and its foundation in the doctrine of reason and natural rights, Mary Wollstonecraft, an impoverished 'gentlewoman', published in 1792 her pioneering work *A Vindication of the Rights of Woman*. The book was dedicated to Talleyrand (a member of the French Constituent Assembly charged with writing a new constitution) to whom she wrote an open letter in which she asks him to

> Consider ... whether, when men contend for their freedom, and be allowed to judge for themselves respecting their own happiness, it be not inconsistent and unjust to subjugate women .....Who made man the exclusive judge, if woman partake with him of the gift of reason?[1]

'All tyrants are eager to crush reason', she says, but then goes on to challenge him with acting in a similar manner when 'you force all women, by denying them civil and political rights, to remain immured in their families groping in the dark'. Women, she asserts, 'may be convenient slaves, but slavery will have its constant effect, degrading the master and the abject dependant'. So runs the central argument of the book, the remainder of which is a refutation of all the dogma which is used to justify women's subjugation. Its challenge still remains largely unanswered. In her unfinished novel *Maria, or the Wrongs of Women*, Wollstonecraft showed

1   Mary Wollstonecraft, *Vindication of the Rights of Woman* (1929).

that she was aware of the link between women's oppression and class exploitation and that both were given spurious legitimacy by organised religion, in this case Methodism. Had she simply confined herself to championing the cause of the few educated and articulate women, it is unlikely that she would have met with such furious opposition, dubbed by them 'a hyena in petticoats'. It is also evident that some among the (male) radical intelligentsia supported her views and followed William Godwin's attack on the conventional family form in which women were forever doomed to a life of submission. In the wake of the fierce anti-Jacobinism that followed Britain's declaration of war on France, such advanced radical views were countered with the main ideological weapon in the armoury of the establishment, that of an evangelical Christian religious revival. Not only was religion an antidote to revolution, but it was also the means by which women could be restored to their 'proper place' at the centre of family life.

The Corresponding Societies

Thus it was that Paine and Wollstonecraft provided much of the ideological inspiration for English radicalism, though it is undoubtedly true that the former was more widely read than the latter. Their ideas clearly influenced the fledgling radical movement during this period. The most important of the radical organisations were the Corresponding Societies, formed in almost every major (and sometimes minor) English and Scottish town during 1792. The largest, although not the first of these societies was the London Corresponding Society (the LCS), the founder and secretary of which was a shoemaker, Thomas Hardy. It became the centre of a loose federation of similar bodies nationwide (literally 'corresponding' with each other), the main aims of which were to campaign for social reform and political democracy (including manhood suffrage), along the lines of Paine's programme outlined in Part Two of his *Rights of Man*. (This was published as a separate 6d pamphlet and was said to be 'in almost every hand'.)

Some have claimed that the LCS was the first working-class political organisation to have been formed in Britain. Others (e.g.

E. P. Thompson in the *Making of the English Working Class*)
say that the description 'popular radical' is more accurate. The
uniqueness of the organisation is not dependent on the truth
of either of these descriptions. What makes the Corresponding
Societies so important, aside from the fear which they engendered
in the ruling class, is the fact that they were truly independent
organisations, formed by and for working people. The term
working people, rather than working class, more accurately
expresses the fluidity of class relations existing at this time of
rapid economic change. The membership of the Corresponding
Societies reflected this, being composed as they were of artisans
– small masters and journeymen, shopkeepers, clerks. A conscious
decision was made to base the LCS on the 'lower orders'. This was
done by making the organisation as open as possible, as enshrined
in one of the rules, which laid down 'that the number of members
be unlimited', and also by keeping the subscription rates low at
a penny a week. This might not seem particularly noteworthy by
twenty-first-century standards, but it was an important departure
in the eighteenth century when politics and political organisations
were the exclusive domain of rich and powerful interest groups
often plotting in secret.

Repression

In 1793 Britain went to war with France – a war that lasted until
1815 with the final defeat of Napoleon at the battle of Waterloo.
This meant that the activities of the Corresponding Societies
were not only deemed to be seditious, but also treasonable.
Paine escaped to France to avoid certain arrest. Whilst there, he
was elected as a deputy to the French Convention, for the Pas
de Calais constituency. In Britain the radicals were harried by
state and more 'unofficial' agencies. The latter consisted of so-
called 'Church and King' mobs, who were left free (and freely
encouraged) to abuse and attack the followers of Paine and to
rampage through the streets burning his effigy. State persecution
started by banning Paine's works, followed by the trials and transportation of leading Scottish radicals, among them Thomas Muir.

A similar attempt in 1794 to convict seven leading members of the LCS, including Hardy himself, backfired on the government when the jury acquitted the men.

Despite persecution and infiltration by government agents, membership of the societies continued to grow at least until 1795. The defeat of the Jacobins in France in 1794, ending as it did the period of revolutionary advance, combined with the fact that the war itself enabled the government to capitalise on anti-French feeling and launch the harshest weapon in its repressive anti-radical armoury. This took the form of two Acts in 1795 – the Treasonable Practices Act and the Seditious Meetings Act. The former redefined treason to include words as well as deeds, while the latter so narrowed the right of assembly as to make political meetings impossible. This was coupled with the growth and more efficient organisation of the repressive apparatus of the state, as seen by the import of German mercenaries and the housing of troops in barracks in order to distance them from the radical influences of the civilian population. The effect, as intended, was to drive the Corresponding Societies underground. By 1797 the LCS had collapsed.

The apparent success of government repression and war fever in smothering the Corresponding Societies was not enough to douse the spirit of rebellion, which now took new forms. Most threatening to the government in view of the war with France were the naval mutinies at Nore and Spithead in 1797, and the Irish Rising of 1798. The latter was led by the Society of United Irishmen, an organisation inspired by Jacobin ideas, formed in 1791 (a year before the LCS), which united Catholics and Protestants in its ranks. Indeed its leader, Wolf Tone, was a Protestant lawyer. He and others saw in the French war a chance to rid Ireland of English control. To this end Tone went to France to plan for a French invasion to coincide with a rising of the Irish people. Three attempts were made between 1796 and 1797, but by the time the French finally arrived in August 1798 it was too late. (The French delay was caused by a change in foreign policy initiated by their new leader, Napoleon Bonaparte.) The Irish leaders had all been arrested, due in the main to the work of a government informer, Thomas Reynolds, but anyway the most favourable opportunity – the time of the naval mutinies the previous year – had been missed.

Trade Unionism

Such events inspired terror among the propertied classes and resulted in further repression. However, the economic impact of the war and the more profound and destabilising effects of industrialisation ensured that protest was never far beneath the surface. Much of this protest took the form of industrial action or 'combination' of one form or another at the point of production. This, of course, implies the existence of trade union organisation.

There has been much debate among historians as to the origins of trade unionism. The traditional view, propounded by the first historians of the trade union movement in this country, Sidney and Beatrice Webb (in *A History of Trade Unionism*, 1894), is based on their definition of a trade union as 'a continuous association of wage earners'. With this in mind, they could therefore find no evidence of trade union existence prior to the eighteenth century. Whilst the Webbs do not make the mistake (made by many of their disciples) of assuming that trade unionism was a by-product of industrialisation, their original definition fails to take account of the continuous struggle between labour and capital even during the period of handicraft production. An understanding of capitalist relations of production during the mercantile period has led some modern historians to see the guild system in a new light as they connect it to the increasing evidence being found to substantiate the existence of struggle waged at the point of production in earlier centuries. There were almost 400 labour disputes in the eighteenth century. Most of these did not involve 'continuous associations', but nevertheless they were concerned with such 'trade union' issues as wages and hours of work. It is nonetheless undeniable that more permanent forms of organisation to defend the economic interests of workers originated at a time when the 'the changing conditions of industry ... reduced to an infinitesimal chance the journeyman's prospect of becoming a small master' (S. and B. Webb). In other words, the changes in the means of production meant that an artisan (a worker who owned his or her own tools) could no longer expect to rise in the world.

Thus it was that by 1789 there was a well-established tradition of workplace organisation to defend wages and living standards. Many of the trade societies formed among the artisans were non-political. They had national structures (for example, among shoemakers, brush-makers, tailors and hatters) which facilitated the common practice of 'tramping' (an organised system of finding work in other parts of the country) and enough organisation to maintain members during sickness or periods of unemployment. The immense dislocation caused by industrialisation, exacerbated by 22 years of warfare and huge rises in food prices, gave an added impetus to workplace combination and trade organisation. This took varied forms, not all of them consistent with the Webbs' definition of trade unionism or of the more moderate operations of some of the trade societies. In these conditions the post-1790 industrial organisation of workers amounted to a considerable threat to the propertied classes resulting in drastic state repression, which itself was fuelled by the constant fear of the spread of revolution in Britain. It is simply not possible to chronicle the many examples of protest in almost every craft or trade. Most of it was highly localised and often took the form of 'collective bargaining by riot' or of machine-breaking, later known as Luddism. Luddism was not simply a protest against new technology. Many of those who participated in it were, like the framework knitters, already using complex machinery, usually the property of the employer, but used on the workers' own premises. The machines were broken as a means of coercing employers into awarding pay rises, particularly during periods when, as during the Napoleonic Wars, food prices were especially high. (Machine-breaking in Yorkshire, the subject of Charlotte Brontë's novel *Shirley*, was set in the winter of 1811–12.) In comparison with this form of machine-wrecking, its use as a protest against the new steam-driven technology of the turn of the century was surprisingly limited. It was exaggerated at the time and has been used since to heap abuse on 'backward-looking' workers who oppose 'progress'. Farm labourers destroyed threshing machines in some areas in the 1830s (this is sometimes referred to as the Last Labourers' Revolt). There was protest against the introduction of the power loom in the 1820s and in Lancashire spinning jennies over a certain size were wrecked in 1778–80. Compared to the earlier purposes of machine-wrecking as part of the collective bargaining process, these later examples pale into insignificance.

Understandably, workers were reluctant to leave any written accounts of these well but secretly planned operations, so most of it, including the more conventional strike activity, remains shrouded in mystery. It was all illegal. However, we know it was widespread because employers petitioned parliament to do something about it. They complained that the existing laws against combination and conspiracy were not drastic enough. The master millwrights of London demanded a short Act of parliament to solve the problem once and for all. Parliament obliged in 1799 by passing in great haste the notorious Combination Acts.

The Combination Acts were not simply more of the same repressive dose. They were a draconian measure which banned every kind of combination or meeting leading to combination, and made offenders liable to summary conviction by two magistrates. In addition, offenders, contrary to the principles of English law, were obliged to give evidence against themselves. The whole procedure was designed to avoid the delays in sentencing which were necessitated under the old laws of conspiracy. Although the Acts banned all combinations, they were used primarily against workplace combinations.

Even though the law remained on the statute book for 25 years it did not succeed in eradicating trade unionism or, indeed, industrial strife. The fact that so many unions 'appeared' when the law was repealed in 1824 is proof of this. It is very difficult to get precise information about such unions existing in a period of illegality. Naturally enough, they were not keen to leave written records, nor were they keen to announce their existence as trade unions. More often than not they called themselves friendly societies since such bodies could still maintain a legal existence. The 1794 Friendly Societies Act made a legal distinction between trade unions and friendly societies. The latter were benefit organisations providing some kind of insurance cover to dues-paying members who fell on hard times caused by sickness, injury or old age. However, it is very likely that many friendly societies did far more than this and performed much more of a trade union function. There was a big increase in the number of friendly societies during the last quarter of the eighteenth century and at least a quarter of them did not register with the Registrar for fear that their account books would be officially scrutinised. This increase was concentrated in those areas in which industrialisation was causing maximum upheaval. Many of these unions/friendly societies were small, short-lived and locally based.

Women in the Early Labour Movement

Some of the unions formed in these years, especially among textile workers, involved women – for example, the Manchester Spinners Society (formed in 1795) was predominantly female. This little noted fact reveals something very important about early trade union history, namely, that it was not, as it came later to be, a purely male-dominated affair. Women had always dominated the spinning side of the textile industry. This persisted even after the advent of the spinning jenny (an early form of mechanisation). However, women lost their dominance in spinning when steam-driven mules began to dominate, especially in cotton. The mechanisation of spinning created a huge demand for weavers and it was here that women replaced men on the new power looms. Nonetheless, women continued to be employed as spinners and weavers in the silk industry in the factories established by Courtaulds in Essex. In addition, they continued as carders and piecers in the spinning process in the factory system in the industrial towns. The mill owners thus showed a decided preference for female labour, and women were among the first factory workers. It would thus not be too wild to assume that women might have been among the pioneers of the trade union movement. Difficulties in finding reliable information about early trade unions and political organisations operating in a period of semi- or total illegality are hugely magnified when it comes to knowing, let alone assessing, the role of women. The hypothesis that women as the first factory workers might also have been the pioneers of modern trade unionism cannot thus be adequately tested without painstaking local research beyond the scope of this book. Lack of evidence, however, is no reason for doubting the importance of attempting to find it, especially when it touches on such a crucial gap in our understanding of the development of the labour movement and the place of women in it.

By 1815 it appeared that although there had been nearly two decades of popular protest, there was little tangible or permanent to show for it. The Corresponding Societies, Luddism, trade unionism and the movement for Irish freedom had all been beaten or suppressed – the Old Corruption of church, state and the landed/mercantile oligarchy was still, as ever, firmly in the saddle. Despite this, however, the ideas nourishing radicalism and trade unionism were very vibrant. Repressive legislation, war hysteria and economic hardship all played their part in checking the organisational form, though not the spirit, of revolt. The postwar period witnessed the reinvigoration and revival of both.

Bibliography

Brontë, C. *Shirley* (first published 1849) contains a fictional account of change in the woollen industry and the Luddite response.

Claeys, G. *Thomas Paine – Social and Political Thought* (Unwin Hyman, 1989)

Harmer, H. J. P. *Tom Paine: The Life of a Revolutionary* (Haus, 2006)

Munby, L. (ed.). *The Luddites and Other Essays* (Katanka, 1972)

Rule, J. (ed.). *British Trade Unionism 1780–1850* (Longman, 1988)

Thompson, E. P. *The Making of the English Working Class* (Gollancz, 1963)

Wollstonecraft, M. *A Vindication of the Rights of Woman* (Everyman, 1929; first published 1790)

3

POSTWAR RADICALISM, 1815–1836

The Treaty of Vienna, signed by the five Great Powers in 1815, marked the end of the French Revolutionary and Napoleonic Wars. France was defeated. The revolution was over. Everywhere in Europe kings, princes and aristocrats reclaimed their privileges. Britain, the most consistent partner in the anti-French coalition, was a victor power and emerged stronger than ever. Nonetheless, a powerful opposition movement developed in the postwar period, which although solidly based among artisans in particular, attracted support from a broad alliance which, until 1832, cut across class boundaries. The very fluidity of the class structure, reflecting as it did the still transitional nature of class relations at this time of ongoing industrial change and economic instability, was in turn reflected in new forms of protest inspired by a welter of political ideologies most of which defy characterisation in the parlance of modern socialist or labourist politics. Old traditions of protest were revived and new ones invented. As thinkers and activists on the left struggled to comprehend the immense changes of which they were part, they produced a rich intellectual legacy (much of which has unfortunately been forgotten) which, within the beginnings of a socialist framework, encompassed an analysis of the family and the subjugation of women.

The Old Regime

Unlike Europe, the old order had not been overthrown in Britain. It was business as usual, with the same Tory government pursuing the same narrow and partisan policies in the interest of the landed aristocracy. But for the opposition it was also business as usual.

The radicalism of the previous period, having suffered a temporary setback, re-emerged in the postwar years with a much wider base and a much broader appeal. Its target was the Tory government, which in the years between 1815 and 1822 earned itself the dubious reputation of being the most reactionary administration of the nineteenth century.

Britain in 1815 was the usual playground for the rich and powerful, with the Prince Regent setting the tone for wild extravagance. However, the contrast between the indulgences of the royal entourage and the lives of the mass of people was all the more marked given the postwar escalation in the cost of living. Food prices remained high, but the upward trend was accentuated by the government's decision to tax items of common consumption, like tea and sugar. This was a cold-blooded move to shift the burden of taxation onto those who could afford it least – a fact made more obvious by a simultaneous decision to abolish the more equitable income tax, which had been introduced as a short-term measure during the war. In addition, the postwar recession led to unemployment and savage wage cuts in many industries, exacerbating the dislocation and misery caused by the process of industrialisation.

The Radicalism of the Intelligentsia

For about five years after the signing of the Treaty of Vienna, the government was seriously troubled by a torrent of popular radical revolt assailing it from diverse and sometimes unexpected quarters. Whilst the causes of protest were not hard to find, the fact that it was so widespread is perhaps somewhat surprising given that, unlike the war years, there was no coherent national organising focus other than a few small and relatively obscure sects. Individuals rather than organisations acquired a mass following. Names like Francis Burdett, William Cobbett, Henry Hunt and John Cartwright were better known and remembered than organisations like the Society of Spencean Philanthropists. The written word in the form of a periodical, a political tract or a poem exercised a powerful appeal, especially when illustrated with a cartoon. This was the golden age of political caricature and satirical writing. The considerable talent of such artists and writers as William Hone, George Cruikshank and James Gillray were so successfully put to the service of the radical movement that the government actually resorted to replying in kind, hence unleashing an amazing pamphlet war. The best example of this was Hone's *The Political House that Jack Built*, a radical lampoon of the clergy, government and monarchy. It was illustrated by Cruikshank and sold in tens of thousands. *The Constitutional House that Jack Built* was the 'official' pro-government response – a parody of a parody. The sheer intellectual onslaught of the supporters of radical reform could not be matched by government scribes. The poets Percy Shelley, William Wordsworth, Lord Byron and Samuel Taylor Coleridge were all overtly politically active in the radical cause in this period, a fact often glossed over in the sanitised selection and interpretation of their works that has subsequently found its way into the canons of English literature. Coleridge and Wordsworth changed their views in later life, Byron died young in the battle to free Greece from its domination by the Ottoman Empire. Shelley also died at an early age, but it is unlikely that he would have moved to the right politically. His politics went beyond radicalism and towards socialism as an honest reading of 'Queen Mab' indicates. He married the daughter of Mary Wollstonecraft (child of her union with the socialist theorist William Godwin) and this undoubtedly helped to develop his support of women's rights. Support for women's liberation and opposition to the conventional family form provided a link between pre- and post-(Napoleonic) war radical thought in that, uniquely, new forms of non-oppressive personal social relations were a major plank in the deliberations of both.

The Radical Revolt, 1815–22

An intellectual revolt on its own could have been contained. The real threat to the government lay in the protest of 'the people all tatter'd and torn' (Hone) which surfaced with force on several occasions during these five years. Such events as the Derbyshire

Rising, the Pentridge Rising, the March of the Blanketeers, the Spa Fields meeting and the huge demonstration in St Peter's Field, Manchester ('Peterloo') all serve to indicate the breadth, diversity and widespread geographical scale of the demand for economic and political reform. There was little ideological conformity – handloom weavers protested against the loss of their livelihoods caused by the introduction of the power loom, William Cobbett, the popular writer and editor of *Twopenny Trash*, looked back nostalgically to the days of pre-industrial England, while the Spenceans (followers of Thomas Spence), the most socialistic in outlook, campaigned for England to be declared 'the people's common farm'. Such evidence as exists shows that women played an important part in the radical movement. Female Reform Societies were formed in many Lancashire towns, following the example of Alice Kitchin in setting up the first one in Blackburn, probably in 1818. These Female Reform Societies mustered large contingents to send to the Peterloo meeting at which many women as well as men bore the brunt of the violence of the yeomanry. The more 'respectable' middle-class elements organised in the Hampden clubs (named after John Hampden who, together with Francis Pym, was a leader of the parliamentary cause in the seventeenth century) and attempted to exert peaceful pressure for reform as an antidote to the more violent protests of the masses. Such violence undoubtedly did occur, as at Spa Fields in London in 1816, but mostly it was greatly over-exaggerated and sometimes directly inspired by government *agents provocateurs*, as in Derbyshire in 1817 and in the Cato Street conspiracy of 1820, in an effort to discredit the radical cause. But however much the government tried to fool others it could not fool itself as to the extent of the popular protest, hence its recourse to draconian repressive measures and state-ordered violence, like the massacre of peaceful protesters at Peterloo in 1819. (This outrage caused Shelley to write one of the best poems of political protest, 'The Mask of Anarchy'.) Habeus corpus (the right not to be imprisoned without trial) was suspended in 1816 and efforts were made to eliminate the radical press by the introduction in 1819 of the notorious Stamp Duty (a 4d tax on all cheap pamphlets and newspapers). This was dubbed a 'tax on knowledge' and inaugurated the 'war of the unstamped press'. The Gagging Act of 1817 forbade all meetings.

The Anti Slavery Movement and the Black Radicals

By the end of the eighteenth century there was considerable opposition to the slave trade for both economic and humanitarian reasons. It was the radicals, however, like John Thelwall of the London Corresponding Society, who linked the struggle against slavery with the fight against a corrupt ruling class at home. In the post-1815 period opposition to the slave trade was a powerful and popular force within the radical movement. When a proposal was made at the Congress of Vienna in 1815 to renew the rights of French slave traders a massive petition containing more than 1½ *million* signatures was handed to parliament. The majority of the signatories were working people.

By 1815 there were upwards of 10,000 black people living in Britain. From their ranks sprang two prominent radical leaders, both members of the most left-wing of the radical groups – the Spenceans. One of these, Robert Wedderburn, the son of a slave, was jailed for two years for his political activities; the other, William Davidson, was hanged and beheaded for his part in the Cato Street conspiracy of 1820. This conspiracy was a plot to blow up the cabinet and was infiltrated and probably inspired by *agents provocateurs*.

Owenism and Co-operation

Robert Owen is the personification of the ideological confusion which characterised radical reformers in the opening decades of the nineteenth century. He distanced himself from and was thus sometimes unpopular with the mainstream of the post-1815 radical movement. Owen was a paradox. As a wealthy and successful mill owner he was a product of the industrial revolution. As a thinker he was the product of eighteenth-century rationalism, but at the same time was influenced by the writings of French utopian socialists, in particular, Charles Fourier. He was a social reformer and as such his work falls into three distinct phases, only the last of which brought him into direct contact with the labour movement. Owen's theory that man's character is created for and not by him led him to take a direct and practical interest in social reform and education for the masses. He attempted to put his ideas into practice in his own factory at New Lanark and then appealed to the rich and powerful to follow his example. He made direct personal approaches to the Prince Regent, to Lord Sidmouth, the Duke of Wellington and even to some of the crowned heads of Europe to become agents of social change. Such appeals to reason in an attempt to transcend class interest fell, unsurprisingly, on deaf ears. This led him to go it alone – to create his own model society by establishing model co-operative communities in America and Britain. All of these communities were short-lived. They represented a rejection of all that was bad in society, but at the same time offered a misplaced hope that it was possible to opt out and survive. The failure of these experiments led him and his followers to see the necessity of fighting from within – first through more practical forms of co-operation and then through trade unionism.

Owen is often hailed as the father of the co-operative movement. This is not strictly true, especially if we acknowledge that the modern movement is based on consumer co-operatives. Consumer co-operatives (many of them short-lived) grew rapidly in the 1820s while Owen was in America. These co-operative shops were often closely connected with the trade union movement. William Lovett, one of the founders of the London Co-operative Society in 1824, wrote:

> When Mr. Owen first came over from America (1829) he looked somewhat coolly on those 'trading associations' and very candidly declared that mere buying and selling formed no part of his 'grand co-operative scheme'; but when he found that great numbers among them were disposed to entertain his views, he took them more in favour, and ultimately took an active part among them.[1]

1   W. Lovett, *Life and Struggles of William Lovett* (1967).

Owen was more disposed towards producer co-ops. He initiated an interesting experiment in the practical application of the labour theory of value by establishing a 'labour exchange' in 1832 in premises in Gray's Inn Road, London. An exchange of labour literally took place in the form of labour notes being issued for items produced by individuals. These labour notes could then be exchanged for other articles of an equivalent value. Value was determined by the cost of materials and labour time necessary for production. It is interesting to note that one of the first examples of the demand for equal pay was articulated in 1832 by women who worked in Owen's 'labour exchange' in Grays Inn Road. These women were supported by male trade unionists, members of the United Trades Association. Success of the labour exchange concept was short-lived as the amount of 'comparatively useless articles ... preponderated over the useful' (Lovett) and the value of the labour notes depreciated.

Communitarianism (the establishment of model communities run along socialist lines in which all property was held in common) and co-operation were just two examples in the 1820s of the efforts of radical thinkers to find solutions for the oppressed in a rapidly changing society, the workings of which they had not yet fully understood. The failure of these experiments led to an awareness of the need for a much more direct form of workers' organisation – trade unionism. Owen recognised this and played a leading role in attempts at general unionism in the early 1830s.

The worsening of living standards during the long-term economic crisis of the 1830s and 1840s gave greater urgency to a more practical way of fighting back. Industrialisation was as yet incomplete. Cotton still dominated the economy, and yet cotton goods fell in price. Employers adopted the classic remedy of cutting wages, with devastating results given that there was no fall in price of the basic necessities of life.

Trade Unionism

It is difficult to separate political and trade union activity in the first half of the nineteenth century. Unions themselves were highly political organisations bearing little resemblance to their modern inheritors. That they appeared as organisationally separate is due to the fact that radical political organisation was all but extinguished by 1820 by repressive legislation and state brutality. Trade unions continued the radical tradition through different organisational forms, but with one important difference: namely that they, rather than the radical clubs, were the vehicles for the development of a specifically working-class (often anti-capitalist) consciousness. This can be seen in the twin developments within trade unionism in these years. One such development was the steady progress of trade union organisation within individual trades, which also involved the attempt to weld the various small trade clubs into some kind of unified (in some cases national) organisation. Second, there were attempts to form general unions of all workers irrespective of trade. These two initiatives were not in conflict – often the leaders of the former were involved in the latter. John Doherty, leader of the cotton spinners, is the most obvious example. Men like Doherty, William Benbow (a Lancashire shoemaker), Owen and many others looked on trade unionism not just as a means for protecting and improving workers' living standards, but also as a vehicle for changing the entire political and economic order. In order to achieve this Benbow popularised the strategy of the 'national holiday' (a general strike). In essence he and others were beginning to appreciate, well before Marx revealed it more precisely, that political power, being based on economic wealth, could only be dislodged by workers at the point of production. The inescapable logic of this argument inevitably produced a potentially very revolutionary variant of trade unionism, jettisoned in the second half of the nineteenth century.

Before the depression of the 1830s there was a short period of relative economic stability in the 1820s with something approaching a boom in the middle years of the decade. In these conditions the newly remodelled Tory government was persuaded by men like Francis Place that trade unions were not the dangerous beasts that they seemed during the war years. Hence in 1824 the Combination Acts were repealed. Place's argument was that legalising trade unions would serve to *discourage* them. He, and other political economists like him, believed that wages were ruled by the law of the market and that allowing workers the freedom to combine would teach them how futile it was to wage a war that was impossible to win. Workers obviously did not share Place's view, as witnessed by the immense increase in union activity, including strike action, following repeal. The fact that so many seemed suddenly to appear came as a surprise only to those who thought that the Combination Acts had succeeded in abolishing unions rather than driving them underground. The government was so worried by this development that it rushed through the 1825 Trade Union Act. Its purpose, very much like that of contemporary legislation, was to reduce the effectiveness of trade unions by making it difficult to organise strikes without falling foul of the law. The clauses forbidding 'molestation' or 'obstruction' to persuade workers to 'abstain' from work gave judges such wide powers of interpretation that even peaceful picketing could be criminalised.

Nonetheless, trade unions themselves remained legal. There is evidence of considerable organisation among spinners, potters, shoemakers, brush-makers, shipwrights and even domestic servants (a short-lived Union of Maidservants was formed in Edinburgh in 1825). The factory-based cotton spinning industry was probably the best organised in trade union terms. At first the associations of mule spinners were locally based with many local strikes, but intermittent attempts were made to establish federations with the aim of equalising piece rates. John Doherty, secretary of the Manchester cotton spinners, led a successful attempt to achieve unity, resulting in the formation of the Grand General Union of Cotton Spinners in 1829. This, though short-lived, was the springboard for further attempts at general unionism.

Today we associate the attempt to form 'one big union' for all workers of all trades with syndicalism, which as a theory was a much later development. Whatever label we attach to attempts to form general unions of all trades in the early nineteenth century, there is no escaping the fact that they were all founded on the premise that the industrial might of the working class could be used to change the political system. Three attempts were made to unite workers in this way. One was as early as 1818 with the formation of the Philanthropic Hercules. The next – the National Association for the Protection of Labour – was initiated by Doherty in 1829 and survived until 1831. Finally, perhaps the most famous was the Grand National Consolidated Trades Union (1833–34).

The attempts by the state and the employers to crush the GNCTU is well known, culminating as it did in 1834 with the transportation of the Tolpuddle Martyrs, six agricultural labourers from the village of Tolpuddle in Dorset who, having joined the GNCTU, were accused and found guilty in a show trial of 'administering illegal oaths'. This ancient piece of legislation was dredged up as the means of defeating trade unionism, given its now legal status, in an attempt to discourage others. There was a mass campaign to prevent the sentences being carried out, and although unsuccessful in its immediate aim, succeeded in pressuring the government to commute the sentences. It is probable, however, that internal divisions within the GNCTU would have caused its demise despite state repression. Although Owen occupied an influential position within the union he was in constant disagreement with two of its more militant and class-conscious leaders – J. E. Smith and James Morrison. The withdrawal of the GNCTU's largest affiliate, the Tailors' Union, following its strike in April 1834 in which the employers cleverly exploited sexual divisions in the industry, was another major factor contributing to the collapse of the umbrella organisation.

Women, Socialism and Trade Unionism

The feminist ideas of Mary Wollstonecraft had a greater influence in the radical and trade union movement of the postwar period than during her own lifetime. (She died from complications arising from the birth of her daughter in 1797.) Owen actively supported the ideas of women's emancipation, and the communitarianism of the 1820s sought to give practical expression to new and non-oppressive ways of living. However, it was not until the

1830s that such ideas emerged in a more popular form from the comparatively tiny intellectual glasshouse in which they had been nurtured. Women themselves played an active role, campaigning for sexual equality and publicly promoting socialism as the only means for its achievement. This period is unique in the extent to which male leaders of the labour movement were open and supportive of such initiatives. Such women as Anna Wheeler, Fanny Wright, Eliza Macauley, Emma Martin, Eliza Sharples and Frances Morrison were all prepared to transgress social convention in campaigning against sexual oppression and class exploitation. Frances Morrison was married to James Morrison the editor of the GNCTU newspaper, *The Pioneer*. This not only had a regular women's page (initially entitled a 'Page for the Ladies', which changed its name, following protests, to 'Women's Page'), but also contained editorials jointly written by the Morrisons in which the demand for equal pay for work of equal value was raised, probably for the very first time. Other issues covered in the Women's Page and elsewhere in *The Pioneer* have a similar contemporary ring to them – drunken husbands, women's responsibility for housework, male hostility to women in the trade union movement, the sexual division of labour and much else.

The GNCTU had a large female membership and women were encouraged to organise in separate 'lodges of industrious females' (women's branches). The pages of *The Pioneer* record the activity of such branches as well as the concerns of male trade unionists (for example, the tailors) that women's low pay dragged down the male rate, but on the other hand it was feared that if women were to gain equal pay, men's livelihoods would be threatened. The response of the male tailors was to argue that women should not be allowed to work in the trade. This line met with great protest from women correspondents and from the paper's editor, James Morrison. Thus GNCTU policy both served the purposes and reflected two antagonistic trends in the labour movement which persisted long after the demise of that organisation. On the one hand, the traditional and probably majority view was that women in an era of technological change were a threat to men's jobs and pay rates and that trade unionism was in being to protect the existing situation. Given the prevalence of the sexual division of labour within and between industries it made sense, according to this argument, to maintain separate spheres for women in trade unions too. On the other hand, there was a dawning recognition that sexual divisions were in the interest of the employer and that the way to overcome the super-exploitation of women was through trade union organisation. Given that no women were in the leadership of sexually mixed unions, Morrison and others in the GNCTU thought that separate women's organisations would encourage more women to become self-mobilising, thereby lessening their reliance on men.

The Reform of Parliament

All radicals, whatever else divided them, had been united for decades in their opposition to the corrupt aristocratic club which passed itself off as the legitimate government of the British Isles. Out of a population of around 14 million in 1831 (in England and Wales), only about 400,000 men had the vote. There was no uniform electoral law applying to the whole country but in general (saving some anomalous exceptions in the borough franchise), only wealthy landowners could vote and be elected. Even in the odd seat where this general rule did not apply, corruption was so rife that votes were easily bought and sold. Apart from the size and composition of the electorate, the most glaring anomaly lay in the distribution of the 558 House of Commons seats which, by the 1830s, bore almost no relationship to where people actually lived. Populous industrial towns like Manchester, Birmingham, Leeds and Sheffield were entirely unrepresented. Seventy per cent of MPs were returned from the southern counties of England – Cornwall returned 42. Gatton in Wiltshire returned two MPs, yet had only one voter! Old Sarum, an uninhabited hill in the same county, enjoyed a similar privilege of double representa- tion. The phrase 'rotten borough', in widespread use at the time, is a good description of these and many other similar examples of the deformed parliamentary system which, according to the

Duke of Wellington, 'was beyond the wit of man to consider ... more perfect'.

The vast majority of the population, rich and poor, were unenfranchised but had more 'wit' than Wellington. The existing reform societies were given a huge boost by two coincidental events in 1830. One was a general election brought about by the death of George IV; the other was news of the revolution in France resulting in the downfall of the hated Charles X. A wave of revolt spread across Europe, Britain included. The reform societies were organised mainly on class lines. The middle class joined the Political Unions, the various working-class groups eventually cohered around the National Union of the Working Classes formed in 1830.

The 1830 election produced the first Whig government for about 50 years. Grey, the new prime minister, described himself as an 'aristocrat both by position and nature ... with a predilection for old institutions'. Nonetheless, such was the nature of the forces for reform outside parliament that even he was forced to see the writing on the wall. He therefore produced a reform bill which would, he hoped, 'afford sure grounds of resistance to further innovation'. Even this modest measure took two years to get through the mother of parliaments and even then only because the strength of the mass movement was powerful enough to create a near-revolutionary situation. The shock troops and the backbone of this movement were the workers. Well organised and often armed, they struck fear into the owners of property, including their erstwhile middle-class allies organised in the Political Unions. In 1831 when the House of Lords rejected the bill, revolutionary outbreaks occurred in many towns – Bath, Derby, Worcester, Nottingham. In Merthyr, the scene of serious 'disturbances', the red flag was raised for the first time in Britain as a symbol of revolt. Bristol was actually taken over for some days by the rebels. Learning the European lesson of a failure to compromise, a frightened British establishment was forced, in June 1832, to pass the Reform Bill. The compromise was just enough to split the reform movement. It satisfied only the industrialists – they were enfranchised (about 217,000 of them were the only additions to the electoral register). Many of the more heinous abuses in the borough franchise and the distribution of seats were cleared up. The Reform Act gave nothing to the working class who had made the whole thing possible. For them the Act was 'The Great Betrayal' and was popularly referred to as such in the years to come. Their masters in the factories now joined the aristocracy as their political masters in Westminster. The goal of the workers' movement was and remained adult (male) suffrage. Even before the fight for parliamentary reform regrouped with greater clarity, it was clear that the movement was strong enough to force its will on the new system. A device known as 'exclusive dealing' was used to elect radical MPs in areas like Oldham where the movement was very strong. A list of electors was published along with their voting preferences. Those who refused to support the radical candidates (in Oldham's case, Cobbett and Fielden) were boycotted by the unenfranchised working class. This took the form of refusing to buy the products or patronise the shops of Tory or Whig voters. A handbill issued in Oldham in the 1832 election spelled out this novel strategy:

> The enemies of reform are everywhere alarmed at the non electors adopting exclusive dealing. The nation and your enemies know the immense power of the working class ... Therefore, workingmen, if you wish well to yourselves, layout your money with those electors of Oldham who support ... Fielden and Cobbett ... The electors' franchise is a trust to be used for your benefit, and not a right to be used against you.[2]

After 1832 the lessons learned by the activists about the connection between economic and political power were more obvious than hitherto. Before the Reform Act the industrialists who exploited labour economically could nonetheless pose as the workers' friends politically. Being excluded from political power themselves, the bourgeoisie were as vehement in their condemnation of the aristocracy as any working-class radical. Indeed, they could also be very radical themselves. In broad terms 1832 changed all this. The strangely contradictory role of the

2   Quoted in John Foster, *Class Struggle and the Industrial Revolution* (1977).

industrialists was ended even if, owing to the fluidity of the class structure and the prevalence for many years to come of many very small-scale capitalists, there remained some blurring at the edges. From now on political protest was largely the preserve of the working class, led by organisations free from middle-class leadership.

The fact that all women remained unenfranchised was relatively unremarked at the time given the exclusion of the vast majority of the population. However, women remained an integral part of most movements of political and economic protest, at least until mid century, when the nature of such protest began to assume a decidedly less revolutionary character. Meanwhile, the 'Great Betrayal' inspired rather than dampened the labour movement and ensured that in the coming two decades, with the absence of middle-class radicalism, it became more class-conscious than ever.

Bibliography

Butt, J. (ed.). *Robert Owen: Prince of Cotton Spinners* (David & Charles, 1971)

Chase, M. *Early Trade Unionism: Fraternity, Skill and the Politics of Labour* (Ashgate, 2000)

Cole, G. D. H. *Attempts at General Union 1818–1834* (Macmillan, 1953)

Cruikshank, G. and Hone, W. *Radical Squibs and Loyal Ripostes: Satirical Pamphlets of the Regency Period 1819–21*, selected and annotated by Edgell Rickword (Adams & Dart, 1971)

Foot, P. *Red Shelley* (Bookmarks, 1984)

Foster, J. *Class Struggle and the Industrial Revolution* (University Paperback, 1977)

Frow, R. and E. *Political Women 1800–1850* (Pluto Press, 1989)

Kirby, R. G. and Musson, A. E. *The Voice of the People: John Doherty 1798–1854* (Manchester University Press, 1975)

Lovett, W. *Life and Struggles* (Macgibbon & Kee, 1967; first published 1876)

Stedman-Jones, G. *Languages of Class* (Cambridge University Press, 1983)

Taylor, B. *Eve and the New Jerusalem* (Virago, 1983)

4
THE AGE OF CHARTISM

The temporary demise of the trade union movement after Tolpuddle, and the 'Great Betrayal' of 1832, had the effect of focusing activity more sharply on other issues. Two campaigns in particular attracted a mass working-class following in the 1820s and 1830s. One was to reduce the hours of work in the factories and improve working conditions generally; the other was to oppose the hated Poor Law Amendment Act of 1834. Thereafter, from 1836 onward, these campaigns, along with other more long-standing elements of workers' organisation, coalesced into one mighty, all-embracing movement – Chartism.

Living Standards

The issues of poor relief and factory reform were not new for the labour movement. How could they be? The latter was a direct product of the process of industrialisation and the former was sharply accentuated by it. There is continuing debate among economic historians about 'the standard of living question'. Put simply, the protagonists (known as the optimists and the pessimists) argue the toss about whether industrialisation in the years up to (roughly) the mid nineteenth century had the effect of raising (optimist view) or lowering (pessimist view) working-class living standards. Without here examining the mass of conflicting evidence, suffice it to say that almost all *contemporary* observers, whatever their political allegiance, were convinced that the hardship of the masses was acute. Victorian novelists like Charles Dickens, Elizabeth Gaskell and even Benjamin Disraeli (in *Sybil*) wrote about the condition of the urban working class in stark, even horrifying terms, as did contemporary observers like Friedrich Engels (in *The Condition of the Working Class in England in 1844*). Numerous government enquiries (known as 'Blue Books') attested to urban squalor producing alarming mortality rates and health defects. Reports of the Factory Commissioners (after 1833) also provide ample evidence of the extent of child labour, horrifyingly long working hours and abysmal working conditions. Their reports do not, of course, cover the even worse conditions of employment not covered by the jurisdiction of the very limited factory legislation. In 1842, an official government enquiry headed by Edwin Chadwick published its *Report on the Sanitary Condition of the Labouring Population of Great Britain*. It too made dismal reading and even spurred the government into limited public health reform.

Factory Reform

Most historians of the factory reform movement date its genesis from the 1830s. It is certainly true that the movement was very strong and active after that date, but this happened only because it was able to build on the solid foundations which had been laid 20 years earlier. There are two reasons why more attention is paid to the later rather than the earlier period. One is that the factory system had, by the 1830s, extended to other branches of textile manufacture, in particular to one of the oldest industries – woollen cloth. The second is that the movement had acquired some powerful support from diverse and unexpected quarters outside the ranks of the working class. Two names illustrate this diversity. The first is Richard Oastler, a Tory of the old school who had never come to terms with industrialisation and the new social order to which it gave rise. He wrote a series of letters in 1830 for the *Leeds Mercury* denouncing what he called 'Yorkshire Slavery' – a damning indictment of conditions in the worsted mills of Bradford. The other was a cotton mill owner and Radical MP for Oldham, John Fielden. Important though men like these were to the cause of factory reform, their contribution, which because of their class position attracted much publicity, is minimal in comparison to that of the much less celebrated, but far deeper and more consistent mass campaigns led and waged by working men and women whose very lives were threatened by the inhuman exploitation to which they were subjected in the early factories.

The first signs of the movement for factory reform are to be found as early as 1814 among the cotton spinners of Manchester who formed what was known as 'short time committees'. Although these and other similarly named committees were closely allied to the cotton trade unions, they existed independently of them and hence carried on their campaign for shorter working hours at times when their unions may have been temporarily broken. This campaign spread throughout the factory districts, led and organised by working men and women long before Oastler's or Fielden's appearance on the scene. Putting the record straight on this point is necessary not just for the sake of historical accuracy. It is also important because it helps to counter the widespread and still prevalent belief that the workers are their own worst enemies and the hardship they suffer is brought about by their own greed and stupidity. Child labour, so this argument runs, existed only because avaricious parents wanted the extra income their offspring could earn. In this fashion the key role played by the workers themselves, through their trade unions, in enforcing factory legislation is also obscured. Until 1833, the absence of a Factory Inspectorate meant that the only means of enforcing the very limited factory legislation was by means of the 'common informer'. Such individuals were invariably trade union officers or representatives who, of course, had firsthand experience of the widespread abuses perpetrated by the factory owners. The 1833 Factory Act ended this system by establishing inspectors to police the new legislation which dealt in the main with limiting the hours of women and children. It was the owners themselves who found ways to circumvent this by enforcing a relay system, a kind of double shift. Most factories were anyway rarely checked and it was this and the flouting of the law which gave rise to the general demand of the short time committees for a ten-hour day for all workers, which was finally partially implemented in 1844.

Blaming the workers for what was in essence the stupendous greed of their masters does little justice to the fact that they were the initiators of reform. The same argument would have us believe that infant mortality was widespread in the factory districts because mothers chose to go out to work, leaving their babies with old women or young children who gave them 'mother's little comforter' (laudanum) and sops (bread soaked in unpasteurised milk), in the absence of any safe substitute for breast milk. The alarmingly high infant mortality rates in the factory districts attracted a great deal of attention in the 1820s and 1830s, but no practical help was given to working mothers whose labour was so attractive to the mill owners. The absence of any kind of child care provision, let alone maternity leave, meant that women often gave birth on the factory floor and returned to work within days of their 'confinement'. It was much easier for Victorian moralists to blame the mother than tackle the problem, for to do so would have meant publicly acknowledging that women played a role outside the home – a fact which the factory system had brought out into the open for perhaps the first time, exposing the huge contradictions in the prevalent ideology of the sanctity of home, hearth and family. Within this construct the idealised notions of femininity and 'women's place' sat uncomfortably with the now publicly exposed reality of the lot of working-class women.

The Poor Law

Until 1834 the system of poor relief in Britain was based on principles established 300 years earlier during the reign of Elizabeth I. There had been many changes in the form and administration of poor relief during this long period, but essentially the principles established by the Poor Law Act of 1601 remained. These were that society had a duty to provide work for the able-bodied poor and to provide subsistence for those who, through age or infirmity, could not work. It all sounds very humane, but in practice it was not. This was because the finance and implementation of any scheme based on these principles fell to the smallest administrative unit of society – the parish. In order to fulfil its commitments, the parish had to levy a special poor rate, the amount of which depended on the scale of the problem. There was thus, in the absence of any state responsibility, a direct local material incentive to devise various stratagems to play down or hide poverty in order to reduce the poor rate. Chief among the devices used were laws forbidding vagrancy and defining 'settlement'. The aim was to ensure that the poor of one parish could not become a burden to the overseers of the poor in another parish.

By the end of the eighteenth century it was evident that the system was not only stretched to its limit, but had become inoperable. With the steady rise in population and the effects of enclosures some came to realise that the causes of the resulting widespread poverty were to be found in low wages and high food prices. The only way to alleviate this without depopulating the agricultural areas was to use the poor rate to provide some form of supplementary allowance. Many different schemes embodying this principle of 'outdoor relief' were tried. The most famous was the Speenhamland system first introduced in Berkshire in 1795 and spreading later to many southern counties. Under this system insufficient wages were supplemented on a sliding scale based on the price of bread and taking into account the number of dependants supported by each applicant. The relief obtained through this and other similar systems was certainly not generous, nor was it inspired by humanitarian or altruistic motives. However, in contrast to what was to come, any form of outdoor relief seemed kind.

The political economists of the industrial era developed a new social philosophy, the echoes of which are similar to the 'two nation' Toryism and New Labourism of today. For them the only way to help the nation's poor was to increase the nation's capital – a job to be left to the wealth creators (the capitalists). Within the framework of classical political economy, the theories of over-population expounded by Thomas Malthus, and of Utilitarianism, developed by Jeremy Bentham, were the foundation of a massive attack on the old Poor Law, culminating in the 1834 Report of the Royal Commission on the Poor Law. Imbued with the ideological dogma of Malthus and Bentham, the commissioners set out to prove that the effect of subsidising wages was to make the working class demoralised and lazy by encouraging, to quote the report of the commission, 'a bounty on indolence and vice'. They also tried to prove that the system resulted in population growth since the 'child benefit' element encouraged the poor to 'breed recklessly'. Many other similarly unproven (and unprovable) excuses masquerading as reasons were given by the commissioners for ditching the old system. Underlying all the dogma, the real concern of the critics of the old Poor Law was its mounting cost – a cost borne by the wealth creators who had better things to do with their money than subsidise the poor.

So, given the impossibility of denying the existence of poverty, what was the alternative to outdoor relief? The Poor Law Amendment Act of 1834, based on the recommendations of the commissioners, offered a simple solution resting on the limited aim of relieving only the 'deserving poor' rather than poverty itself. The Act abolished all forms of outdoor relief and instead sanctioned only 'indoor relief' administered through a network of workhouses under the control of central government. Those applying for help would be deemed to be deserving if they passed the workhouse test, which was based on the principle of 'less eligibility'. This meant that if anyone was granted relief 'his situation on the whole shall not be made really or apparently so eligible as the situation of the independent labourer of the lowest class'. In other words, workhouses were to be made as uncomfortable as possible in order to deter the poor in favour of the utterly destitute. Thus the choice for the poor was stark – the workhouse or starve. The regime of the workhouse was intolerably harsh, almost penal. Families were separated, food was sparse, accommodation dismal and all but the very sick were forced into harsh, unrewarding work. The undeserving poor who failed the workhouse test had, according to this utilitarian philosophy, only themselves to blame for their situation. They were left to their own devices and the whims of private charity. Poverty, if it could not be cured by 'self-help', was to be punished. The spectre of the workhouse haunted the poor for the next hundred years and helps explain the fear and shame of the very admission of poverty.

It was easy enough to pass a law like this, but not as easy to enforce it. Opposition was on a scale never before witnessed on any other issue. When the commissioners turned their attention, in 1837, to implementing the Act in the North the opposition was so strong and so widespread that they were forced, in some cases, to give up entirely. Over a quarter of a million people joined a demonstration near Bradford in 1837. Over the whole West Riding of Yorkshire and especially in Huddersfield the implementation of the Act was delayed. This was also the case in the factory districts of Lancashire. The short time committees were used as the basis of opposition. The later involvement of the Chartists frightened off some of the 'respectable' support from Tories like Disraeli and *The Times* which had initially opposed the New Poor Law. The government's timing was bad. It was attempting to introduce the law during a time of severe trade depression when many workers had been laid off or were on short time. Any form of indoor relief (let alone the dreaded workhouse) was inappropriate in these circumstances – a temporary problem did not require a permanent 'solution'. Even some employers recognised this: they did not want their labour force to be lost permanently to the workhouse. The opposition remained strong until the mid 1840s, by which time the government was forced to give way and allow outdoor relief to continue in the North, even though workhouses there were finally built.

Chartism

To describe Chartism simply as a political movement based on the demands contained in a six-point Charter is both correct and misleading at the same time. The Charter itself, launched in 1838 by members of the London Working Men's Association, was not the product of new or original thinking. It contained the standard radical demands which had been articulated in one form or another for the past 40 years. Thus this simple description of Chartism gives us no clue as to its real significance.

So, wherein lies the significance of Chartism? First, it would not be an exaggeration to say that Chartism was the single most important working-class political movement of the nineteenth century. Its mass support was clearly visible in the presentation of three 'monster' petitions to parliament in 1839, 1842 and 1848, all containing literally millions of signatures. From this mass support came the formation of the first ever working-class political party, the National Charter Association, founded in 1840. Second, Chartism was the culmination and highest point of a long radical tradition, but although it was a product of that tradition it also represented something qualitatively new. Within it, its most class-conscious elements were gravitating away from radicalism and towards socialism. Guided by such theoreticians as Bronterre O'Brien ('the schoolmaster of Chartism') and later George Julian Harney and Ernest Jones (both of whom were closely associated with Karl Marx and Friedrich Engels, both resident in Britain from 1848 onwards as political exiles from their native Germany), an important 'left' trend within Chartism, which later became the leadership, made connections between political oppression and economic exploitation. Despite its divisions and tactical errors, Chartism posed an enormous threat to the established order precisely because it was able to weld together (at times) and articulate class consciousness with political consciousness – a potent mixture. But even more than this, it managed, in the early years at least, to form alliances with small property owners in a huge anti-government alliance, the uniqueness of which lay in the fact that it was led by class-conscious workers. The defeat of Chartism in the 1850s represented a massive defeat for the working-class movement and ushered in a new phase in the history of the British labour movement. Chartism was a turning point in this history in both a positive and a negative sense: its existence promised much; its eclipse turned those promises into far-off dreams, still unfulfilled.

Chartism cannot be said to have failed. After all, its very existence as a movement capable of mobilising such mass support over 14 years is a sign of success. The more important question is why it did not fulfil its potential. To explain this involves looking beyond the conventionally labelled divisions between the so-called 'moral force' versus 'physical force' wings of Chartism and instead analysing the social composition of the movement on which rested its different political perspectives. The fact that Chartism was a uniquely working-class movement is not a sufficient explanation of its social composition. The working class was still in the process of formation and cannot be considered then, as now, to be a homogeneous whole. The elements comprising Chartism in the early stages were wide-ranging, reflecting social diversity. The demands of the Charter were broad enough to win support from factory workers, from artisans (skilled workers who owned their own tools), from workers like the handloom weavers, whose manual skills were in the process of being rendered obsolete by industrialisation, from women workers and from black and Irish workers. There was even support early on from lower-middle-class radicals – shopkeepers, professional people and owners of small workshops. The Charter provided a means by which a fragile unity could be built, but such unity could not weather the turbulent storms of the revolutionary insurgency of 1839. In that year, after parliament had rejected the first petition, the delegates to the Chartist Convention gave confused messages as to the next stage in the campaign. They first accepted and then rejected a call for a general rising and planned instead for strike activity. Nonetheless, armed risings did take place, the most notable of which was in Newport under the leadership of the former mayor of the town, John Frost. There were outbreaks in other towns, but given the forcible dispersal of the Convention, there was no central co-ordination and each individual revolt was suppressed by the military. Mass arrests followed and many of the Chartist leaders were subsequently imprisoned. By 1840 when the insurrectionary mood had subsided and the movement regrouped, the more 'respectable' elements, notably the middle-class faction around the Birmingham banker Joseph Attwood and an artisan group led by William Lovett, had dropped out altogether. This could have led to greater ideological clarity and unity of the remaining forces had there been a more profound understanding of the key importance of struggles of the factory workers. However, the militancy of the industrial struggle took the leadership of the National Charter Association (formed in 1840 as a political party organisation) by surprise. This was clearly seen in 1842 when the hesitancy and divisions among the Chartist leaders resulted in a tragic lost opportunity.

The General Strike of 1842

1842 was the year in which the first ever general strike took place. The momentous events of August and September of that year are usually referred to by historians disparagingly as the 'Plug Riots'. The implication behind such a description is that the episode was the work of half-starved, half-crazed, desperate workers who spontaneously travelled the length and breadth of the country pulling out the plugs of the steam boilers which operated the machinery, forcing other mindless workers to walk out and join them. Such a description bears no relation to the facts. The strike was well planned and organised by the trade unions and involved nearly half a million workers throughout Britain, spreading from its nucleus in the heart of the cotton industry in Lancashire and involving workers in almost every other major trade. Whilst it is true that the immediate cause of the strike was the proposal of the cotton manufacturers to cut wages by 25 per cent in response to the severe trade depression, the strike was also highly political in character, involving the demand for the Charter as its central aim. In fact, at countless meetings the strikers passed resolutions declaring that they would not return to work 'until the People's Charter is the law of the land'.

The signs were good. The political and industrial wings of the movement had come together and the mood was militant. Sales of the Chartist newspaper, the *Northern Star*, were high and over three million signatures were collected on the second Chartist petition presented to Parliament in 1842. So, what went wrong? The main problem was one of central leadership and direction. The strikers had their own leaders, almost all of whom were Chartists and some, like Richard Pilling (leader of the Ashton weavers) and Alexander Hutchinson (general secretary of the smiths' union and editor of the *Trades Journal*), were socialists. However, although various trade conferences were called during the course of the strike, and despite much meticulous local planning, there was little in the way of central co-ordination given the absence of a nationally organised trade union movement. So why didn't the National Charter Association fill the breach? After all, the strike was for the Charter. The answer is that the Chartist leadership was not only taken by surprise by the strike, but was also divided in its attitude towards it. In general terms it expressed support, especially as time went on. However, expressing support is easy, charting a strategy is much more difficult, especially when it became clear that some of the Chartist leaders including William Hill (editor of the *Northern Star*) and at times Feargus O'Connor (the paper's owner) viewed the strike as an employer-inspired diversion from the fight for the Charter. Given O'Connor's idiosyncratic politics it is not all that surprising that he vacillated. More surprising was Harney's inexplicable outright opposition to the strike in view of his left-wing credentials. In short, the Chartist leadership at this stage was at best incapable of grasping the full significance of this truly momentous display of working-class power, and at worst unable to give it the central direction it so badly needed. Thus it was that by September, after numerous bloody confrontations with the troops and more than 1,500 arrests, the strike was finally broken.

There is little doubt as to the significance with which the strike was viewed by the forces of law and order. It was a critical and unique moment in which both the economic *and* political power of capital was threatened. Lord Abinger, the judge at the mass show trial of those charged with sedition for their participation in the strike, expressed the establishment view succinctly:

> The establishment of the Charter would become an odious tyranny devoted to democratic principles, and elected by persons a vast majority of whom have no property and depend on manual labour... The first thing such an assembly would do would be to aim at the destruction of property.[1]

1   Quoted in M. Jenkins, *The General Strike of 1842* (1980).

The Chartist Land Plan

The defeat of 1842 had very important consequences for the future of Chartism. O'Connor sought to revive it by taking it in a new and, as it turned out, unproductive direction. He turned his back on the temporarily defeated factory workers and instead sought to base Chartism's support on the permanently defeated pre-industrial hand trades like the handloom weavers. Given that the future direction of industrial Britain held little for such workers, O'Connor (echoing William Cobbett almost 30 years earlier) conjured up for them dreams of the past – of a 'golden age' of rural Britain untainted by factories and grimy towns where sturdy peasant proprietors retained their independence. The fact that such an age had never existed did not lessen its romantic appeal and hence the attraction of the proposal to re-create something like it in the form of the Chartist Land Plan's vision of model rural communities. This was a grand scheme of O'Connor's launched in 1843 to which workers were invited to take shares. Its objects, as stated in the *Northern Star*, were

> to purchase land on which to locate its members, in order to demonstrate to the working classes of the kingdom, firstly, the value of the land as a means of making them independent of the grinding capitalist; and, secondly to show them the necessity of securing the speedy enactment of the People's Charter ...

Land was bought and several settlements started on this basis with lots being drawn to determine which of the shareholders would be given a house and a smallholding. The pages of the *Northern Star* bear witness to the enormous effort and energy consumed by this utopian scheme – and all to no avail, since the whole enterprise failed miserably within a few years.

Socialism and Internationalism

Whilst O'Connor was preoccupied with his dreams of peasant proprietorship, the political leadership of Chartism gravitated in an increasingly socialist direction under the influence of Harney.

He was the effective editor of the *Northern Star* from 1843 onwards and exercised even greater control of the paper when its offices moved to London the following year. London at this time was the centre for European revolutionary exiles forced to flee from their own countries in the wake of the failure of the revolutions of 1830 and subsequent imposition of reactionary regimes. Marx and Engels were at the centre of the network of émigrés and Harney not only made their acquaintance and moved in their circle, but in 1845 helped to form the Society of Fraternal Democrats. This was an organisation of representatives of the socialist and workers' movements of European countries aiming to give practical meaning to the principles of proletarian internationalism. It is widely regarded as the forerunner and indeed the prototype of the First International. Harney ensured that its activities, along with reports of the struggles of workers in other countries, received wide coverage in the *Northern Star*.

Thus it was that in the mid 1840s, the leadership of the Chartist movement, whilst not completely united, was increasingly socialist in orientation. Positive though this was, it came too late. The special conditions which had facilitated such wide working-class unity around the Charter were now passing and were only fleetingly resurrected in 1847–48. The new leadership had little appeal to those groups that had already defected, and the Land Plan absorbed the interest of the declining hand trades. Skilled workers, after the defeat of 1842, turned increasingly to trade unionism of a more sectional type. Within the most important and the most militant industry, cotton textiles, the employers had begun to recognise trade unions and to establish a system of collective bargaining. This meant that the best organised and potentially most dangerous section of workers could obtain concessions through legal and peaceable means, provided they mended their ways and divorced themselves from the old traditions. Hence Chartism's support base was much narrower, resting as it now did on unskilled workers and politically advanced artisans and others.

1848

The government had learned much from the working-class upheavals of previous decades and had taken steps to prepare itself for fresh outbursts. This was clearly seen during the third and final revival of Chartism in 1847–48. This revival, coinciding as it did with the international slump of 1847, was given an immense boost by the news of the revolution in France in 1848. The fact that Britain was one of the very few European states whose government remained intact in that year was due in part to its successful mobilisation of troops and special constables (consisting of property owners and even of some better paid skilled workers), which threatened to massacre the huge demonstration massed in Kennington Common, London on 10 April 1848. The demonstrators had planned to march to Westminster to present the third Chartist petition which contained almost two million signatures. In the event, caution and fear (in particular on the part of O'Connor) prevailed. The demonstration was dispersed and a small deputation was sent to parliament instead. The government followed its 'victory' with a wave of repression and mass arrests of Chartist leaders, included among whom was William Cuffay, a black man, the son of a slave. Cuffay was a tailor and had emerged as one of the most prominent leaders of London Chartism. He was the main organiser of the Kennington Common meeting and vehemently opposed the decision to disband it. He was later put on trial for 'levying war against the Queen' and sentenced to transportation for life to Van Diemen's Land (now Tasmania). If historians have failed to acknowledge that a respected Chartist leader was black, contemporary observers did not. *The Times* described him as 'half a "nigger"'. A more sympathetic account in *Reynolds' Political Instructor* said of him that he was 'loved by his own order' and that he was 'a scion of Africa's oppressed race'.

After 1848

Chartism was not defeated in 1848, but it never again became the national mass movement that it had been. This is partly due to bitter internal divisions, which finally resulted in a complete break between the socialists led by Harney and Ernest Jones from O'Connor and his followers, who favoured an alliance with the middle-class National Parliamentary and Financial Reform Association, a body which advocated a ratepayers' franchise. The split was complete by 1850, with the socialists in control. Harney launched a new paper, *The Red Republican*, which stated in its first issue that Chartism had 'progressed from the idea of simple political reform to the idea of social revolution'. In the same year the *Red Republican* carried the first English translation of *The Manifesto of the Communist Party*, written in 1848 in German by Marx and Engels.

However, the internal divisions and government repression are not sufficient reasons to explain the inability of Chartism to sustain itself in the 1850s. The appeal of 'the Charter and something more' (the detailed programme of social reform adopted in 1851) withered on the vine. Mention has already been made of the contracting base of Chartism's support already in evidence in the mid 1840s. The underlying reasons for divisions within the working class, which the temporary revival of Chartism in the year of revolution (1848) was unable to overcome, have to be sought outside the 'subjective' arena of the movement itself. These underlying or 'objective' factors are related to developments within the British economy, which, by the mid nineteenth century, had overcome many of the problems associated with the first phase of industrialisation. These changes will be examined more closely in Chapter 5. For now suffice to say that the great ensuing Victorian prosperity not only cast a rosy glow over the self-made capitalist, but also enabled a section of the working class to bask in the reflected rays. In other words, the material conditions were established whereby skilled male workers could make a reasonable living and even prosper. Hence for them the attraction of Chartism, particularly in its socialist phase, continued to decline in inverse ratio to the attraction of the new-style, more defensive trade unions. These workers no longer had an interest in overthrowing a system that was now capable of rewarding them. The changes they sought were *within* the system, not outside it. The divisions that thus emerged within the working class had a profound impact on the development of the labour movement. In the short term it meant that the decline of Chartism was to be permanent as the conditions passed which give rise to the development of revolutionary class consciousness. It was this developing consciousness which characterised the labour movement in the first half of the nineteenth century and which found its highest expression in Chartism. It was almost 50 years before the working class was to form another political party of its own.

The Role of Women

Although the Charter called for manhood rather than universal suffrage, this did not mean that all Chartists were opposed to women's suffrage, or that women were uninvolved or inactive in the Chartist movement. Quite the opposite is true. Building on the already considerable female involvement in the reform, Owenite and trade union struggles of the previous two decades, women emerged as a considerable force within Chartism as activists, theoreticians and sometimes as leaders. Many female Charter Associations were established after 1840, and such women as Mathilda Roalfe, Mary Ann Walker, Ann Knight, Helen McFarlane, Catherine Barmby and others were well known nationally as speakers, propagandists and organisers. Helen McFarlane produced the first English translation of Marx and Engels' *Communist Manifesto*, the first translation from the original German to appear anywhere in the world. Catherine Barmby and Ann Knight were both socialist feminists. In 1847 Ann Knight, a Chartist leader in Sheffield, published a pamphlet demanding votes for women. This followed a possibly earlier demand for the same right from Catherine Barmby, who, in an undated essay entitled 'The Demand for the Emancipation of Women Politically and Socially', called for the Charter to be amended to include female suffrage and argued that women must be emancipated domestically as well as politically. She called for economic independence and freedom from 'household drudgery'.

In a later article, 'Women's Industrial Independence' (published in 1848 in the *Apostle and Chronicle of the Communist Church*), she prefigured some of the arguments of the twentieth-century women's liberation movement when she demanded 'associative arrangements' to lessen women's enslavement within the home. She also argued, earlier than anyone else, for the necessity of a novel form of consciousness-raising for women in an all-female environment. For this reason, although she herself was an atheist, she proposed that women should be permitted to become priests and thereby, using the power of their office, facilitate the coming together of women to share their common problems and experiences.

The full extent of women's involvement in Chartism is still under-researched and the above account is but a sample of what we already know. Even this fragment is sufficient to illustrate the point that within the radical and socialist tradition of the late eighteenth and first half of the nineteenth centuries, working-class women were at last beginning to find a voice in the public political arena and that this voice forms the foundation of the socialist feminist tradition. It also serves to illustrate the point made earlier, in chapter 2, that there was a direct link between the emergence of such consciousness among working-class women and that of the general level of political class consciousness in the labour movement. The defiant and daring nature of the movement in both its theory and its practice, its willingness to challenge the dominant norms and values of the bourgeoisie and aristocracy, created a space for women to extend this challenge to the usually private and sacrosanct areas of family life and personal relationships. The socialist and radical challenge was all the richer, and more frightening to the establishment, for such an intervention. The decline of Chartism marked the temporary halt to this kind of politics and with it the active participation of women in the labour movement for at least three decades. The recollection of the radical and socialist origins of the labour movement must also acknowledge its feminist tradition. Both are as much part of its legacy as the later labourist alternative.

Bibliography

Ashton, O. and Pickering, P. *Friends of the People: Uneasy Radicals in the Age of the Chartists* (Merlin, 2002)

Briggs, A. (ed.). *Chartist Studies* (Papermac, 1967)

Chadwick, E. *Report on the Sanitary Conditions of the Labouring Population of Great Britain* (Edinburgh University Press, 1965; first published 1842)

Dickens, C. *Hard Times* (Dent, 1907; first published 1854)

Disraeli, B. *Sybil: or the Two Nations* (Oxford University Press, 1956; first published 1845)

Driver, C. *Richard Oastler: A Tory Radical* (Octagon Books, 1970)

Engels, F. *Condition of the Working Class in England in 1844* (Allen & Unwin, 1968; first published 1892)

Gaskell, E. *Mary Barton: A Tale of Manchester Life* (Penguin Books, 1970; first published 1848)

Jenkins, M. *The General Strike of 1842* (Lawrence & Wishart, 1980)

Jones, E. C. and Saville, J. *Ernest Jones, Chartist* (Lawrence & Wishart, 1952)

Schoyen, A. R. *The Chartist Challenge: A Portrait of George Julian Harney* (Heinemann, 1958)

Thompson, D. *The Chartists* (Wildwood, 1984)

Thompson, D. *Outsiders: Class, Gender, and Nation* (Verso, 1993)

Ward, J. T. *The Factory Movement 1830–55* (Macmillan, 1960)

Ward, J. T. (ed.). *Popular Movements c. 1830–1850* (Macmillan, 1970)

Part 2

The Workshop of the World and Beyond, 1850–1920

5

ECONOMIC AND POLITICAL BACKGROUND, 1850–1918

The economic development of Britain from the mid nineteenth century until the end of the First World War falls into two distinct phases, although taken together, their unifying feature is the continued prevalence of unusually high rates of profit. The source of such profit was firmly based on Britain's well-established lead in industrial production. By the 1870s, however, this early lead was being overtaken by other countries, with the consequence that Britain became increasingly reliant on her colonial empire.

The Economy

c. 1850–c. 1873: 'The Great Victorian Boom'

By mid century, having overcome the dislocation associated with being the first country to industrialise, Britain began to reap the benefit of her early lead. By the late 1840s she entered into a second phase of industrialisation, one that was much more broadly based than the first, dominated as it had been by the cotton industry. The construction of the railway network, almost complete by 1847, had stimulated the growth of a huge capital goods industry based on coal, iron and (later) steel and, of course, engineering. The development of various branches of the engineering industry (in this period, machine tools, machinery, locomotive construction, shipbuilding and marine engineering) would not have been possible without the expansion of the capital goods sector. Iron was both the agent and the symbol of mid-nineteenth-century industrialisation. Coal was its source of motive power, used to supply first steam and then gas as the prime generators of the machine age. Together with cotton, these formed Britain's staple industries. Until the 1870s they flourished in a unique period of steady, uninterrupted growth, punctuated only by the two short depressions, in 1857 and 1866.

Alongside textiles, the manufactured goods produced in this second phase found not only an expanding home market, due to a rise in real wages and a continued increase in population, but also lucrative markets overseas, especially in America and later in Europe. By 1850 Britain had acquired a monopoly of world trade – she had literally become 'the workshop of the world'. By 1870 Britain accounted for two-thirds of the world's production of cotton goods and half the world's output of coal and iron. Her dominance of world trade was complemented by a policy of free trade which was officially espoused after 1846, from which date tariff duties on imports and exports were gradually removed. During the 1860s many European countries also removed their tariff duties, thereby allowing Britain access to some of the most profitable markets on the most advantageous terms, since at this stage she had no rival industrial competitors. The fact that America and parts of continental Europe were in the process of industrialising was at this stage a great advantage to Britain since it increased their dependence on the kind of British products essential to their own economic development, machinery in particular. Outside Europe and America the market for British manufactured goods, especially cotton textiles, was extensive and worldwide. In fact, whether they liked it or not, these countries were forced to trade with Britain. The colonies were an obvious case in point, but no country could escape Britain's trading and economic hegemony. Those, like China, that resisted by closing their ports or levying high import duties were forced into submission by war (1840–42) and by gunboat (1856).

Apart from cotton, the staple industries did not require much in the way of technical innovation and labour-saving devices. Coal was mined in the traditional way, but more intensively and extensively than hitherto. The techniques for iron extraction and manufacture had already developed in the first half of the century;

now this period saw their wider application with a great increase in the number of blast furnaces. The major technical innovation of this period was the Bessemer converter (1856) for the production of steel.

Taken as a whole, and in comparison to the previous 50 years, the main industrial changes in these years (and for the rest of the century) are not marked by great technical progress in the forces of production. Rather, the main change is to be found in the scale and extent of industry (mining, manufacturing and building) and in the way such operations were organised and managed. In general, with the exception of engineering, the following trends emerge. First, there was a tendency towards concentration in ownership and an increase in the size of the firm. This happened in engineering, but 20 or so years after cotton, coal and iron. Nonetheless, a surprisingly large number of small employers continued to operate in the capital goods industries, buttressed presumably by the boom conditions. Second, there was a very marked pattern of geographical concentration and local specialisation. Some of this was obvious – mining industries are located where the raw material is found; shipyards are usually sited on the coast, though in Britain the concentration was on Tyneside and Clydeside. The cotton industry demands damp climatic conditions and for this and other reasons had established itself in Lancashire, but within that relatively small area there was further specialisation. Spinning was established in a circle of towns around Manchester, with Bolton specialising in fine yarns, Oldham and Rochdale concentrating on medium and coarse. Weaving was carried out in the North-West, again with different towns specialising – patterned cloths in Nelson and Colne, shirtings and sheetings in Preston, etc. Such specialisation was an inevitable feature of the division of labour characterising mature industrial capitalism. It meant that whole towns were dependent for employment on a single branch of one industry – not a problem when the industry concerned was thriving, but the consequences of a slump were dire.

The third industrial trend was the emergence of more intensive methods of profit-making. The first half of the century had witnessed the almost genocidal tendency of the manufacturers to extend the working day beyond the limits of human endurance in order to maximise their profits. Factory legislation mainly directed at limiting working hours put a brake on such 'extensive' methods. Given the lack of any major new technology, the only way to maintain profitability was to get more productivity over the legislative imperative of a shorting working day and week. This was accomplished by a variety of methods, the most prominent being the speed-up of machinery, tighter labour discipline and the introduction of piecework payment systems.

c. 1873–c. 1896 'The Great Depression'

The boom conditions of the middle years of the nineteenth century could not last indefinitely, if only because the economies of Britain's trading partners were bound to develop to a point at which they no longer required British manufactured goods and were even able to rival her in the production of such goods. Just when precisely this happened and whether we can call the period following the boom years the 'great depression' is still the subject of intense historical debate. Terminology aside, there can be no doubt that first, by the last quarter of the nineteenth century many of Britain's most lucrative markets were closed to her, second, that Britain was facing serious competition from Europe and America, and third, that prices, in the wake of a surfeit of mass production, were falling.

By 1870 the phase of economic liberalism and progressive drive for national identity in continental Europe (denied by the Great Powers' carve-up exemplified by the Vienna Settlement) was over. From a mass of small states, Germany and Italy both completed their unification and the theory and practice of a more chauvinistic kind of nationalism surfaced. (The word 'nationalist' was used for the first time at the end of the nineteenth century.) This, combined with the depression which threatened the newly growing industries of continental Europe, induced almost all of their national governments to impose protective tariffs.

The competition that Britain now faced in manufactured goods was much more serious than contemporaries thought. Certainly, there was a great awareness of the problem at the time as government enquiries and the publication of such books as E. E. Williams' *Made in Germany* (1896) and Frederick Mackenzie's *American Invaders* (1902) clearly showed. It wasn't simply that other countries had, by industrialising, caught up with Britain. The real problem lay in the fact that Britain had been overtaken by them, and no matter how much she increased her production (which she did), she could never make up the lost ground without massive capital investment, now or in the future, because they had industrialised on the basis of newer and superior technology. The great irony was that many of the inventions underlying this new technology were actually pioneered in Britain, but were not used there. The most obvious example was in the iron and steel industry in which Gilchrist and Thomas's development of the 'basic' process for the mass production of steel (1878) was used to revolutionise steel production in France, America and Germany. It could be argued that the causes of Britain's industrial decline lay in her too narrow concentration on her basic industries. But again the major technological inventions for the industries of the future were also British. Faraday's pioneering discoveries could have led to the British, rather than the Germans or Americans, developing the electricity industry. The same story can be told of the chemical industry where the Germans were quick to exploit the British invention (by W. H. Perkin) of synthetic dyes. Hence Britain failed to keep pace on the old ground and did not even try, despite the opportunity, to set foot on the new until well after others had become established.

From the 1870s the general trend of all prices, not just those of manufactured goods, was downwards. Improved communication systems throughout the world and the use of refrigeration stimulated the growth of agricultural production on a vast scale in the Americas and Australasia. Meat and grain were imported cheaply, free of tariffs, with the result that food prices were significantly reduced. This, combined with a series of poor harvests in Britain, had a ruinous effect on agriculture, resulting in a dramatic decline in the area of land under cultivation and the reduction of the agricultural labour force by about a half. The fall in prices of agricultural goods had an adverse effect on the terms of trade for Britain because it meant that her non-European markets had less purchasing power to buy British manufactured exports. In addition, Britain was faced with foreign competition from her new trading rivals in these markets at prices which often undercut her less technologically advanced industries.

1896–1918

By the closing years of the nineteenth century prices had begun to rise again, but the underlying causes of the chronic problems faced by the British economy in the preceding period remained. The tendency was to paper over the cracks with a variety of short- and medium-term expedients. The real solution then as now would have meant a vast amount of capital investment in domestic industry in order both to re-equip the declining and technologically backward basic industries and to set up the newer, science-based industries using the known technology pioneered in Britain. Neither happened in the period before the First World War. Instead, this period saw an accentuation of the trends begun during the depression.

The Empire

Faced with the loss of her markets in Europe and America, Britain became increasingly reliant on her colonial empire. During the boom years and before, British colonies had been exploited for their raw materials; now they were as important as markets for British exports. Their great advantage was that as 'wholly owned' territories they had no say in their own economic destinies. Whereas in the 1850s and 1860s many prominent politicians following the free trade, laissez-faire line of the Colonial Reform Society had argued for a freer relationship between Britain and the Empire, by the last quarter of the nineteenth century their tune had changed. Benjamin Disraeli's attitude mirrors this change precisely. In 1852 he referred in a speech at the Crystal Palace to 'these dammed colonies' being 'millstones round our neck'. This pre-1870 approach was not motivated by a liberal or humanitarian concern for the colonised. It simply reflected the fact that in the absence of serious rivalry from any other Great Power, the objective of the colonial 'reformers' was to incur the minimum possible administrative and military expense without jeopardising Britain's economic domination. Certainly, no colonies were relinquished in this period and any attempt at self-determination was brutally repressed, as in the case of India in 1857. From the 1870s onwards, however, British policy was dominated by the twin imperatives of ever-tighter control of existing colonies and the relentless drive to conquer and annex new ones. She was not alone in this objective – the drive for protected markets propelled other European countries on the same course, leading to the aggressive imperialism which characterised the 1880s onwards. This resulted in many 'small' wars between the colonisers and the colonised and heightened international tension between the colonising 'great' powers (and not so great powers, e.g. Italy, Belgium), culminating in the First World War. Britain, in this field if in no other, maintained her early lead. By 1914 the total of British colonial territory amounted to some 12.7 million square miles in Asia, Africa, the Far and Near East and Europe (i.e. Ireland).

The Export of Capital

However, manufactured goods were not the only British exports to the colonies. More important than this was the export of capital. British capital, like any other, is not necessarily patriotic. It will be invested anywhere or in any activity which yields a high rate of return. In the early period of industrialisation and railway building, the domestic economy provided just such an outlet for the already large capital accumulations of Britain. Later, and until the 1870s, the majority of British capital exports were invested in the newly industrialising economies of continental Europe and America. Due to the growing abundance of supplies of capital in those areas, British capital was forced to find other profitable outlets. Hence capital was exported in vast amounts to other parts of the world, including her own colonies. This typically involved investment in mining, oil, plantations and railways. In 1870 British capital assets abroad were about £700 million; by 1913 this had risen to an astronomical £4,000 million. The highly profitable return on these investments was the most important aspect of Britain's 'invisible' export earnings. Other 'invisibles' including the profits from the carrying trade (the British maritime fleet was the largest in the world and was used by other countries) and her dominant position in world insurance and banking. All of this ensured that the City of London retained its early lead as the world's financial centre, despite Britain's stagnation and loss of leadership in productive manufacturing. However, this financial hegemony also served to mask and perpetuate her industrial stagnation in two ways. First, because her invisible trade distorted what was actually a balance of payments crisis (i.e. the gap between imports and exports), and second, because it drew investment capital away from where it was most needed – in domestic industry.

Further Labour Intensification

So, although the world market was expanding, Britain's share of it was only guaranteed in her own colonies. Elsewhere, Britain had to compete with more efficient producers. She expanded her sales of her traditional manufactured products in her domestic and oversees markets only slowly. The exception to this was in coal exports and the export of machinery – both being products essential to any country's future industrial development. Hence it is no accident that in coal and heavy machine engineering the industrial trends observed during the period of the depression were most accentuated. Given the failure to invest in new technology, the only way to maintain profit and increase productivity to meet growing demand was by a further intensification of labour. Nowhere was this more apparent than in the coal industry, where the crudest and most brutal strategies were adopted, involving attempts to lengthen the hours of work and cut wages (sometimes at the same time). In engineering (and elsewhere) the more sophisticated techniques of 'scientific management' were applied. The turret and capstan lathes had the effect of breaking down the job into minute specialisms, all of which could be timed. This enabled all sorts of payment systems to be introduced, the most common being the premium bonus as an incentive to speed up. The main obstacle to all types of labour intensification, was, of course, the trade union and it is no accident that some of the most bitter industrial battles were fought in these industries during this period.

Other Industries

Any survey of the British economy which concentrated solely on the staple industries will have missed (at least) two crucial points. The first is that these industries, despite their importance in the industrial and trading pattern of Britain, employed at their height less than half the workforce (roughly 40 per cent). Second, because (with the exception of the cotton industry) the workforce in the staple industries was male, the impression would be given that women hardly worked at all. Other industries (like pottery, tailoring, boot- and shoemaking and printing) were based either in small factories or workshops and relied on craft skills with relatively little large-scale mechanisation. This did not mean that machines were not used – for example, power-driven sewing machines in the tailoring trade and monotype and linotype machines in the printing industry were widespread by the end of the century. Other industries employing labour on a large scale remained unmechanised, including the building trade, agriculture and some of the service industries such as retailing and road transport, the latter remaining horse-driven until well into the twentieth century. In fact, even as late as 1914 firms employing fewer than 100 workers were responsible for almost all (roughly 97 per cent) of production.

Women in the Labour Force

Evidence of women's participation rates in the labour force is notoriously unreliable. The main sources are census returns, useful for this purpose only from 1851 onwards. Then as now, official statistics took no account of the fact that women's work patterns differed from those of men owing to the fact that their working lives had to accommodate the contradictions imposed by their domestic roles. Women often worked part-time or on a seasonal basis. But a woman does not cease to be a worker simply because she is forced to work in non-traditional (for men at least) work patterns. The greatest problem of evidence is in the area of married women's work. For both ideological and financial reasons the work of married women was grossly under-recorded, so much so that it throws the official evidence into doubt. The Victorians wanted to maintain the pretence that married women did not work – it upset the conventional morality of the sanctity of family life as the shocking revelations about women in the cotton industry in the first half of the century had shown. However, the very fact of job segregation is a clear indication that women were still needed in the workforce. The only way to overcome the contradiction between the needs of capital and its ideological moralism was by literally and figuratively hiding women's work, particularly the work of married women. The notion of the 'family wage' encouraged even male trade unionists to collude in this duplicity (see Chapter 6). Married women continued of necessity, sometimes for limited periods, to supplement (or even supply) the family income by doing paid work in their own homes, like sewing or taking in other people's washing or child minding. Such homeworking was the most hidden (and possibly fastest growing) area of employment, which then as now was never recorded in the official statistics. In times of unemployment, sickness or death of the 'male breadwinner' such earnings may have been the only way to avoid the workhouse. Women themselves may well have colluded in hiding the fact of their employment either because they, or indeed their husbands, saw it as a mark of shame or because they did not want a visit from the tax collector. A slightly less hidden, but nonetheless unrecorded, aspect of women's employment was their work in the sweated trades or as industrial outworkers or in small, dingy unregulated workshops escaping the notice of the inspectorate and hence of any factory legislation.

So, although the census data show that the percentage of 'economically active' women declined towards the end of the century, this is improbable, especially given the growth in male unemployment even among the better paid workers from the 1870s onwards. The official figures show that between 1871 and 1931 the rate of women legally entitled to work ranged between 27 per cent and 35 per cent. The table below shows the 'industries' in which these (recorded) women worked.

Distribution of Women in Major Occupational Groups in Britain, 1851–1911

	1851	1871	1891	1911
Domestic servants	1,224,419	1,664,195	1,959,195	1,822,169
Textile workers	506,492	519,110	576,536	604,253
Dressmakers, milliners, tailoresses		469,519		
Clerical workers			182,782	
Agricultural workers	70,470	55,687	46,196	19,341

Politics and Ideology

1850–67

Until 1867, when the better-off section of the male working class was enfranchised by the Second Reform Act, the electorate remained very small and the party system (Whig and Tory) retained the character of rival and exclusive interest groups unsure of the precise differences between them. The emergence of 100 or so unattached Peelites (followers of Robert Peel who had broken the ranks of the Tory Party over the Corn Law issue in 1846) added to the fluidity of the party system. Both parties knew that they had to appease the *nouveau riche* industrialists by not rocking the free trade boat and at the same time retain their traditional aristocratic bases. William Gladstone summed it up succinctly in 1858 when the Tories, under Lord Derby, formed a government: 'It would be hard to show the broad differences of public principle between the government and the bench opposite.' Between 1846 and 1867 there were nine governments, very few of them having stable majorities, and so it was safest to concentrate on that which within ruling circles was uncontroversial – foreign policy; that is, the maintenance of British interests abroad.

Great efforts were made in this period to instil in the working class a sense of the Victorian values of thrift, sobriety, hard work and discipline. The Church played an important part in this – as witnessed by the feverish Church of England building programme of the mid 1840s as an antidote to Chartism. Apart from organised religion, the spirit of the attempt to incorporate the working class (or at least the better-off section of it) into the dominant value system is best represented by the work of Samuel Smiles. Smiles' best-known book, *Self-Help: with Illustrations of Character and Conduct*, was published in 1859. It continued to be read throughout the century and by 1900 its sales had exceeded a quarter of a million. It represented and advocated the self-confident spirit and individualism of the self-made men of the industrial age. The book was based on a series of lectures delivered by Smiles to a Leeds mutual improvement society (one of many similar organisations established by better paid, usually skilled, workers for social betterment). The opening sentence of *Self-Help*, 'Heaven helps them who help themselves', was illustrated with examples of the rags-to-riches high achievers of Victorian Britain – men like George Stephenson, James Watt, Josiah Wedgwood, Richard Cobden and countless others. (Examples from history also served to prove Smiles' point – Shakespeare, Copernicus, Titian, Joshua Reynolds, etc.) They all, according to Smiles, came from humble backgrounds, but by dint of hard work and perseverance in the face of adversity they all made their pile. So the message was clear to all working men – don't rock the boat, don't ask the state to help you get on, do it yourself by persistent effort and endeavour. No message could be better suited to an era of economic expansion which allegedly provided great opportunities for all, but at the same time was founded on the unfettered free play of market forces which almost made a virtue of the fittest surviving and the weakest being pushed to the wall. The weakest could neither demand nor expect any help since their predicament was due to their own character deficiencies. (For people in Britain today, there is no difficulty in recognising this message; it has been resurrected, while collectivism has been systematically abolished in favour of the individualism of rediscovered Victorian values, the only difference being that then it was founded on economic progress!)

1867–1906

Both the Tory and Liberal Parties from 1867 were conscious of the need to capture the albeit limited newly enfranchised male working-class vote. The 1867 Reform Act gave the vote to every male adult householder living in a borough constituency and to male lodgers paying at least £10 p.a. for unfurnished rooms. This gave the vote to about 1,500,000 men. It appeared initially that the Liberals had the natural advantage, having masterminded the phenomenon of 'lib-labism'. This was a means by which the Liberals graciously permitted working men to present themselves as parliamentary candidates in predominantly working-class constituencies. Needless to say such an altruistic attempt to slightly modify the class composition of the House of Commons was destined to benefit the Liberal cause, since these candidates stood as Liberals and, if elected, took the Liberal whip. Hence the first 'cloth-cap' Members of Parliament were not Labour men. In fact, the very success of lib-labism was one of the reasons for the great delay in forming an independent, working-class political party. This phenomenon continued when the franchise was extended further in 1884. Essentially, the third Reform Act extended the franchise to the counties on the same terms as those accorded to the boroughs by the 1867 Act.

What of the Tories? If the Liberals seemed to be doing so well in incorporating those workers who had the vote, how do we explain the fact that a Tory government was ever elected again, especially given that they feared that the extension of the county franchise in 1884 would undermine their traditional base of support? In fact, the question is even more pertinent given that the years between 1885 and 1906 witnessed a period of almost uninterrupted Conservative rule (the interruptions were provided by two brief Liberal administrations – one in 1886 and the other from 1892 to 1895), and all at the very time when the electorate had just been massively enlarged (1884).

The strictly political explanation points to an analysis of the great difficulties facing the Liberal Party during this period. This included (among other policy differences) a split in the ranks in 1886 over the question of Home Rule for Ireland which led to a motley breakaway group of Liberal Unionists (i.e. the union with Ireland – nothing to do with trades unionists) led by Joseph Chamberlain, who eventually joined the Conservative Party. (Hence the name change of that party to the one it still holds – the Conservative and Unionist Party.) When the Labour Representation Committee was established in 1900, the old lib-labism was formally ended, and in the longer term, the Liberal revival of 1906 aside, the Liberal Party was virtually extinguished. On the other hand, although the Tories had their differences, especially on the question of the future of free trade, an open rupture was not apparent until 1903. In that year Chamberlain (that great wrecker of parties) formed the Tariff Reform League and blew open the simmering rift within the capitalist class on how best to respond to the crisis-torn British economy. Once again the old battleground of free trade versus protection (now modified by preferential treatment for the Empire) threatened temporarily to split the Conservative Party as it had done in 1846. This division was in part responsible for the Liberal election victory of 1906.

The Tories were far too patrician to foster their own tame cloth-cap MPs. They were nonetheless very well organised in working-class areas. Traditionally, their main base of support had been the counties, but very early on Disraeli realised the importance of securing a base in the boroughs. In the 1870s he had established Working Men's Conservative Associations. Randolph Churchill continued in a similar vein with the foundation of the

Primrose League, although this was more successful in rural areas than among the urban working class. One of the successes of the more democratic appeal of the Tories was to secure a substantial part of the textile workers' vote in Lancashire (the cotton towns especially) and in Yorkshire.

However, an analysis of the working-class vote in purely political terms presupposes great differences of principle between the two main political parties. In fact, none such existed in overall orientation, especially since the post-Gladstonian Liberal Party increasingly identified itself with the dominant imperialist ethos of the age. Both parties were prepared to make concessions to secure the working-class vote by offering social and trade union reform. It would be invidious and hair-splitting to say which party was more generous in this sphere. They were both motivated by the same tactical imperative – to do just enough to secure the vote of the workers whilst at the same time not alienating the men of property.

Racism

So although the extension of the franchise in 1867 and 1884 produced a great sea change in British politics, and in particular a more recognisable party system, the strength of the system was not (and still is not) a matter of party politics alone. In the era of the masses, more subtle forms of social influence and social control emerged. The last quarter of the nineteenth century witnessed a great expansion, formally and informally, of the ideological apparatus of the state which was both prompted and facilitated by the rise in literacy. By 1890 elementary education was free and compulsory for all and thus the use of school geography and history textbooks was seen as an important mechanism for inculcating the dominant ideology, especially that of racial superiority. The following extract from *A History of England*, a standard text book by C. R. L. Fletcher and Rudyard Kipling, in use for many years in elementary schools, shows that such racist ideas were not confined to a few quirky intellectuals. Part of the section on the West Indies reads:

> The prosperity of the West Indies, once our richest possession, has very
> largely declined since slavery was abolished in 1833. There is little market
> for their chief products, and yet a large population, mainly descended from
> slaves imported in previous centuries, or of mixed black and white races, is
> lazy, vicious and incapable of any serious improvement, or of work except
> under compulsion. In such a climate a few bananas will sustain the life
> of a negro quite sufficiently: why should he work to get more than this?
> He is quite happy and quite useless and spends any extra money he has
> upon finery.[1]

This was the era of the birth, or the more wide-scale development,
of the popular press (dominated by the Conservative magnate, Lord
Harmsworth), the propaganda poster, the music hall, the Scout
movement (and other similar youth movements), the working
men's club, cheaper and more popular literature (the novels of
G. A. Henty and Rudyard Kipling) and great national pageants
like Queen Victoria's Diamond Jubilee and Empire Day. The
significance of this expanded mass culture was that it coincided
with the new mass ideology of jingoistic imperialism. Whereas
'self-help' ideology reflected the self-confidence of the booming
mid-Victorian economy, the Empire and its benefits in the form
of social imperialism provided the new unifying antidote to the
emerging socialist consciousness of the 1880s which threatened
to expose the possible class conflict of a declining economy. The
popular culture directed at the masses both reflected and provided
great opportunities to win the workers over to the national, as
opposed to the class, cause. Of course, ideology alone could not
accomplish this; this is why social imperialism was so important.
Social imperialism, a term first used by the Austrian marxist Karl
Renner in 1917, was summed up by Disraeli's famous dictum,
'sanitas et imperium' – by which he meant that the profits from
the Empire could be used in part to finance social reform. It was
recognised that a mass electorate could not be wooed by self-
help alone and that imperial expansion, which of itself demanded
popular support if only to provide soldiers to conquer new

1   C. R. L. Fletcher and R. Kipling, *A History of England* (1911).

colonies and defend existing ones from rival imperialisms, could play a key role in winning votes for either of the two parties if it was linked materially to social betterment. The writings of all the major imperialist statesmen (Chamberlain, Cecil Rhodes, Viscount Milner, to name but a few) all made this connection. The point was made earliest and clearest by the Tories, which may help to account for their ascendancy in the latter part of the nineteenth century.

The ideology of racism had underpinned slavery and hence was not a new phenomenon. In the period of imperialist expansion, however, it was dressed up in a new, pseudo-scientific garb and given popular mass appeal. Hitler was later to draw on the writing of the British white supremacists of this period, men like Benjamin Kidd and Karl Pearson who subverted Darwin's theory of evolution by crudely using his ideas on the 'survival of the fittest' and applying them to the struggle between races. Pearson, whose only objection to socialism was the theory of class struggle, substituted instead the struggle between races as the mechanism of progress. The black races had already lost out in this struggle, having been conquered by the whites, hence proving the racial superiority of the conqueror. Despite the finer points of 'theory' which divided the two men, their central concern, born out of England's declining economic position as a world power, was the question of the national 'struggle for existence', which for them was synonymous with racial superiority. Pearson associated himself with the biologist Francis Galton, a cousin of Charles Darwin and professor of eugenics at London University. Galton discovered the new 'science' of eugenics, the practical application of which could, by means of selective breeding, regulate heredity and produce a (white) super-race, capable of surviving the struggle for existence.[2] Eugenics became an established and virtually unquestioned orthodoxy. It was allied to the prevalent fear that the survival of the imperial super-race was jeopardised by two problems: first, the birth rate, which had fallen steadily,

2   For a full discussion of this, see Bernard Semmel, *Imperialism and Social Reform* (1960).

especially among the middle class, since the 1880s, and second, the 'degenerated' condition of the masses.[3]

1906–20

The arrival of the Labour Party on the political scene (see Chapter 8), the culmination of the long campaign to enfranchise women and the First World War all had profound repercussions, in the long or short term, on the political system. The birth of the Labour Party led ultimately to the demise of the Liberals, despite the latter's stunning election victory of 1906, thereby altering the form, if not the content, of Britain's two-party politics. Meanwhile, the 1906 Liberal government did all it could to head off the Labour challenge with a series of collectivist social reforms, the funding of which led to the great constitutional crisis of 1910–11, resulting in the restriction of the veto power of the House of Lords. By 1918 all adult males over 21 and women over 30 who were householders, or married to householders or graduates were enfranchised. (Women had to wait until 1928 to be enfranchised on the same terms as men.) The war produced a coalition government in 1915 (which included Labour until 1917) under the premiership of David Lloyd George, who managed to retain this position with Conservative support until 1922. Hence the first election in 1918 under the new franchise produced another coalition government, but the Tory participants in it were clear that they called the tune. As Bonar Law, their leader, said of Lloyd George: 'It is not his Liberal friends, it is the Unionist Party which has made him prime minister.'

Ireland

No survey of English politics over the last eight centuries could be complete without mentioning Ireland – England's first and probably last colony. And yet, as with all subjugated nations, it is usually overlooked by constitutional historians, save for the

---

3 This eugenic fear was realised when, in 1899, so many working-class recruits for the Boer War were rejected as medically unfit.

occasional reference to the suppression of a local rising. Ireland, however, unlike the more far-flung reaches of the Empire, forced its way onto the agenda of English politics in the last quarter of the nineteenth century in particular, when the nationalist cause gate-crashed the portals of Westminster and insinuated itself into the very fabric of the parliamentary system. Since the famine of 1845, the Irish economy had been steadily reduced to that of a supplier of livestock for the tables of the English, but by the 1870s even this was threatened by the import of refrigerated meat from South America and Australasia. Constant resistance to forced rural impoverishment was met by savage coercion. Such resistance formed the backbone of the unity of all shades of nationalist opinion, regardless of religious affiliation, which was expressed in the formation of Home Rule movement in the 1870s under the leadership of first Isaac Butt and later Charles Stewart Parnell. Home Rule candidates stood for election to the English House of Commons and their success in returning a fluctuating group of around 60 MPs had a dramatic effect on the English party system in general, but at two moments in particular, 1885 and 1910, the votes of these MPs held the balance between the Liberal and Tory Parties and hence determined the fate of governments. In the nineteenth century this Irish influence resulted not in the victory of the Home Rule cause, but rather in the defeat of the Gladstonian Liberal Party. Gladstone was 'converted' to the idea of Home Rule as the only realistic alternative to the demonstrably unworkable traditional policy of coercion. Gladstone's 'conversion' was as much motivated by pragmatism as idealism since the power of the House of Lords with its safe Tory majority would never have allowed the bill to pass. Nonetheless his *realpolitik* was a miscalculation since the Home Rule bill introduced in 1886 was defeated in the Commons and his party was split. In 1911 Asquith's Liberal government was once again forced to pay the price for Irish support by introducing another Home Rule bill. The possibility that this attempt would be successful, in parliament at least given the now reduced power of the Lords, fuelled the fire of Loyalist opposition based in the northern Irish provinces. Ulster Unionism was based on the interests of the settler, mainly

Protestant, population of the north which by now, linked with English capital, had acquired dominance in the cotton, linen and shipbuilding industries. Unwilling to lose this lucrative base of capital investment, English Tories (and the anti-Home Rule defectors from the Liberal Party), now led by Bonar Law, were prepared to condone and assist the open rebellion of Ulster Loyalists in order to prevent Irish independence. Under the slogan 'Ulster will fight and Ulster will be right', the interests of capital on both sides of the Irish Sea conspired to pervert one of the most sacred and time-honoured principles of the establishment – the rule of law. Were it not for the fact that the establishment itself was engaged in this conspiracy it would have been viewed as treason. But the forces which organised around 'The Covenant' (a document signed by Ulster Protestants as a binding oath pledging resistance to Home Rule) were too powerful to be dealt with as traitors. Apart from the panoply of establishment figures, statesmen and politicians (Viscount Milner, Walter Long, Rudyard Kipling, Edward Elgar and the entire Tory Party) who actively supported the Ulster Unionists, it was clear that the forces of law and order in Ireland did so too. In an act of unpunished mutiny, Brigadier Gough, commander of the British cavalry brigade stationed in Ireland at the Curragh, along with 60 other officers resigned rather than be forced to fight the Covenanters, who had themselves in 1913 organised their own military wing, the Ulster Volunteer Force.

Against this background Asquith capitulated. The Home Rule bill was amended to exclude the province of Ulster, and although in this form it was passed, its implementation was delayed until the end of First World War. The war provided a convenient diversion from the Irish Question, in parliament at least. But in Ireland the struggle continued. The moderation of the parliamentary Nationalist Party (successor to the Home Rule Party) led by John Redmond was challenged in Ireland by an alliance of Republican nationalists, who not only rejected Redmond's support for the British in the First World War, but saw it as Ireland's opportunity to win her own war against the English. The Irish Republican Brotherhood (an alliance of the

Fenians and the Gaelic Republicans) organised their own fighting wing, the Volunteers, to fight against the terrorism launched by the British forces and the Orange Order. This was supplemented by the Socialist Republicans led by James Connolly, whose Citizen Army contained recruits who had to be (where eligible) trade union members. Not content with waiting on the pleasure of the English to deliver Home Rule, the combined Republican forces planned to liberate Ireland by their own efforts and to this end organised the remarkable Irish Rising in Easter week 1916. Although this took the English authorities by surprise, it was, after a brief moment of glory, brutally suppressed and its leaders, including Connolly, were executed. The impact of the Rising had repercussions far beyond the event itself. This was clearly shown in the elections of 1918 when Redmond's party was routed in the polls and the Republican forces, except in Ulster, were triumphantly returned and constituted themselves the governing body of 'the Republic established in Easter Week'. The coalition government in Westminster, which was by now strongly influenced by Unionist diehards like Edward Carson and F. E. Smith, did everything possible to counter this act of rebellion short of recognising the obvious fact of the existence in practice of the Irish Republic. A reign of terror was launched by paramilitary irregulars (the Black and Tans), whilst at the same time the Government of Ireland Act was passed in 1920, which attempted to impose the Home Rule solution of 1914. Such a 'solution' was unacceptable to those who really ruled Ireland and the undeclared war continued between the Irish forces (now organised in the Irish Republican Army) and the Black and Tans. The truce and treaty signed in 1921 gave Ireland Dominion status, apart from the six (not the original nine) counties of Ulster, which could and did choose to be excluded. This compromise, although accepted, found little favour with the Unionists. However, a section of the nationalist Republicans remained bitterly opposed and a civil war ensued in the South between the pro- and anti-treaty factions. Britain had 'solved' the Irish Question at the expense of the Irish people, and although the South (the Free State) did become a republic in 1925, the price paid was high. The civil war had taken its toll, but even greater was the permanent reminder of British and Orange dominance of the economically lucrative North, enshrined by Partition. The legacy of the as yet unfinished struggle for Irish freedom is a devastating fact of political life today.

Bibliography

Ashworth, W. *An Economic History of England* (Methuen, 1960)

Chancellor, V. *History for Their Masters* (Adams & Dart, 1970)

Eliot, G. *Felix Holt* (Penguin Books, 1987; first published 1866, a novel set against the background of the 1867 Reform Act)

Floud, R. *The People and the British Economy, 1830–1914* (Oxford University Press, 1997)

Goldby, J. M. (ed.) *Culture and Society in Britain 1850–1890* (Oxford University Press, 1991)

Hobsbawm, E. J. *The Age of Capital 1848–1975* (Cardinal, 1991)

Jackson, T. A. *Ireland Her Own* (Lawrence & Wishart, 1971)

Kemp, T. *Industrialisation in 19th Century Europe* (Longman, 1985)

Marsden, G. (ed.) *Victorian Values* (Longman, 1990)

Sayers, R. S. *A History of Economic Change in England 1880–1939* (Oxford University Press, 1967)

Semmel, B. *Imperialism and Social Reform* (George Allen & Unwin, 1960)

Thompson, A. *Imperial Britain: The Empire in British Politics, c. 1880–1932* (Longman, 2000)

Young, G. M. *Portrait of an Age: Victorian England* (Oxford University Press, 1989; first published 1936)

6

TRADE UNIONS, POLITICS AND THE LABOUR ARISTOCRACY, 1850–1880

There is little doubt that there was a change in both the orientation and the organisation of the labour movement in the 1850s. The form of these changes was represented by the growth of the Amalgamated Unions (see below), but it would be misleading to see these as a superimposed alien creation. These kinds of union had their roots in the previous period. So, what was new? Is it valid to see the Chartist period as a watershed and the 1850s as labour's turning point?

Apart from the fact that Amalgamated Unions gained in strength and importance, two other factors give this period its distinguishing features. First, the organisational base of the movement was much narrower than hitherto, hence it is as instructive to analyse what kind of workers were left on the outside of the labour movement as it is to look at who was organised by it. Second, we must note the undoubted triumph within the labour movement of a particular kind of ideology, best summarised by the engineers' slogan, 'Defence not Defiance'. The contrast between this and the emerging socialism of the Owenite and Chartist movements before 1850 was very stark.

Put simply, how do we explain the fact the labour movement appeared for at least 20 years to be content to exclude from its ranks the majority of workers (women, the lesser skilled and the lower paid) and to find for itself a niche within the capitalist system, the very system which had once been the object of such hatred? Part of the explanation is to be found in an analysis of the decline of Chartism (see Chapter 4), which was greatly affected by the spectacular growth of the economy in the boom years (see

Chapter 5). But, while this might help to explain the initial shift in orientation and ideology, it cannot explain its long-term success or the mechanism for achieving it.

The Labour Aristocracy

The great prosperity of the mid-Victorian period touched even the 'lower orders', but not all of them. Had capitalism been able to accomplish such a miracle, poverty, unemployment and homelessness would all have been eradicated. In fact, for the vast majority of the working population conditions remained almost as bleak as ever, except perhaps that there was more regularity of employment. However, a section of the working class experienced an appreciable change in terms of a considerable rise in real wages and a vast improvement in living, as well as often in working conditions. Contemporaries like the trade unionist George Potter used the term 'aristocracy' to describe this group of workers, who could be easily distinguished from labourers by their habits of dress, manners and lifestyle. Tom Mann, in his *Memoirs*, describes his comrade John Burns thus: 'He always wore a serge suit, a white shirt, a black tie, and a bowler hat. He looked the engineer all over.' The general use, then and now, of the term 'labour aristocracy' to describe the better-off section of the working class is uncontroversial, although there are differences as to whom the term could be justifiably applied. This aside, the real controversy lies in the theory which makes use of such a category of workers to explain the move away from the more revolutionary traditions of the labour movement associated with the previous period.

So, who were the labour aristocrats? A combination of factors separately or together determined the prosperity of this group of workers. Of overriding importance was the profitability of the particular industry in which they were employed. The most prosperous undertakings were the staple industries (coal, iron and steel, and cotton), together with the building industry, which experienced boom conditions in this period. But that did not mean that all workers in these industries were labour aristocrats. In some cases (e.g. engineering), higher pay was determined by skill (usually achieved after serving an apprenticeship). However, in industries like coal mining and cotton manufacture apprenticeships were rare, but nonetheless there existed discernible groups of higher paid workers. In mining the hewers were the best paid and in cotton it was the adult male spinners. There is no particularly good reason for this other than custom, practice and prejudice in the industries themselves. (Prejudice because it will be remembered that the first cotton spinners in the industrialised mills were women, and very poorly paid.) If we are to find any logic in such payment systems it is probably better explained by the employers' desire for social control, which could be achieved by creating a divided and hierarchical workforce. Given the immense prosperity of these industries in this period, it was now possible to create such hierarchies much more consistently than hitherto through pay differentials. Finally, higher paid workers could be found in industries which were unmechanised and still depended in part on artisan skill. Masons and joiners in the building trade fitted into this category, as did printers. The skilled craftsmen in the luxury or bespoke trades (e.g. tailoring, shoemaking, jewellery) could also be counted in this group. Underlying all this is the stark fact of a blatant sexual division of labour which automatically excluded women workers from the higher earnings league.

Given the absence of a white-collar managerial stratum and also the small-scale nature of many industrial undertakings, it is hardly surprising that groups of privileged workers were receptive to the self-improvement ideas of the Samuel Smiles type (Chapter 5). Social advancement, even to the point of becoming a small master, seemed well within the grasp of any hard-working and thrifty man, provided his passions were not roused by drink or 'dangerous' politics. Thus it was that the economic and social boundaries between the labour aristocrats and their 'betters' were seen by the former as more blurred, with the inevitable consequence that the gulf between the aristocrats and the rest of the working class widened.

It is not possible to say what those who were left behind thought of the new situation, but it was quite clear that the boom years having created for the first time the promise (or maybe just the dream) of upward social mobility had a profound impact on the thinking and lifestyle of the group of favoured workers. In one sense there is nothing particularly remarkable about this – ingrained habits of subservience and deference have always meant that the 'lower orders' tend to ape their betters. The remarkable, though controversial, aspect is the extent to which such attitudes and ideas penetrated the labour movement. This is not to deny their force earlier – it was not the case that one day in 1850 the working class awoke to find that it had become a reactionary mass, whereas the day before it had been revolutionary. However, after 1850, the 'Defence not Defiance' philosophy was the *dominant* trend for the simple reason that it made sense to those who advocated it.

Given the coincidence of the labour aristocracy and the organised labour movement, it would be hard to deny the ideological influence of the former on the latter. Of course, there were periods of militancy during these 20 or so years, just as there were quiet years in the preceding turbulent period. But it is also true that the dominant characteristic of each period was markedly different, despite obvious continuities. It stands to reason that those groups who dominate the movement also dominate its ideas and orientation, and it was undoubtedly the case that the labour aristocracy dominated almost exclusively.

Trade Unionism – the New Model

Although trade unionism revived after the demise of Chartism, it was clear from the start that in important respects it was very different from the trade unionism of the earlier period. Most notably the earlier experiments in general unionism were discontinued, as was its general outlook as expressed in the objective of the GNCTU: 'bringing about a different order of things, in which the really useful and intelligent part of society only shall have the direction of its affairs'. That said, most of the so-called new model unions were re-formations of (usually) already existing craft organisations. For example, the most famous, the Amalgamated Society of Engineers (1851), was a grouping of smaller societies around the largest of the engineering unions, the Journeymen Steam-Engine, Machine Makers and Millwrights Friendly Society, formed in 1826. Many of these older (and now amalgamated or revitalised) unions were already craft-dominated and fairly cautious in that they concentrated more on friendly society benefits than class confrontation. So, are the Webbs correct in their description of the unions formed between 1850 and 1870 as 'new model'?

The 'newness' of trade unionism in this period resides in their contrast with the older societies from which they evolved. These were usually smaller, more local and often impermanent. The new formations were nationally based, highly centralised and much stronger. Their high membership subscription made them richer too, and hence better placed to continue the already established trend of employing full-time officials and offering improved benefits. To this extent, the Amalgamated Society of Engineers did form a model national organisation on which many others were based (for example, the Amalgamated Society of Carpenters and Joiners).

The other novel feature was linked to the more favourable economic circumstances which permitted those more favourably placed workers to engage more productively, through their unions, in forms of collective bargaining which were very rare in the earlier years of industrial capitalism. Negotiation and arbitration gradually came to be accepted practices and were a much more common means of securing improvements in wages and conditions than strike action. The first conciliation and arbitration board, consisting of equal numbers of employers and workers, was established in 1860 for the Nottingham hosiery trade. This found imitators in many other industries and regions. Not that strikes did not take place (for example, the engineers' strike of 1852 and the protracted London builders' strike of 1859–60), but caution was to be exercised in the use of the 'double-edged (strike) weapon' (Applegarth, secretary of the Amalgamated Society of Carpenters and Joiners). William Allen, secretary of the ASE, informed the 1867 Royal Commission on Trade Unions that in his union, 'The Executive Council and the members, generally speaking, are averse to strikes. They think that matters ought to be settled in a different way than coming to strikes or lock-outs.'

Whilst the economy was buoyant and expanding and the provision of key labour (often skilled) was in short supply (owing to union control), a 'different way', in the form of collective bargaining, could be used and yielded rich rewards. The prosperity of the individual enterprise thus came to be seen to be as important to the worker as to the employer. When trade was good and profits high, the well-placed worker expected to share the good fortune. Hence a boilermaker's song of 1872, after expressing sympathy with the risks capital had to run, ended

> So 'tis just and meet
> Labour should co-operate,
> And to help with all their might
> The masters to compete.

Of course, this meant jettisoning the notions of class consciousness in favour of a more sectional and exclusive trade (or at best trade union) consciousness, the former appearing as old-fashioned rhetoric, whereas the latter could, literally and figuratively, deliver the goods.

Finally, the other new feature of trade unionism was the fact that apart from the co-operative movement, it was virtually the only form of working-class organisation. Gone, therefore, was the *independent* political dimension of the labour movement which had so characterised it in its formative years. Apart from some smaller, less centralised and often more militant unions in the North of England, this was the *only* form of trade unionism, whereas in the past it had existed as but one tendency among others. The smaller craft unions, like those of the tailors and shoemakers, whilst not 'new model' in their organisational form, shared a similar ideology. George Potter, editor of the trade union paper *The Beehive*, was the spokesman for these and the northern unions. So, although we know that new model unionism was symbolised by its exclusiveness, being the organisations of the labour aristocracy, the fact is that trade unionism in general did not exist for the vast mass of British workers. Hence it was exclusive in itself and by virtue of its dominance. It was nonetheless very successful in its own terms. In 1850 there were roughly 100,000 trade union members. By 1874 this figure had risen to over one million. Thereafter there was a sharp decline in membership, reflecting the strong associations of this type of trade unionism with Britain's economic fortunes.

Despite the decline in the years of the depression, most of the unions established in this period survived. Indeed, many of the craft-based unions in existence today can trace their history back to the 1850s. Other organisations like the Trades Councils and the Trade Union Congress were also established at this time. The TUC itself had very inauspicious beginnings and its first meeting in 1868, whilst having an historical significance, passed virtually unnoticed at the time. Convened by the Manchester and Salford Trades Council, it was proposed that

> the congress shall assume the character of the annual meetings of the British Association for the Advancement of Science and the Social Science Association, in the transactions of which Societies the artisan class are almost entirely excluded. (circular issued in February 1868 by the Manchester and Salford Trades Council)[1]

In other words, the presumption was that the annual congress should be little more than a debating society dealing with the 'merits and demerits' of 'papers, previously carefully prepared' on a twelve-point list of subjects broadly connected with labour and trade union interests. Other than agreeing to meet annually, no permanent structure or organisation was established after the first congress. Greater cohesion and immediacy were given to these leisurely and somewhat scholarly proceedings by the fear that the government's sudden interest in trade unionism in the 1870s might produce hostile legislation.

Women and Trade Unionism

What happened to the vast mass of workers who were excluded from the unions of the labour aristocracy? Why didn't those

---

1 Reprinted in V. L. Allen, *The Sociology of Industrial Relations* (1971).

workers, the low paid and lesser skilled who gained little or nothing from Britain's prosperity, organise themselves? They, the most exploited, were only divided by a generation from the revolutionary traditions of Chartism, Owenism and early trade unionism. Other than the evidence we have of their misery, through contemporary novels and social surveys, we know next to nothing about this majority group. There were some tentative attempts to organise unskilled labour, including agricultural workers, in the 1870s in the wake of the strike wave inspired by the engineers' fight for a nine-hour day in the North-East. Despite the efforts of the Labour Protection League the only survival of this was the Stevedores Union (which later played a key role in the London dock strike of 1889).

Women workers were a special case. The dominant sexist ideology, punctured slightly in the previous period, now permeated fully the more class-collaborationist mood of the labour movement. Women workers suffered a great defeat. The only trade in which they remained organised in any numbers was weaving. The aim of trade unionism, according to Henry Broadhurst, secretary of the TUC, speaking in 1875, was

> to bring about a condition ... where wives and daughters would be in their proper sphere at home, instead of being dragged into competition for livelihood against the great and strong men of the world.[2]

From this kind of thinking sprang the widespread acceptance of the notion of the 'family wage' to be earned by the male breadwinner. Hence not only was unequal pay accepted as the norm, but women's work was tolerated only if it did not threaten that of men. In any case it was seen as a stigma if a man permitted his wife to work, hence the widespread practice, hardly contested by the unions until the twentieth century, of barring married women from employment altogether. Such attitudes and practices help to explain women's increasing job segregation and the fact that so much female labour was literally hidden (see Chapter 5). It is not surprising, therefore, that the unions of this period

2   TUC Congress Report 1875, p. 14.

demonstrated a studied indifference if not downright hostility to women workers. Any attempts to organise women in this period came from outside the labour movement, often through the work of philanthropic women. The most notable example is the formation in 1874 of the Women's Protective and Provident League (later the Women's Trade Union League). The League, under the leadership of Emma Paterson, fostered the growth of separate associations of women working in such trades as dressmaking, millinery and upholstering. Between 1874 and 1886 over 30 such associations were formed on the same plan, using a model constitution devised by the League. Most of these societies were very small, weak and short lived. They hardly merit the description 'trade union' since their stated aim was to 'to promote an entente cordiale between the labourer, the employer and the consumer'. Strike action was deprecated as 'rash and mistaken' and instead emphasis was placed on friendly society benefits. But such attitudes were derived from the craft unions, so perhaps our judgement should be more even-handed. The difference was that in the women's case their unions were not nearly as successful and the impetus to organise came from the outside. The only matter of real controversy was the League's opposition to protective legislation for women on the grounds that it restricted their choice of employment and earning capacity. Apart from the still topical debate on this question, the lasting achievement of the League was to get the first women delegates to the TUC.

Co-operation and Friendly Societies

In a way, the trade unionism that evolved can be seen, and indeed was seen by the governing class, as part of a legitimate attempt by law-abiding workers to better themselves in the approved self-help tradition. This partly explains the improvements in the legal status of trade unions achieved in the 1870s (see section on 'politics' below).

The development of the co-operative movement provides an even clearer indication of this trend in the labour movement to self-improvement through self-organisation. Co-operation in the first half of the nineteenth century, whilst it took many forms, was essentially political in character in that it was inspired by a vision of a different and better society. Although consumer co-ops existed, this was not the only, nor indeed the dominant trend. In the second half of the century it was. The establishment of the Rochdale Pioneers Equitable Society in 1844 heralded a great expansion of co-operative shops throughout Britain, which followed the Rochdale model of inviting custom by paying dividends on purchases. Later, in 1863 in England and 1868 in Scotland, wholesale societies were established on sound business principles. At one level these developments were a practical and very successful way of encouraging workers' self-improvement by encouraging the saving and investment habit whilst at the same time satisfying material needs in the form of better quality and usually cheaper items of common consumption. However, at another level this movement in its very pragmatism marked a turning away from the 'new moral world' ideals of earlier co-operation. This was reflected in the changed aims and objects of the Rochdale Manufacturing Society, which by 1860 stated: 'the present co-operative movement does not seek to level the inequalities which exist in society as regards wealth', but rather according to Abraham Howarth (president of Pioneers' Society), unites individual talent 'for the mutual benefit of each' through 'a common bond of self-interest'. The spirit of this kind of co-operation was very much in keeping with the spirit of trade unionism in the same period – both were in tune with the spirit of the age.

Closely connected, in fact symbolic of this spirit, was the spectacular growth of friendly societies. The origin of friendly societies goes back much further but their growth in the second half of the nineteenth century reflects the increasing need of an urban population wholly dependent on their own purchasing power unsupported by any form of self-sufficiency to sustain them when they fell on hard times through sickness, old age or unemployment. The lack of any state support whatsoever rendered the friendly society the ideal type of self-help organisation through which the ideal type of thrifty, sober worker could make provision for himself without being a burden to others and avoiding the threat of the hated Poor Law. As a result the ruling classes were quite prepared to look kindly on friendly societies, seeing them for what they were – agents of social accommodation rather than agents of social change. Thus it was that such strangely named organisations (with strange rituals to match), like the Independent Order of Oddfellows, the Loyal Order of Ancient Britons, the Antideluvian Buffaloes, became the fastest growing working-class organisations, far outstripping in membership both trade unions and co-operative societies. By 1872 they could claim around four million members. Of course, it was only the better-paid workers who had the spare cash to invest in such organisations.

Politics

Although no independent working-class political organisation was yet formed or even contemplated, trade unions did exert some political influence in these years. The fluid state of the party system in the mid-Victorian period witnessed the development of middle-class-inspired popular radicalism which cut across class boundaries. The more forward-looking of British capitalists, together with their parliamentary allies, captured progressive sentiment with a new form of internationalism that welcomed the national movements in the Italian and German states. Hostility was shown to the autocratic and semi-feudal governments of the Austrian and Russian Empires. General Haynau, the Austrian 'butcher' of the 1848 Hungarian revolution, was given a rough reception by British workers when he visited Britain in 1850. The Foreign Secretary, Lord Palmerston, having already labelled the Austrians 'the greatest brutes that ever called themselves by the undeserved title of civilised men', now added fuel to the fire by saying of the Haynau incident that the workers should have 'tossed him in a blanket, rolled him in the kennel and sent him home in a cab'.

The fact that most British trade union leaders affiliated their organisations to the First International (1864–72) was little more that a continuation of this already acceptable type of internationalism, born during a period when Britain reckoned she had much to teach a world emerging from feudalism about democracy. When the issue of working-class state power arose as a result of the Paris Commune of 1871, the leaders of Britain's trade unions recoiled in horror and were the first to turn tail, thereby precipitating the downfall of the International.

Sections of the middle class, including prominent 'captains of industry' like the cotton magnate John Bright, favoured the extension of the franchise. They formed the Reform Union for this purpose to campaign for household suffrage and in so doing the more radical and working-class Reform League, which advocated manhood suffrage, was emasculated. Trade unions were quick to exploit the new opportunities presented by the extension of the franchise in 1867 to better paid urban male workers by taking on some of the functions of a parliamentary pressure group. This was exemplified by the formation in 1871 of the TUC's Parliamentary Committee – forerunner of the General Council and successor to the informal grouping of general secretaries of Amalgamated Unions based in London (dubbed the 'Junta' by the Webbs). The very name of this body described its function: to exert pressure on MPs to pass legislation favourable to the functioning of trade unions and collective bargaining. There was ample opportunity in the 1860s and 1870s. A flurry of interest and attention was showered on the trade unions. Two Royal Commissions were established in the space of seven years. The first, in 1867, was to enquire into the trade unions, following the so-called Sheffield 'outrages'; and the second, on Labour Laws, was appointed in 1874. Of the six major pieces of factory/trade union/industrial relations legislation passed as a result, the main consequence was that the status of trade unions, although not their power, was accentuated. The old Master and Servant Law was modified by the Employers and Workmen Act 1875, which meant that not only employers could be sued for breach of contract, but that such an offence was now a civil and not a criminal one. The 1874 Factory Act set a ten-hour limit on the working day (the unions were campaigning for eight). The 1871 Trade Union Act recognised unions as legal entities as corporations and as such they were entitled to protection under the law. (This provided an end to the anomaly revealed by the *Hornby v. Close* case in which it was deemed *not* to be unlawful to abscond with the funds of a union – in this case the boilermakers'.) The question as to whether unions could in practice take effective strike action by picketing the workplace was the subject of much controversy. Interestingly, it was a Liberal government which criminalised picketing (by the Conspiracy and Protection of Property Act 1871) and a Tory government which decriminalised it (by the Criminal Law Amendment Act 1875).

So, had the ruling class been converted to the trade union cause? George Howell, secretary of the TUC Parliamentary Committee, appeared to think so. In 1875 he resigned his post on the grounds that the 'work of emancipation' was now 'full and complete'. Two factors combined to make the ruling class look more favourably on trade unions than they had done at almost any other time (the 1824 repeal excepted). One was that despite their historical paranoia of workers' combinations, they could see that the unions formed after 1850 were quite different from their predecessors and that in some senses they were positively advantageous. The Majority Report of the 1869 Royal Commission expressed it thus:

> the habitual code of sentiment which prevailed between employers and workmen in times when the former were regarded both by law and usage as the governing class is now greatly relaxed, and cannot be revived. A substitute has now been found for it, arising from the feelings of equity, and enlightened self interest, and mutual forbearance, which should exist between contracting parties who can best promote their several chances of advantage by aiding and accommodating each other.

This substitute was trade unionism.

Second, it was clear that the working-class vote was important to both parties and that the Tories were as keen as the Liberals were to use it to their advantage. The phenomenon of lib-labism has already been mentioned (see Chapter 5). It yielded its first results in the 1874 election with the return of a miner, Thomas Burt, as the Liberal MP for Morpeth, and Alexander McDonald (secretary of the National Miners' Association) as the Liberal MP for Stafford. The Tory government that took office under Disraeli after the election saw the danger of working-class Liberalism and hence remedied the defects of Gladstone's trade union legislation. This came as something of a surprise to the TUC, which had declined to give evidence to the 1874 Royal Commission on the grounds that its establishment was a delaying tactic. In fact, the recommendations of the Commission were unhelpful, but the ensuing legislation, which ignored its findings, was not.

So, although lib-labism was a force, the Tory strategy to combat it must have worked, otherwise Liberal governments would have been a permanent fixture. In any case the TUC Parliamentary Committee advised tactical voting at election time by submitting a series of 'test questions' to the candidates seeking their attitudes on current questions of concern to trade unionists. Thus it was that modern trade unionism had discovered that its economic and political interests could be accommodated within the framework of the existing system and that the system was expansive and pragmatic enough to incorporate those interests. In this sense the British labour movement was unique in Europe. In almost every other European country, with the possible exception of Belgium, the development of trade unions was a product of the political activity of the working class, usually in the form of the creation of a socialist party. In Britain the reverse was the case. By the 1880s a strong, although narrowly based trade union movement had been created, the very success of which, in its interdependent harmony with the existing economic and political system, banished all thoughts, let alone practical steps, of political independence. The surprise is that such a situation remained so long after the material conditions to which it had given rise passed. However, by the 1880s there were the stirrings of a challenge. The boom was over and the ensuing depression questioned the complacency of the self-help ideal.

Bibliography

Allen, V. L. *The Sociology of Industrial Relations* (Longman, 1971)

Gray, R. *The Labour Aristocracy in 19th Century Britain* (Macmillan, 1981)

Hobsbawm, E. J. 'The Labour Aristocracy in 19th Century Britain', in *Labouring Men* (Weidenfeld & Nicolson, 1968)

Hobsbawm, E. J. 'Trends in the British Labour Movement since 1850', in *Labouring Men* (Weidenfeld & Nicolson, 1968)

Hutt, A. *British Trade Unionism – A Short History* (Lawrence & Wishart, 1975; first published 1941)

More, C. *Skill and the English Working Class 1970–1914* (Croom Helm, 1980)

Rothstein, T. *From Chartism to Labourism* (Martin Lawrence, 1929)

Simon, B. *Studies in the History of Education* (Lawrence & Wishart, 1964)

7

THE RISE OF A MASS LABOUR MOVEMENT – TRADE UNIONISM, 1880s–1914

The years up to and including the First World War witnessed the rise of a mass labour movement. Trade unionism spread to previously unorganised workers and its initial militancy rocked the complacency of the old leadership. The new mood was inspired by a revival in socialist activity, beginning in the 1880s. This presented a challenge to the dominant reformist ideology of the movement but was not strong enough to displace reformism completely, although it seemed close to doing so, despite the turn in the economic tide. Ultimately, this political challenge was emasculated, leaving the strange British paradox of militant trade unionism with a very weak political voice (apart from small and often sectarian socialist sects) in the form of the Labour Representation Committee (1900). This latter body, which was the forerunner of the Labour Party, was the child of the trade unions, but reflected the reformist ideology of their cautious leaderships. Whereas in much of continental Europe mass marxist/socialist parties were in the vanguard of similar pre-war militant struggles, in Britain not only was the reverse the case, but such a political party barely existed. Hence apart from the socialist groups, and later the Communist Party, the mass movement was left without the kind of political leadership which reflected its growing militancy. This partly explains why syndicalism (see section on syndicalism below), especially in the immediate pre-war years, was such a force.

The trade unions were not the only mass movement. The women's movement, almost unnoticed by the labour movement, had attracted a mass following by the turn of the century. The importance of its early allegiances to the labour movement and its roots among working-class women failed to be fully recognised industrially or politically by the male-dominated labour leadership (with a few notable exceptions). Syndicalism too, despite its socialist inclinations, offered little to women industrially or politically in an era when their main struggle was for the franchise. Thus it was that the opportunities offered by the 'Votes for Women' campaign was lost by the labour movement and hence the Women's Social and Political Union eventually, in 1903, severed its links with organised labour.

So, were these the decades of lost opportunity in which the reactionary and chauvinistic male leaders of the labour movement, desperate to hang on to their power and privilege, squandered the immense revolutionary prospects offered by an increasingly powerful and class-conscious movement of women and men? This may well be a descriptive picture, but it offers no real explanation beyond the 'evil men' approach to history. The fact is that although politics does not obediently follow economics, the ending of Britain's boom, whilst upsetting the Victorian equipoise of the previous period, did not mean that the material conditions for the continued advancement for at least a section of the working class had finally come to an end. This period was one of adjustment rather than breakdown in which the old labour–capital consensus was ultimately renewed.

Imperialism and the Labour Movement

The renewal of the consensus was dependent on a renewal of its supportive ideology. The expansion of the British Empire provided the material basis for this. It helped to maintain low prices, especially of food, at a time of economic adversity, thus preventing a drastic drop in real wages for those who had jobs. By providing protected markets it assisted in the maintenance of high profits in certain traditional export industries (the staples) which had lost their competitive edge elsewhere. Those industries thereby, albeit with difficulty and in an altered form, retained a privileged sector of workers who continued to identify their interests with those of the fortunes of their own firm against 'foreign' encroachment. The increased importance of capital exports to the colonies and elsewhere assisted in the creation of further class divisions as a growing army of white-collar clerical workers mushroomed to staff the finance sector of the economy. Finally, there was some truth in the social imperialist argument that the profits from the Empire could be used to finance social reform in Britain. The real substance of the limited social reforms introduced should not be exaggerated, but for those who were unconvinced by the socialist alternative, they gave continued hope of further improvement within the existing system.

Of equal importance, however, was the fact that imperialist ideology, with its outspoken racist overtones, made skilful use of popular culture (see Chapter 5) and undoubtedly, in an atmosphere of heightened national and racial chauvinism, made it much harder for a comparatively weak socialist movement to gain much ground. Whether or not imperialist and racist ideology penetrated the collective psyche of the labour movement is hard to determine and is the subject of continued debate. It would be difficult to imagine that it had no impact, given its prevalence in every walk of life and the fact that the working class was the special target of the social imperialists, who were quick to spot the dangers of the appeal of socialism at a time when the majority of male workers were enfranchised (1884) and the economy was in the doldrums. The following, oft-quoted statement made in 1895 by Cecil Rhodes illustrates perfectly the concerns of the social imperialists.

I was in the East End of London yesterday and attended a meeting of the unemployed. I listened to the wild speeches which were just a cry for 'bread, bread, bread' and on my way home I pondered over the scene and I became more than ever convinced of the importance of imperialism ... My cherished idea is a solution for the social problem i.e. in order to save the 40,000,000 inhabitants of the United Kingdom from a bloody civil war, we colonial statesmen must acquire new lands to settle the surplus population, to provide new markets for the goods produced by them in factories and mines. The Empire, as I have always said, is a bread and butter question. If you want to avoid civil war, you must become imperialists.[1]

Apart from the anti-imperialist stance taken by some (although by no means all) of the socialist organisations, the attitude of the mainstream labour movement leadership to the Empire was at best silent on the issue and at worst aggressively pro-imperialist. The partition of Africa appeared to escape the notice of the TUC. Its only comment on the enslavement of India was a resolution asking for factory legislation to be introduced in the subcontinent. In 1899 the TUC 'took note' of the Boer War. Its 1901 Congress decided to support the war and in 1902 criticised the government for its 'clumsy handling' of the issue. A surprising array of pro-imperialists appeared as opinion formers on the intellectual left. The non-marxist Fabian Society, formed in 1884 (the 'think-tank' of reformism and later of the Labour right wing), was aggressively pro-imperialist. Its classic text on the subject, *Fabianism and the Empire*, drafted by Bernard Shaw and published in 1900, could have been written by Rhodes or Chamberlain. For the Fabians, the Empire provided the means of accomplishing the social reforms they consistently championed and it led them, not in the direction of labour independence, but rather towards political unity with all those who wanted to promote the 'national interest', as opposed to sectional or class interests. Many of them, like H. G. Wells and Shaw himself, were outspokenly racist and accepted without question the prevalent white supremacist ideology. Hence they were the prime movers behind a project to form a new party of 'National Efficiency'. Ultimately, they contented themselves with regular meetings of the Coefficients, a 'brains trust' formed by the Fabians (notably the Webbs), consisting of leading Liberal and Tory imperialists, to discuss the 'aims and methods of Imperial policy'.

Although it might be suspected that the rarefied middle-class intellectualism of the Fabian Society was hardly representative in thought or deed of the labour movement as a whole, the trend it reflected had far-reaching resonances. It was imperialism,

1   Quoted in V. I. Lenin *Imperialism: the Highest Stage of Capitalism* (1917).

particularly social imperialism, rather than the Fabians which gave credence to the idea of the 'the national interest' and 'the white man's burden'. This was most sharply expressed in times of war and affected even those with more respectable left-wing credentials than the Fabians. In this connection the Boer War and later the First World War were testing grounds and turning points for the politically conscious section of the labour movement. The leader of the Social Democratic Federation, H. M. Hyndman, opposed the Boer War, as did the Independent Labour Party (founded in 1893). However, their grounds for doing so had nothing to do with any recognition of the interests of the indigenous black population. Their pro-Boer sentiment was based on their dislike of 'Rand capitalists', who were frequently referred to as 'financial Jews'. Later, Hyndman and Robert Blatchford, editor of the popular socialist paper *The Clarion*, became ardent supporters of Britain's 'big navy' programme – the policy of increasing naval expenditure to protect the Empire from rival European imperialism. Hyndman's views did not reflect the majority opinion within his own party, but the fact that he, as its leader, articulated them, meant that valuable time and energy were spent waging an internal struggle rather than in conducting an anti-imperialist crusade.

The attitude to imperialism of the majority within the leadership of the British labour movement was not that much worse than the labour movements of other European countries, the main difference being that the wave of tub-thumping, flag-waving chauvinism caught independent labour politics in Britain in its very infancy and gave the older incorporated political tradition a new lease of life. All over Europe there were rifts on the issue, usually dividing hitherto united socialist parties into pro- and anti-marxist groupings, so that by the time of the First World War the scene was set for the breakdown of international class solidarity, expressed in organisational form through the Second International, into national labour movements, all to varying degrees supporting the war efforts of their own country's governments.

New Unionism

It is against this background that political (see Chapter 8) and trade union developments of the years 1880–1914 must be understood. Between 1888 and 1918 trade unions grew at a faster rate than at any time in their history. The estimated membership figure stood at roughly 750,000 at the beginning of the period, rising to 6,500,000 in 1918. This spectacular growth took place in three main periods: 1888–91; 1910–14 during 'the great unrest', a period of extensive strike action largely inspired by syndicalism; and during the war years, 1914–18, which not only continued the militancy of the previous four years but witnessed the development of the shop stewards' movement.

1888–91

Inspired by the successes of the women match workers' strike at the Bryant & May factory in 1888 (known somewhat belittlingly as the match girls' strike),[2] and the gas workers' and dockers' strike of 1889, trade unionism among unskilled, semi-skilled, white-collar and professional workers spread rapidly. The term 'new unionism' is properly applied to this short period. It does not simply refer to the fact that many new unions were formed, but that a new approach to trade unionism permeated both the older and the new organisations. Tom Mann and Ben Tillett criticised

2   This strike was significant not just because it was organised and led by women. In itself this was not unique. Its importance lay in the fact that it took place in one of the notorious 'sweated trades' and that the involvement of 'outsiders' like Annie Besant ensured that it achieved wide publicity. It is perhaps a sign of the tendency to regard women as victims rather than as fighters that the popular historical representation of the strike consists of faded photographs of waif-like women suffering from the occupational disease 'phossy jaw' (the debilitating effect of the phosphorous component of the match tip which eroded the women's facial bones). The Bryant & May factory, in use until the 1970s, still stands today in Bow, East London. Its exterior remains for those who know or care – a stark and gaunt reminder of their suffering and their brief moment of victory. Despite this, save for a small and easily missed plaque, no memorial remains, and the stain of the past is now buried, symbolically, in the building's current use as 'concept dwellings' for the stylish new incomers to today's East End. The noise and smell of the unsanitary factory has presumably been masked by the whir of the jacuzzi, the gentle ripple of the swimming pool and the aroma of the sauna, all of which the residents may enjoy exclusively at their leisure.

the old outlook in a penny pamphlet, 'The New Trades Unionism – a Reply to Mr. George Shipton', published in 1891:

> many of the older unions are very reluctant to engage in a labour struggle, no matter how great the necessity, because they are hemmed in by sick and funeral claims, so that to a large extent they have lost their true characteristic of being fighting organisations ...

Why was it that this outlook was finally challenged at the end of the 1880s? It had been clear since the mid 1870s that 'old unionism' had not been successful even in its own limited terms. Only the very largest and richest unions had been able to withstand the pressures of the depression and the drain on their funds due to unemployment. Many craft unions now fell by the wayside, and of the two mining unions, one was dead and the other moribund. The example of the initially successful, although short-lived attempt to organise agricultural labourers in 1872 may have served to indicate that trying to organise among the unskilled was fruitless, especially at a time when trade unionism for the skilled was beginning to experience difficulties. The key factor in explaining the change in outlook in the 1880s is a political one.

The outlook of old unionism was challenged by class-conscious socialists (see Chapter 8), some of whom, like Tom Mann and John Burns, were already, as ASE members, experienced trade unionists. Indeed, there was a growing left opposition within some of the craft unions which was to have important repercussions later. The strike activity which led to the breakthrough among the unskilled was often led or inspired by socialists. Mann and Burns, both of whom played a key role among the dockers, were members of the Social Democratic Federation, as was Will Thorne, the gas workers' leader. Prominent socialists outside the trade union movement, like Eleanor Marx, Keir Hardie and H. H. Champion, were frequent speakers at mass meetings of trade unionists and also assisted in recruitment drives. The organising principle was that of mass recruitment. Whereas old unionism had relied on the skill and scarcity value of labour, new unionism was dependent on sheer force of numbers for its success. Thus women were welcomed as members from the start, and this accounted for the first recorded real increase in women's trade union membership, from roughly 50,000 in 1888 to about 432,000 in 1913 (however, the gains for women should not be over-emphasised; see section on women below). The central slogan of this forward movement was the demand for an eight-hour working day – a demand of the international labour movement, popularised by the newly formed Second International (1889–1914). The huge May Day 1890 demonstration in favour of the eight-hour day took even its organisers by surprise. So effective was this agitation that it penetrated the bastions of the old unionism; the ASE declared itself in favour in 1889, as did the TUC at its 1890 Congress.

Many of the unions among the unskilled did not survive beyond 1891, although the collapse of some of them was temporary. The irony was that the new unions which survived the 1890s often did so by becoming more like the older unions. They concentrated their efforts on particular groups of workers, rather than spreading themselves generally, and consolidated their gains where they were already strong. During the 1890s the only new unions to be formed and to weather the storm were among white-collar and professional workers. Three unions formed in 1891 are indicative of this trend: the Post Office Workers' Union, the National Amalgamated Union of Shop Assistants and the Postmen's Federation. The National Union of Teachers was formed in 1889.

In fact, the more tangible achievements of the spirit of new unionism were to be found within the older unions. In 1891 Mann came within 1,000 votes of winning the general secretaryship of the ASE, and in 1892 that union began to recruit more widely among less skilled engineers. In 1889, a new, initially more militant miners' union, the Miners Federation of Great Britain, emerged from the collapse of the older societies. It recruited more widely than just among the hewers (the base of the old miners' unions) and declared itself in favour of the eight-hour day from its inception. The Amalgamated Society of Railway Servants abandoned much of its exclusiveness in the 1890s and began to recruit from all grades.

The Employers' Counter-offensive

Part of the reason for the collapse of so many of the newly formed unions was the resistance of the employers, aided by state legislative action. This was the period in which determined efforts were made to counter trade union growth by more effective and coordinated employers' strategies, as witnessed by the formation of employers' associations within, and ultimately across, industries and their widespread adoption of the tactics of the lockout and the use of 'scab' labour. The first of their targets were the new unions. By these means even the biggest of the new unions, the London gas workers and the dockers, were smashed. The job of breaking the older unions was not as easy, but it was even more vital for the employers to do so. Trade union resistance in the staple industries was impeding employers' determination to introduce new working methods and wage-cutting associated with the drive for labour intensification – their preferred strategy, in the absence of capital investment, to ensure the maintenance of their profits in an increasingly competitive world market (see Chapter 5). Thus it was that attempts were made by the employers to reduce wages in the cotton and mining industries in 1893 and to defeat the engineers' struggle for the eight-hour day following the national lockout of 1897. The settlement which ended the cotton spinners' strike and the engineers' lockout resulted in a form of collective bargaining which incorporated the unions' leaderships in an industrial truce which implicitly acknowledged the main objective of the employers – the 'right to manage' at a time of great internal change in their industries. The 1893 Brooklands Agreement in cotton was the prototype. It established a National Procedure Agreement whereby all disputes, whether at a national or local level, had to be referred to a central joint council of the industry (consisting of union and management sides) before strike action was 'permitted'. Other industries (apart from engineering) followed suit – the boot and shoe industry in 1895, the building industry in 1904 and shipbuilding in 1908. This new departure in industrial relations also helps to explain the period of industrial peace between 1888 and 1907.

Thus although the employers had met with determined resistance, the great forward push of trade unionism appeared to have halted. This strengthened the hand of the 'old guard' of union leaders whose outlook had been temporarily challenged but who remained in post despite the militancy of the rank and file. They, having entered into these novel forms of national collective bargaining, were as keen as the employers to see the system work. Furthermore, they took advantage of the lull in militancy to consolidate their own position. The change in the standing orders of the TUC in 1895 symbolised this. The block vote was introduced and Trades Councils were barred from sending delegates to Congress, as were those not working at their trade. This last was a move to bar socialist 'agitators' from attending future Congresses.

The hostility of the employers to trade unionism was reinforced by two infamous legal decisions which challenged the legislative gains made by the respectable leadership in the 1870s. The case of *Lyons v. Wilkins* in 1896, upheld by the High Court and the Court of Appeal in 1897, set a precedent by outlawing even peaceful picketing. In 1901 the Taff Vale judgment, whilst not outlawing strike action directly, enabled the employer, the Taff Vale Railway Company, to sue the union (in this case the Amalgamated Society of Railway Servants) for losses sustained during a strike. The fact that the decision was upheld by the House of Lords, thereby reversing a ruling of the Court of Appeal, indicated that in essence this action, inspired as it was by the Employers' Parliamentary Council, was intended to prevent strike action altogether.

Syndicalism

On the face of it, therefore, it seemed that by the beginning of the twentieth century, trade unionism had achieved very little. The gains of the old leadership had been overturned by the courts and by the vicissitudes of the economy, and the new unions had little to show for themselves with the exception of the continued organisation of white-collar and professional workers. The only new union to be formed during the period of industrial peace was an unlikely but significant one in that it foreshadowed the ideas which inspired 'the great unrest'. This was the as yet tiny Workers' Union formed in 1898 by Tom Mann as a general union along the lines of the old GNCTU. Trade union membership, which stood at just over two million in 1900, actually declined slightly between 1903 and 1906. Thereafter, however, its rise was steady until 1914, with spectacular increases recorded from 1910. This growth was a product of the extraordinary militancy of the pre-war years, which exploded in a huge wave of strike action, dubbed 'the great unrest'. It owed little to the leadership of the industrial and political wings of labour movement; indeed, its very hostility to such leadership, which was condemned as class collaborationist, inspired its alternative, syndicalism. Syndicalism, whilst being the inspiration, was not necessarily the cause of the massive strike wave, rooted as it was in the worsening material conditions of employed workers. Syndicalists were a minority current in the labour movement, but nonetheless offered a simple alternative to the continued employers' offensive – that of direct action in order to regain some form of workers' control over workplace pay and conditions utilising the strategy of the mass strike and rapid trade union recruitment.

At a deeper level syndicalism represented the much grander project of winning, through industrial action, workers' control of the means of production as a whole, thereby consigning capitalism to the dustbin of history. Although within it there were different and cross-fertilising ideological currents, syndicalism was an international phenomenon which took hold in many European countries and in the US during roughly the same period. Whereas in Britain syndicalists operated as a force *within* the existing already strong trade unions, in France, Spain, Italy and the US, they broke away from a much weaker and divided movement to form their own trade union confederations. Small anarchist and socialist political groups, like the Industrial League, the Central Labour College and the Plebs League (the last two both a product of a breakaway from Ruskin College), popularised syndicalist ideas in Britain. However, had it not attracted the support of trade unionists such as Mann, James Connolly and Jim Larkin it is likely that syndicalism would have remained the property of small sects without mass influence. Mann, Connolly and Larkin all learned the syndicalist message in their travels abroad and all three rejected the notion of 'dual unionism' – the establishment of separate syndicalist unions alongside the existing ones. Rather, they sought to change the existing trade unions from within, whilst rejecting the ineffective political forum of parliament and labourist politics. The South Wales Miners Federation gave practical form to syndicalist theory. In the wake of the defeat of the often violent (e.g. Tonypandy) strike movement in the South Wales coalfield of 1910–11, syndicalist miners led by Noah Ablett (a former Ruskin student) set about reconstructing the union along the lines contained in a pamphlet widely discussed by rank-and-file miners and published in 1912 under the title *The Miners' Next Step*. This was the best and most popular expression of the syndicalist tradition. Its opposition to the encrusted and collabo-rationist miners' union leadership was matched only by its class hatred of the mine owners. It advocated a wholesale repudiation of the existing system of conciliation and collective bargaining in favour of rank-and-file control of the union and workers' control of industry. To this end it proclaimed the syndicalist tenet that,

> an industrial vote will affect the lives and happiness of workmen far more than a political vote ... Hence it should be more sought after and its privileges more jealously guarded.[3]

The vacuum created by the absence of political leadership, together with the ineffectiveness of old unionism, meant that syndicalism, with its clarion call to direct action by the rank and file, found a ready response within the conditions of pre-war industrial militancy.

Women, New Unionism and Syndicalism

Despite the fact that the number of women trade unionists had increased by 1914, 90 per cent of all trade unionists were men

---

3   *The Miners' Next Step: Being a Suggested Scheme for the Reorganisation of the Federation*, p. 9. Issued by the Unofficial Reform Committee, Tonypandy, 1912.

and over 90 per cent of women workers remained unorganised. Of the 10 per cent of organised women almost half were members of unions in the textile industry (the only industry in which they had maintained continuous organisation), and a high proportion of the remainder were members of teaching, clerical and shop workers' unions.

Although the periods of growth in women's trade union membership usually coincided with overall union expansion, the unions themselves cannot claim sole credit for organising women workers. As in the previous period, that task fell to women themselves. This time, however, the new unions of the late 1880s actually admitted women members, although they did little to attract them. The open access policy of the new unions and the general militancy giving rise to their creation had an effect on the existing organisations promoting women's trade union membership. The Women's Trade Union League (formerly the Women's Protective and Provident League 1874, renamed the Women's Trade Union and Provident League in 1891) became more militant and abandoned some of the policies of its predecessors. The League supported strikes and encouraged women to join existing trade unions. Far from opposing protective legislation as the WPPL had done, the League campaigned for its extension. Other organisations were formed in this period which championed the cause of working women and campaigned for their unionisation. A member of one of them, Clementina Black of the Women's Industrial Council, moved the first successful equal pay resolution at the 1888 TUC. This was not such a victory for women's rights as it might have seemed. Quite apart from the fact that nothing was done to campaign for it, it was hoped that in the unlikely event of its implementation, women would price themselves out of the labour market, thereby ceasing 'competition for livelihood against the great and strong men of the world' (Henry Broadhurst).

In membership terms, the two most important women's organisations were the Co-operative Women's Guild (formed in 1883, with 67,000 members by 1931 organised in 1,400 branches) and the National Federation of Women Workers, founded in 1906.

The Guilds were very active in the North – their membership was drawn from working-class women. They campaigned to improve the conditions for women at work and at home, as well as being a vital educator and mobiliser in the fight for the vote (see Chapter 8). The National Federation of Women Workers under the leadership of Mary Macarthur probably did more than any other organisation, including the unions, to unionise women, especially during the mass strike wave of 1910–14. The Federation saw strikes as the chief means of unionising unorganised workers. The NFWW was entirely altruistic in that its efforts were purely for the benefit of the unions rather than its own prestige. Although its membership had risen to 20,000 by 1914, its leaders never intended that the NFWW should remain permanently as a women's union. In fact, in 1920 it quietly merged with the General Workers' Union (now the GMB). The Federation also played another role which was seen by some as contrary to the interests of trade unions. It, along with many of the other women's organisations, campaigned to expose the evils of the sweated trades. Their propaganda was very effective and played a major part in inducing the Liberal government to pass the 1909 Trade Boards Act, which was an attempt to fix minimum wages in certain of the most exploitative trades, usually the ones in which women predominated. This was seen by some trade union purists as an attempt to bypass union organisation and rely instead on state regulation. The fact that the unions had ignored such trades for so long presumably meant that the women were supposed to be content with nothing forever. Even those male trade unionists like Will Thorne, whose politics should have taught them better, persisted in writing off such reforms as the work of middle-class do-gooders. Such a hardly justified attitude to the trade board system blinded male activists to the union recruitment side of the NFWW's work, which had in any case been particularly successful in some of the small 'sweated' factories in London, like biscuit-, jam- and pickle-making, bottle washing and a host of others. But for the work of the NFWW such women would have been ignored, even by the more revolutionary syndicalists. Syndicalism, for all its successes in promoting the massive spread of trade unionism in the immediate pre-war years, concerned itself by its very nature with large concentrations of labour in factories and mines, and these tended to be male-dominated. The ideal of industrial unionism leading to workers' control of industry had very little to offer women workers in small workplaces and in industries which were hardly central to the motor of the capitalist system. A strike in a pickle factory, in syndicalist terms, could not be equated with a strike in an industry at the heart of the productive process like mining or engineering.

Thus it was that syndicalism was a mixed blessing. Whilst it captured the mood of and inspired the trade union militants of the pre-war years in a way that the small socialist sects failed to do, its appeal was nonetheless limited to the big industrial battalions from which women were largely excluded. But in any case its total focus on workplace struggles meant an explicit rejection of wider political issues, like the franchise for women. It confused a healthy cynicism of the existing political system, with a disregard for all those who sought to work within it regardless of their political standpoint. The political vacuum created by the left in the labour movement was readily filled by the right wing, thus fuelling the syndicalist prophesy of the corruption of established politics.

Bibliography

Ablett, N. and others. *The Miners' Next Step* (South Wales Miners' Federation, 1912)

Bell, T. *Pioneering Days* (Lawrence & Wishart, 1941)

Holton, B. *British Syndicalism 1900–1914* (Pluto Press, 1976)

Hyman, R. *The Workers Union* (Oxford University Press, 1971)

Lenin, V. I. *Imperialism: the Highest Stage of Capitalism* (Progress, 1968; first published 1917)

Lenin, V. I. *British Labour and British Imperialism* (Lawrence & Wishart, 1969)

Lovell, J. *British Trade Unions 1875–1933* (Macmillan, 1977)

Mann, T. *Memoirs* (MacGibbon & Kee, 1967; first published 1923)

Mann, T. *Social and Economic Writings* (Spokesman, 1988)

Mann, T. (ed.) *The Industrial Syndicalist*, vol. 1, nos. 1–11 (July 1910– May 1911) (Spokesman Books, 1974)

Morris, J. *Women Workers and the Sweated Trades: The Origins of Minimum Wage Legislation* (Gower, 1986)
For histories of women's involvement in trade unions see, for example:

Boston, S. *Women Workers and the Trade Unions* (Davies-Poynter, 1980)
Lewenhak, S. *Women and Trade Unions: An Outline History of Women in the British Trade Union Movement* (Ernest Benn, 1977)
Pinchbeck, I. *Women in Trade Unions* (Virago, 1984; first published 1920)

8

THE RISE OF A MASS LABOUR MOVEMENT – SOCIALIST POLITICS, 1880s–1914

The three decades before the First World War witnessed a socialist revival. Socialism was one of the chief factors in inspiring the trade union expansion and militancy of these years, while the fact of mass industrial struggle undoubtedly increased the appeal of socialism. Hence the stage appeared to be set for a political counterpart to the industrial unrest. Yet the early political promise of socialism remained largely unfulfilled. Aside from the underlying influences of social imperialism (see Chapter 7), British socialism emerged as a peculiarly eclectic and contradictory product of Christian moralism, militant class consciousness, radical individualism, deferential conformity, reformism and marxism. These trends were represented by the plethora of organisations which emerged between the 1880s and 1920, but they could also be found *within* individual organisations. Apart from the Fabian Society, and later the Communist Party, no single organisation could be said to be a pure reflection of any single variety of socialist thought. Hence when it was clear by 1900 that a dominant organisation had emerged in the form of the Labour Representation Committee (known from 1906 as the Labour Party) its only distinctiveness was that it championed parliamentarianism. It did not, as yet, represent a distinct socialist current, it was not even a party in the accepted sense of the term, it was rather a federal organisation – a broad church. However, through it and its successor, the Labour Party, parliamentary socialism stamped its imprint on the entire labour movement.

This was accomplished despite, or possibly because of, doctrinal inertia, which, tempered by the parliamentary obsession, was able to accomplish something unique to Britain – the unification in one organisation of the industrial and political wings of the labour movement. However, although such a merger, achieved as it was during a period of heightened class consciousness, was a potentially revolutionary achievement, this was far from its purpose. Rather, it sought accommodation within the parliamentary system so that through it the best possible deal for the workers could be won. Thus doctrinal inertia, via the medium of parliamentary socialism and by sleight of hand, was converted, almost without knowing it, into reformism.

Marxism

The fact that reformist parliamentary socialism ultimately became the distinguishing political hallmark of the British labour movement (and remains so to this day) would have surprised socialist activists of the 1880s and 1890s for two very different reasons. First, because in the beginning the ideological appeal of marxism was strongly counterposed to reformism; and second, because the attachment of the leadership of the main trade unions to liberalism was opposed altogether to the notion of independent labour representation. When, by 1901, most of the trade union leaders were eventually won round to the idea of an independent workers' party, the resulting compromise produced in the form of the LRC was further evidence to the marxists of the bankruptcy of reformism and induced in them and their rank-and-file militant supporters a distrust, and even hatred, of the whole parliamentary system. Mass extra-parliamentary activity, especially during the syndicalist wave, was posed by the trade union militants against participation in 'bourgeois' parliaments – although the political left was not averse to standing candidates in local and national elections.

Most of the marxist organisations were small in terms of their membership, but they exercised an influence far beyond their numbers. The first such organisation, the Social Democratic

Federation, was not marxist when it was formed as the Democratic Federation in 1881, but rather was a federation of London radical clubs under the leadership of the former Tory stockbroker H. M. Hyndman, which, by 1883, had gravitated to marxism. Hyndman's brand of marxism was, to say the least, peculiar and the SDF was initially very sectarian both in relation to other labour movement organisations and in its own internal squabbles. Nonetheless, the organisation and its immediate successors had a long history and contained within its ranks at one time or another most of the leading trade union and socialist militants of the next 30 or so years. This is all the more surprising given that the SDF leadership was initially opposed to trade unions, having written them off as bastions of a corrupt labour aristocracy. This view was unmodified even during the new unionism of the late 1880s in which leading militants like Mann, Tillett and Burns were, or had been, SDF members. The SDF's initial attitude to strikes was similarly out of keeping with 'the great unrest' of 1910–14. Strikes were viewed as a waste of time in that they induced in workers the unrevolutionary belief that they could really achieve something within capitalism, the wage system of which was fixed against them anyway. The justification for this was based on the unmarxist theory of the 'iron law of wages' propounded by Ferdinand Lasalle and explicitly rejected by Marx himself in the early 1870s. And yet much of the impetus for the wave of strikes came from militants who had learned their socialism from the SDF. Similarly, Hyndman's attachment to nationalism and imperialism owed nothing to marxism and promoted disunity and ideological confusion at a time when the force of the countervailing jingoistic propaganda demanded clarity from those who had always posed as the educators of the workers. Thus for all that was positive in the other aspects of the agitational and educative role of such groups as the SDF and its splinter group, the Socialist League, the opportunities presented to them of a working class awakened to mass struggle was dissipated on the altar of their sectarianism. *Justice*, the journal of the SDF, and to a lesser extent *Commonweal*, the Socialist League's paper (edited by William Morris), conducted valuable propaganda for the socialist cause in general, but did little to lead or even reflect the day-to-day struggle, except in relation to the important campaign against unemployment in the mid 1880s. Overall, their propaganda was concentrated on the political rather than the economic struggle, and in this they did not reject the campaigns to use parliament and local government to win social reforms, such as free school meals, affordable housing and the eight-hour day. In fact, the breakaway groups – first the Socialist League and then the Socialist Labour Party (1903) – were highly critical of the parent organisation for being too willing to use the existing structures to win reforms. The concentration on the political as opposed to the economic struggle was in itself a product of a much older political tradition dating back to Chartist days, witnessed in particular by the failure of the Chartist leadership to recognise the importance of the 1842 general strike. Nonetheless, given the by now well-established position of the trade unions and their changing nature, it is hard to appreciate avowedly marxist organisations falling into the same trap some 50 years later.

The pressure of syndicalist militancy did, however, by 1911 induce the British Socialist Party (as it was then called, having changed its name again from the Social Democratic Party, which the SDF had named itself in 1909) to modify its attitude to trade unions and strikes. The BSP was later to become the main organisation behind the formation of the Communist Party in 1920. Meanwhile much of the fertile ground of mass militancy had been lost to non-marxist organisations – politically, in the form of the Independent Labour Party; and industrially, in the form of syndicalism. Thus it was that although marxism had been an inspirational force ideologically in popularising socialism, it remained, organisationally, outside the mainstream of the labour movement in these years.

The fact that organisations are usually judged by the stance and characters of their leadership often obscures the reality of the contribution and impact made at grass-roots level on the part of the rank and file. In the case of the SDF its ability to attract, albeit for short periods, almost every subsequently well-known socialist owes more to the consistent propaganda and presence of the branches than to Hyndman. Quite simply, before 1893 the SDF was the only place for class-conscious socialist activists. After 1893, when the Independent Labour Party (ILP) was formed, the SDF retained its status as the only organisation in Britain which professed marxism.

Ethical Socialism

The fact that marxist organisations failed to attract a mass following does not indicate that British workers were solely preoccupied with trade unionism and hostile to marxism in particular or to politics in general. The steady growth of the ILP in the North belies such an assumption. It is probably true, although impossible to prove given the peculiarities of British marxism, that the ground was more fertile for the spread of a non-marxist socialist party. After all, the liberal tradition within the working class was by now deeply embedded. Those to the left of this tradition were, like Keir Hardie in the 1880s, 'advanced' radicals. In popularising socialism, the marxist groups impacted on such radical class-conscious workers to the extent that they developed a moral critique of capitalism and an acceptance of the moral values of socialism, but without necessarily accepting marxist theory. The clearest and most popular expression of this was found in the writings of Robert Blatchford whose paper, *The Clarion* (started in 1891), achieved a circulation of upwards of 30,000 and a readership of thousands more. His book *Merrie England* (1893) was probably the most influential volume since Paine's *Rights of Man*.

Paradoxically, such ethical socialism gained the best reception in regions where strike action had been relatively unsuccessful. This is not to say that trade unionism was weak in such areas, but rather that its traditional strength could no longer be relied on to protect the living standards of the working class at a time when they were under sustained attack by the employers. One such area was the West Riding of Yorkshire where male and female textile workers had a long and continuous history of active trade unionism. The American McKinley tariff of 1886 had a disastrous effect on textile exports and the mill owners had resorted to the old methods of wage reduction, coupled with labour intensification, in order to protect their profits. A wave of strikes resulted, the most famous of which, the Manningham Mills strike of 1890–91 in which women workers played an active role, was a last-ditch attempt by the textile unions, now aroused from their torpor, to halt the employers' attack. The fact that the strike, although well organised and well supported by the community as a whole, ultimately failed did more than anything to induce the workers to turn to politics and may thus be one of the main reasons for the spectacular growth of the ILP, which was founded in 1893 in Bradford, the very heart of the industrial struggle. Liberalism was no longer the answer, it was too closely identified with the employers. Class-conscious workers were increasingly receptive to the kind of independent labour politics which gave expression to their concerns both at work and in the community. Of the 305 ILP branches formed in the first year of its existence, 105 were in Yorkshire. Some of the most active organisers promoting the ILP's growth had been, or still were, members of marxist groups. Tom Maguire and Fred Jowett had joined the Socialist League in the 1880s and Tom Mann of the SDF was elected to the secretaryship of the ILP in 1894. Jowett was also a committed Christian, remaining active in the Congregational chapel in Bradford until at least 1892. The connection between nonconformity and socialism has sometimes been exaggerated, but it remains the case that some of the moral tenets of the Christian gospel inspired the socialist pioneers. In fact, much of the language and practice of socialism was borrowed from religion, with socialist churches, socialist Sunday schools and socialist preachers attracting a wide following and helping to boost ILP membership.

The ILP's brand of socialism was non-sectarian in both a practical and an ideological sense. Women and men came to it from marxist, Christian or radical traditions provided they agreed that

the interests of Labour are paramount to, and must take precedence of,
all other interests, and that the advancement of these interests of Labour
must be sought by political and constitutional action.

This declaration of adherence drawn up by the London ILP gives
the real clue to the historical significance of the ILP – it worked
consistently to win the entire labour movement for the simple
and straightforward project of the creation of a political party
of the working class which would stand its own candidates in
elections independent of existing parliamentary parties. Its lack
of doctrinal consistency was an asset in this campaign, but at the
same time it prefigured its outcome in that its achievement involved
a compromise formula in which socialism itself was a casualty.

The Beginnings of Parliamentary Labourism

The uniqueness of the ILP's early success in bridging the gap
between trade unionists and socialists set its course in the direction
of the much more grandiose task of cementing this unity formally
on a national scale in the form of a political party capable of
fighting elections and giving the labour interest a voice in
parliament. This relatively limited objective was hard to achieve
given the trade union leaderships' attachment to Liberalism
and could only be accomplished by an appeal to pragmatism
rather than to idealism. The Taff Vale decision of 1901 was more
important in a practical sense in convincing the trade unions
of the need for a parliamentary voice than countless socialist
exhortations on the bankruptcy of Liberalism. By this date only
the Miners' Federation remained outside the labour coalition (it
eventually affiliated in 1909). A parliamentary voice was all that
was offered by the LRC. Its purpose, as stated at its founding
conference in 1900, was simply 'to establish a distinct labour
group in parliament who shall have their own whips and agree
upon their own policy'. Affiliated organisations would finance
their own candidates but would receive LRC backing. Keir Hardie
of the ILP characterised the 'philosophy' of the new organisation
not as socialism but *labourism*, which he defined as:

theory and practice which accepted the possibility of social change within the existing framework of society; which rejected the revolutionary violence and action implicit in Chartist ideas of physical force; and which increasingly recognised the working of political democracy of the parliamentary variety as the practical means of achieving its own aims and objectives.[1]

Labourism thus became the successor to nineteenth-century lib-labism, but it did not supersede it entirely as the new lib-lab pact of 1903 was to show. This was a secret electoral agreement between Ramsay MacDonald of the LRC and Herbert Gladstone of the Liberal Party whereby the Liberals agreed to stand down in over 30 constituencies in return for Labour support for other Liberal candidates elsewhere and a promise of support for a future Liberal government. Such cautious tactics may seem surprising in view of the ILP's fervent belief in political independence and the fact that three Independent Labour MPs had been returned without Liberal support in the general election of 1892 (Hardie for West Ham; Havelock Ellis, the seamen's leader for Middlesbrough; and John Burns for Battersea). However, a series of election defeats for Labour thereafter, notably in the 1895 general election and a 1901 by-election, followed. This resulted not in an analysis of the jingoistic atmosphere of those years, which made victory for any progressive candidate a near-impossibility, but rather a conviction that three-cornered fights were the essence of the problem. Thus emerged the unself-confident vision of Labour's future prospects in which not only its socialism but also its independence were to be jettisoned for the sake of its parliamentary ambitions. This did not pose a problem for MacDonald, the new secretary of the LRC, whose vision of the Labour Party from the outset was hardly even labourist. His stated aim in 1903 was for

a united democratic party appealing to the people on behalf of a single, comprehensive belief in social reconstruction. The party may not be called Liberal, and will be as far ahead of Liberalism as Liberalism itself was of its predecessor Whiggism.[2]

1   Quoted in D. Coates, *The Labour Party and the Struggle for Socialism* (1975).
2   Quoted in R. Miliband, *Parliamentary Socialism* (1961).

Even though the ILP might not have shared MacDonald's view, it is clear that Hardie at least knew of the Liberal electoral alliance and went along with it. In fact, implicitly the green light was given to such an alliance in 1900 when the objectives of the LRC also stated that it must 'embrace a readiness to co-operate with any party which for the time being may be engaged in promoting legislation in the direct interest of labour'. This 'readiness to co-operate' was responsible for the disaffiliation of the SDF in 1901, leaving the socialist current in the Labour Party even weaker. The euphoria of the electoral success in the 1906 election in which 29 Labour candidates were returned had the effect of confirming MacDonald's strategy. The landslide Liberal victory, which ushered in a period of long-awaited social reform, also served to justify the uncritical support of Labour for the Liberal legislative programme, blinding it to the significance of the remarkable victory of the Independent Labour candidate, Victor Grayson, in a three-cornered by-election without official Labour support in Colne Valley in 1907.

Although in the two elections of 1910 there was an increase in the number of Labour MPs (42 in January, 44 in December), this was largely due to the transfer of miners' votes rather than to a significant electoral upsurge. Again, most of these seats were won as a result of an accommodation with the Liberals. By now, however, there was a much more outspoken criticism from the left of Labour strategy. The so-called 'green manifesto' published in 1910 (officially entitled *Let Us Reform the Labour Party*), condemned Labour for clinging to the coat-tails of Liberalism. But the die was cast, and Labour's parliamentary leaders were already well entrenched enough to weather the storm, especially since their critics offered little in the way of a viable alternative. Had they managed to make common cause with the industrial militants outside parliament and linked the industrial to the political struggle, socialism rather than syndicalism might have been given a new lease of life.

However, the logic of the parliamentary process locked Labour's left wing into its familiar role of being the socialist conscience of a party firmly committed to a one-dimensional strategy. The left was an irritant within this strategy, but was perforce limited by it as well. MacDonald and Philip Snowden published separate pamphlets in 1912 both attacking syndicalism. Working-class industrial militancy was an embarrassment to them – far from seeking to give it a political voice, it had to be condemned for fear of damaging an electoral strategy which was so closely tied to Liberalism. This was the first of many such episodes in which Labour showed itself to be as hostile to mass extra-parliamentary struggle as any Tory or Liberal. This naturally fuelled in the years before the First World War the syndicalist strategy of direct action and workers' control of industry to bring about socialism, bypassing altogether the parliamentary scene.

Reformism

Unlike reformist social democracy in continental Europe, the British strain emerged without the theoretical underpinnings which characterised the sharp ideological battles of the Second International in general, and of the largest of the European workers' parties, the German SDP, in particular. The Fabian Society, formed in 1884, the most 'theoretical' of the non-marxist organisations, distanced itself initially from Labour politics. Although there was a representative of the Fabian Society, E. R. Pease, on the LRC, the Fabians played only a minor role in the fight for Independent Labour representation, preferring instead their policy of permeating the Liberal Party. Once the Labour Party was up and running, the Fabians acknowledged its possibilities and switched their intellectual efforts in its direction. Their theory and practice provided a suitably harmonious counterpoint for Labour's new parliamentary leaders. The Fabians' track-record was fairly impressive. As a predominantly middle-class organisation much of its effort was devoted to scholarly research into all manner of social and political questions, with leading members like Sidney and Beatrice Webb becoming acknowledged 'experts' in their fields. On a practical level it was the proud Fabian boast that they had defeated marxism in London through their assiduous work in nurturing the Liberal–Labour alliance, which had taken control of the newly formed (1888) London County Council. Their 'gas and water' municipal socialism established a tradition of attention to detail at local government level, which its supporters argued brought more tangible benefits to the working class than all the marxist polemic put together. So, although labourism had already emerged on the national scene in a pragmatic way, Fabianism gave it its reformist intellectual underpinnings, freeing its leaders to get on with less cerebral tasks.

Fabianism itself, however, was not immune to intellectual challenges from within. During the 'great unrest', opposition to its non-revolutionary gradualist philosophy emerged. The main rebel was G. D. H. Cole, whose breakaway group of Guild Socialists took with them the Fabian research department and converted it to the Labour Research Department. (The latter still exists to fulfil its original purpose to provide a service for active trade unionists.)

Women, Politics and Socialism

None of the labour or socialist organisations made the enfranchisement of women, or women's rights in general, a campaigning priority. Indeed, the SDF was for a time downright hostile, while the ILP and the Labour Party were late converts. The issue of votes for women had been debated on countless occasions in labour movement forums but it was always sidelined by the device of passing an alternative resolution (usually proposed by Harry Quelch of the SDF) calling for full adult suffrage. Although there were individual men, like Keir Hardie, George Lansbury and Ben Turner (of the woollen workers' union), who saw through this ploy and supported women's suffrage, it was not until 1907 that the ILP was won over and 1912 that the Labour Party finally followed suit. Apart from the outright misogynists like Belfort Bax of the SDF, the argument which united the whole political spectrum of the labour movement in opposition to the demands of the women's movement varied from one of sheer political expediency advanced by the MacDonald tendency to the 'class politics' line of the SDF leadership. The former reckoned that a bill to enfranchise women was simply unachievable and would alienate Labour's Liberal supporters, while the latter argued that the vote for women was undesirable since it would add too many middle-class votes to the electoral register and hence would work in the interest of the bourgeois parties. The fact that neither the Tories nor the Liberals saw it that way and remained hostile to the demand had little effect on the dubious logic of both camps. The fight for the vote was the single demand around which the disparate strands of the women's movement could rally in the late nineteenth century. There had been many separate challenges to women's non-status as citizens throughout the century. The Victorian ideal of passive womanhood had always been a hollow sham for working-class women, but increasingly women from more well-to-do backgrounds were forced to question a society which conferred humanity on them only if they were dependent wives, daughters or sisters. Unmarried or widowed women, whatever their class background, were often forced to live in dire poverty. Opportunities for 'gentlewomen' to obtain paid work outside the home, other than as governesses, were extremely limited. Within marriage, although they had the status of wives, they were owned by their husbands – it was not until 1888 that the Married Women's Property Act allowed women to retain their own property after marriage. Thus it was that the frequently dismissed 'bourgeois' women's movement, whilst not challenging the dominant sexist ideology as a whole, or even seeking to make common cause with 'lower-class' women, did produce pioneers who broke through the wall of male prejudice and hostility against the odds.

Women novelists like Jane Austen (writing secretly and living in poverty in her brother's house) articulated the plight of such women. All her heroines sought marriage because, as she put it in *Pride and Prejudice*, this 'was the one honourable provision for well educated women of small fortune, and, however uncertain of giving happiness, must be their pleasantest preservative from want'. Other writers like the Brontë sisters and Mary Ann Evans (George Eliot) had to adopt male pseudonyms in order to get their works published. Elizabeth Garrett Anderson, Sophia Jex Blake and others had to undergo appalling male hostility, including physical violence, in order to qualify as doctors. Mary Seacole, a black Jamaican, did as much as the more famous Florence Nightingale to establish nursing as a respectable profession for women, contending with both sexism and racism in the attempt. Josephine Butler did more than any male politician to win, in 1886, the repeal of the notorious Contagious Diseases Acts. (These Acts empowered the authorities in naval and military areas to classify any woman as a 'common prostitute' and thereby subject her to a medical examination which, if refused, would result in her imprisonment.) Dorothea Beale and Frances Mary Buss contended with ignorant prejudice in order to establish the propriety of education for girls outside the home, as did Emily Davies and Jemima Clough in winning the right for women to obtain a university education.

Such initiatives, and many more besides, rarely attracted the interest, let alone the support, of the political wing of the labour movement. Assuming, charitably, that the reason for this was more to do with class hostility than male prejudice, no such similar excuse could be found for failing to support the women's suffrage campaign, which by the end of the century had a mass following among working-class women. Indeed, many of its leaders, like Selina Cooper, Ada Nield Chew, Annie Kenney, Hannah Mitchell, Helen Silcock and many others, were well known as socialists and sometimes as trade unionists, besides having the working-class credentials lacking in some of their lofty male socialist opponents. These women, the radical suffragists, had a dramatic impact on the older and more cautious women's suffrage societies, whose aim was to win the vote for women 'as it is, or may be accorded to men'. Instead, they formulated the demand for 'womanhood suffrage' – the vote without a property qualification for all women over the age of 21.

This demand electrified and mobilised women in the Lancashire cotton towns and beyond. They worked through and with a variety of organisations, including local branches of the ILP, the Women's Co-operative Guilds, the North of England Society for Women's Suffrage and Trades Councils, as well as establishing their own – the Lancashire and Cheshire Women Textile and Other Workers' Representation Committee. By the time the Pankhursts formed the Women's Social and Political Union in 1903, they were already latecomers on the scene. In the years before the WSPU moved from Manchester to London in 1906, it too had strong ILP connections. The fact that the labour movement was so slow to respond to the growing mass movement for women's suffrage provided Emmeline and Christabel Pankhurst with the excuse for severing the link, but in doing so they also turned their backs on working-class women. The WSPU achieved its fame precisely because of this. It concentrated its efforts on influential and 'well-placed' women in a less democratic pressure group style of campaigning differing only from the *salon* style of the older middle-class suffrage societies in its less orthodox tactics. Individual acts of arson and terrorism captured the headlines, as did the strong-arm response of the Liberal government. Despite the heroism of such exploits, they alienated and upstaged the mass campaigns of working-class women with which Charlotte Despard of the SDF and Sylvia Pankhurst (incurring the wrath of both her mother and sister) identified themselves. The division within the women's suffrage movement was more about its class orientation than any question of short-term tactics. This was in evidence when Sylvia was expelled from the WSPU in 1914 because of her activities among working-class women in the East End of London. She reported Christabel's comments on this occasion:

> a working women's movement was of no value; working women were the weaker portion of the sex: how could it be otherwise? Their lives were too hard, their education too meagre to equip them for the struggle! Surely it is a mistake to use the weakest for the struggle! We want picked women, the very strongest and most intelligent! ... we want all our women to take instructions and walk in step like an army.[3]

The military metaphors proved to be appropriate – just a few months later these 'intelligent' women were instructed by their high command to ditch the battle for the vote in order to support

3   Sylvia Pankhurst, *The Suffragette Movement* (1931).

the real army fighting the Germans in the 1914–18 war. Happily, the women of 'meagre education' did not respond to this call and the fact that the first instalment of the women's vote was enacted in 1918 is a tribute to their continued mass campaigning before and after the war. The commonly accepted story that the vote was granted as a reward for women's work in support of the war effort is hardly credible, although a convenient explanation for the government climb-down.

As with the government, the conversion of the Labour Party and the ILP owed little to arson and bombs and more to mass and sustained pressure in working-class areas. However, the lateness of the conversion meant that a golden opportunity of linking this mass women's movement with the predominantly male labour movement was dissipated to the ultimate disadvantage of both. In Germany and Russia the socialists had shown an early understanding of the 'woman question' and had, not without opposition, declared their support for equal rights, the women's franchise and for women's self-organisation within the socialist movement. The writings of Lenin, Bebel and Clara Zetkin consistently advocated such policies and were debated within the Second International. International Women's Day (8 March) was celebrated in 1910 by women in 17 countries (Britain was not one of them) on the initiative of the women's section of the Second International to highlight primarily the demand for the vote. So, the British socialist and labour organisations, had they chosen to support women's rights, had ample international examples to follow.

Bibliography

Cole, M. 'Guild Socialism and the Labour Research Department', in A. Briggs and J. Saville (eds). *Essays in Labour History 1886–1923* (Macmillan, 1971)

Collins, H. 'The Marxism of the SDF', in A. Briggs and J. Saville (eds). *Essays in Labour History 1886–1923* (Macmillan, 1971)

Davis, M. *Sylvia Pankhurst: A Life in Radical Politics* (Pluto Press, 1999)

Hobsbawm, E. J. 'The Fabians Reconsidered', in *Labouring Men* (Weidenfeld & Nicolson, 1968)

Levine, P. *Victorian Feminism 1850–1900* (Hutchinson, 1987)

Liddington, J. *The Life and Times of a Respectable Rebel: Selina Cooper 1864–1946* (Virago, 1984)

Liddington, J. and Norris, J. *One Hand Tied Behind Us: The Rise of the Women's Suffrage Movement* (Virago, 1978)

Miliband, R. *Parliamentary Socialism* (Allen & Unwin, 1961)

Mitchell, H. *The Hard Way Up: Autobiography of Hannah Mitchell: Suffragette and Rebel* (Virago, 1977)

Pankhurst, S. *The Suffragette Movement* (Virago, 1977; first published 1931)

Pelling, H. *The Origins of the Labour Party 1880–1900* (Oxford University Press, 1965)

Pierson, S. *Marxism and the Origins of British Socialism* (Cornell University Press, 1973)

Ramelson, M. *The Petticoat Rebellion* (Lawrence & Wishart, 1972)

Strachey, R. *The Cause: A Short History of the Women's Movement in Britain* (Virago, 1978; first published 1928)

Thompson, E. P. 'Homage to Tom Maguire', in A. Briggs and J. Saville (eds). *Essays in Labour History 1886–1923* (Macmillan, 1971)

Thompson, E. P. *William Morris: Romantic to Revolutionary* (Merlin Press, 1977)

Tsuzuki, C. *H. M. Hyndman and British Socialism* (Oxford University Press, 1961)

9

LABOUR, THE SHOP STEWARDS' MOVEMENT AND THE FIRST WORLD WAR

War disrupts society. The First World War was no exception, but far from disrupting the trends within the labour movement it had the effect of stimulating them. The militancy of labour's rank and file continued unabated, whilst the exigencies of war gave labour's leaders the chance to become fully enmeshed within the state apparatus. The gulf between the two widened to such an extent that it was difficult for both to coexist within the same organisations. The 'unofficial' opposition, reflecting the chasm between leaders, generated its own structures in the form of the Shop Stewards' Movement and Workers' Committees. Although no longer unofficial, the shop stewards of today can trace their origins to this period during which rank-and-file workers kept effective trade unionism alive in the face of their leaders' surrender.

The War and the Labour Leadership

The British labour leadership was not alone in capitulating to the nationalist seduction of a war between rival imperialisms. Similar patterns were repeated throughout the European labour movement, with the exception of Russia and Serbia. The resolutions of the Second International in condemning colonialism (1907 Stuttgart Congress) and calling for workers to oppose war (1910 Copenhagen Congress), were soon forgotten in the rush to arms, and the International itself collapsed. British labour leaders maintained an anti-war stance up until the day that the government declared war on Germany – 4 August 1914. Thereafter, their opposition transformed itself not just into support but to wholesale co-operation in the war effort. At the end of August the Labour Party and the TUC declared an 'industrial truce' for the duration of the war and lent their support to an all-party recruitment campaign. The British Socialist Party led by Hyndman supported this position until the leadership was defeated in 1915–16 and replaced by socialist internationalists in 1916. On a primarily ethical basis, the ILP maintained an anti-war policy from the start, even though some of its leading parliamentary members did not. As an ILP member, Ramsay MacDonald surprised his detractors by opposing the war. In consequence he resigned as leader of the Labour Party. He was succeeded by Arthur Henderson. Labour compliance was more than welcomed by a government faced with the problems of wartime production and mass mobilisation of fighting men. As it became clear that the war would not be 'over by Christmas', the government became more dependent on a compliant labour leadership to act as their conduit to the masses. In order to achieve its wartime aims, it was clearly desirable for the state to operate through a process of consent rather than coercion, even if this meant, from the viewpoint of the leaders of organised labour, a hitherto unimagined degree of status in the machinery of government.

Not that coercion was far below the surface as the draconian measures adopted in 1915 showed. Apart from the Defence of the Realm Act by which the government assumed the right to commandeer any factory and its workers it deemed necessary for war work, the Treasury Agreements and the Munitions of War Act were both concluded with explicit Labour and/or trade union support. By May 1915 there were three Labour MPs in the coalition government, and one of them, Arthur Henderson, was in the cabinet. The two Treasury Agreements signed by government and trade union representatives confirmed labour's promise to abandon strike action for the duration of the war. It also drew the unions, including the ASE, whose members were principally affected, into agreeing to suspend 'restrictive practices' in skilled trades by agreeing to the use of unskilled or semi-skilled labour (particularly that of women) in the war industries, a process known as 'dilution'. To press home their advantage, the government rushed through the Munitions of War Act, which made these agreements legally binding, extended their coverage to other industries and introduced the infamous 'leaving certificate'. This was a device whereby a worker could obtain other employment only on production of such a certificate and was clearly aimed at preventing sacked militants from working again. Promises that the government, in return for these massive concessions, would take steps to clamp down on the enhanced opportunities for profiteering were seen as a fair quid pro quo by the labour leadership, although in practice this turned out to be quite meaningless.

Thus was opened, in Lloyd George's phrase, 'a great new chapter in the history of Labour in its relations with the State'. In a way he was correct. As a result of the war, Labour was transformed from a pressure group struggling to gain a foothold in consensus politics into partial incorporation in the state machine – partial in the sense that although the ambition of the leadership was flattered by the role they were now asked to play, that role was very limited. They were never real insiders in that they had no impact whatsoever in the formulation of policy. Rather, they were tolerated as useful brokers in the execution of policies decided by those who really held power. Provided they accepted that and toed the line, which meant not driving too hard a bargain (even though they had more bargaining strength than they realised), the infinitely flexible British state was prepared to confer prestige on them.

The Labour Movement and the War

The Clyde

As it turned out the Labour leadership proved to be singularly ineffective in delivering a compliant labour movement to serve the nation's war effort. Apart from the ILP there was a considerable body of political opposition to the war which generated a host of anti-war organisations. These included the Union of Democratic Control and the No Conscription Fellowship. Socialists played a part in these alongside radicals from the liberal tradition, whose internationalism and pacifism were affronted by the wasteful carnage inflicted in the name of national self-interest. As the war progressed, the lack of war aims, coupled with the blundering stupidity of the military commanders, made it clear that the price of peace was to be paid through mass slaughter. The 'war to end wars' was reduced to the stalemate of the Western Front, the Gallipoli campaign to open an Eastern Front having ended in ignominious disaster. Ever-increasing supplies of cannon fodder in the form (by 1916) of conscripted soldiers were dumped in trenches where they faced near-certain death when they were ordered to go 'over the top' in futile battles to advance the front a few miles.

The most serious threat to the patriotic consensus came, however, from industry. Wartime industrial struggles were not linked directly to the anti-war movement, and there was no equivalent in Britain to the anti-war strikes which took place in continental Europe. The main effect of the strikes in Britain was that they posed a real challenge to the incorporation of labour, which labour's leaders had attempted, so tamely, to deliver. Whether consciously anti-war or not, it was clear from 1915 that industrial workers were not going to be bound by the surrender of their leadership, nor were they to be cowed by the legal strictures against strike action. J. T. Murphy, a prominent shop steward leader in Sheffield and later nationally, put it thus:

> None of the strikes which took place during the course of the war were anti-war strikes. They were frequently led by men such as myself who wanted to stop the war, but that was not the actual motive. Had the question of stopping the war been put to any strikers' meeting it would have been overwhelmingly defeated. The stoppages had a different origin and a different motive. They arose out of a growing conviction that the workers at home were *the custodians of the conditions of labour for those in the armed forces, as well as for themselves.*[1]

---

1   Murphy's emphasis; cited in J. T. Murphy, *New Horizons* (1941), p. 44.

Even anti-war activists like Sylvia Pankhurst had to accept that in the first year of the war at least her organisation, the East London Federation of Suffragettes (ELFS), could not campaign against the war for fear of offending those whose relatives were fighting at the front. A special committee meeting was called 'to consider what we should do now that war has been declared'[2] at which Sylvia Pankhurst posed three alternatives: to go on as if nothing had happened; to make things better for those who were suffering because of the war; or to make political capital out of the situation. The second was the preferred option, although by implication this also entailed the third option as well. In deference to the sensibilities of ELFS members[3] it was thought that not much could be said directly about the war since so many people had relatives involved 'that they will not listen yet'.[4] There is no question as to Sylvia Pankhurst's anti-war position, but she showed a deal of sensitivity in the way she propounded this view, because as she later wrote, she 'felt sorrow in having to tell the relatives of soldiers that the war was in vain'.[5] Hence it was decided to concentrate on the issues of food supplies and prices and the relief of distress, as well as the vote. Furthermore, it was decided that ELFS members should serve on local distress committees, and argued that such members should make 'the fullest possible use of this opportunity to help our East London neighbours especially the women and children at this time of national crisis. Such opportunities of doing important administrative work are seldom open to working women.'[6] However, this position soon changed as it became obvious that the war was a mismanaged military exercise in senseless sacrifice.

The sharpest and earliest expression of the mood of workers' defiance came from the very engineers whose quiescence was so

---

2 6 August 1914, ELFS minute book, PP Amsterdam.
3 Barbara Winslow, in *Sylvia Pankhurst: Sexual Politics and Political Activism* (1996), points out that even doughty activists like Nora Smyth and Jessie Payne supported 'England's cause' initially and that the ELFS lost members and supporters because of Sylvia Pankhurst's well-known pacifism. This situation changed when the full horror of the war became apparent.
4 Ibid.
5 Autobiographical Notes, handwritten unpublished mss 1937, PP Amsterdam.
6 *Woman's Dreadnought*, 29 August 1914.

vital for wartime production. A strike of engineering workers (ASE members) in February 1915 on the Clyde in support of a wage demand of 2d arising from the expiry of a pre-war agreement, had important repercussions. The strike was, of course, unsupported by the ASE leadership and it was, in addition, of dubious legality, occurring as it did in munitions factories. (The blanket ban on strike action was not in force until July when the Munitions of War Act became law.) Aided by the hastily formed Central Withdrawal of Labour Committee, the strike spread rapidly throughout the Clyde.

Signs of mass defiance were not limited to Scotland. In the same year there was a mass strike of 200,000 miners in South Wales which, like the Clydeside engineers' strike, came from a claim arising from the expiry of a pre-war agreement. The vital need for coal in wartime gave this strike special importance and far from using any of the strong-arm powers at his disposal to crush it, Lloyd George went in person to South Wales to negotiate a settlement by which the miners' demands were, in the main, satisfied.

In themselves there seemed nothing to distinguish these strikes in the early years of the war from the normal run of trade dispute on wages and conditions. Apart from the fact that they occurred in the difficult conditions of war hysteria and repressive legislation, they seemed unremarkable. The Clydeside workers were ultimately defeated and the South Wales miners won no more than the deal that miners elsewhere in the country had achieved without strike action. However, on Clydeside the Central Withdrawal of Labour Committee was replaced by a permanent organisation, the Clyde Workers' Committee, whose aims were:

> to obtain an ever increasing control over workshop conditions, to regulate the terms upon which workers shall be employed, and to organise the workers on a class basis and to maintain the class struggle until the overthrow of the wages system, the freedom of the workers and the establishment of industrial democracy have been attained.

This body provided the model for similar organisations in other urban industrial centres. Its language was syndicalist, but its practice was not in the sense that it sought to link the industrial struggle in which it was firmly rooted to wider, community-based campaigns. Hence it transcended the narrower horizons of syndicalism to include women and unorganised workers in a more general *political* onslaught on capitalism. In this way the often limited and defensive demands of the strike movement were given a broader character in that they acted as mobilisers for the working class as a whole. The new structures developed in the factories in the absence of official union backing aided this process. Narrow sectionalism preserved by individual unions crumbled as new, directly elected workplace representatives took the place of the by now immobilised full-time officials. These representatives, the shop stewards, were not in themselves a new creation – they had existed in some unions, particularly the ASE, for some time, mainly to recruit new members and collect union dues. Now, however, their function changed beyond recognition. They not only dealt with the myriad of problems caused by the abandonment of pre-war industrial practices (especially dilution), but represented workers across the craft and union divide, thereby advancing the process of working-class unity. The fact that the Shop Stewards' Movement was particularly strong among the engineers was significant given their key importance in wartime production and that their union, despite its traditional craft exclusiveness, was well established and well organised. The explanation for this is a political one. Socialists in all unions, albeit a tiny minority, were quick to seize on the vacuum left by the abrogation of their union leaders and acquired an influence out of all proportion to their numbers. The shop stewards on the Clyde, even if they were not already socialists, came under the socialist influence of the Clyde Workers' Committee, the body which united them. The influence of the BSP, the SLP and the ILP was very strong in the west of Scotland, although the ILP did not have the industrial influence enjoyed by the other two. John Maclean's (BSP) marxist education classes attracted hundreds of workers. Socialist militants like Willie Gallacher (BSP, chairman of the Clyde Workers' Committee), Arthur MacManus, J. W. Muir (both of the SLP) and others gave practical and theoretical leadership to the growing mass movement in the factories and the wider community where rent strikes were common.

Dilution

However, it soon became evident that the paradox of socialist militants rooted so strongly in the most skilled and craft-conscious section of the workforce was both a strength and a weakness. The issue of dilution posed the great contradiction between craft and class. By 1916 it tested the ability of socialists to give principled but practical leadership, as distinct from revolutionary phrase-mongering, on an issue of immediate concern. The government for its part clearly saw the importance of the dilution question in Scotland, not just for its own sake, but because they saw it as the chief means of breaking the influence of the CWC. The militant craft union approach to dilution would be to oppose it root and branch on the simple grounds that it would break the long-established craft control of the engineering industry which had been won in the teeth of employer opposition. Maintaining such controls in wartime implied great militancy because it meant opposing the state itself as well as the union leadership. But what of the socialists? They had always railed against craft exclusiveness and had sought to broaden the appeal of their union. Now it seemed that the state and their own previously blinkered leadership were on their side. In addition, there was the little acknowledged question of sexism. Could socialists identify with the backward male chauvinist opposition to the entry of women into the engineering industry? These issues had to be faced elsewhere, but the very strength of the socialist base within Scottish engineering and the predominance of that industry (together with shipbuilding) on the Clyde meant that the dilution issue was particularly sharply focused there.

The CWC showed that it was unafraid to tackle the issue head on, but in doing so it revealed at this stage an internal division and an overestimation of its political (although not its industrial) strength. Courageously, both the SLP and BSP factions in the CWC leadership did not oppose dilution *per se*. The majority position was to call on munitions workers to refuse to negotiate its terms and to campaign instead for the nationalisation of the engineering industry under workers' control. Maclean opposed this line because implicit within it was an acceptance of the unpalatable fact that engineers should be more effectively self-organised to do the government's war work. As it turned out, the government strategy of attempting, through their commissioners especially appointed for the purpose, to go over the heads of the CWC directly to the factories to negotiate individual agreements was at least partially successful. The matter was thus taken out of the hands of the CWC as the dilution agreement at Parkhead Forge showed. This left the CWC to fight a rearguard action on less revolutionary terms not of its own choosing. Revolutionary socialism was temporarily defeated, but militant trade unionism was not. Within weeks of the Parkhead agreement, the workers at that factory went on strike over the right of their convenor, David Kirkwood (an ILP member who negotiated the dilution agreement), to walk freely around the different departments of the factory in the course of his trade union work.

It was richly ironic, therefore, that the very factory which proved to be the weakest link in the CWC's chain turned out to be the one that prompted the second wave of strikes on the Clyde. Sensing their advantage, the government used the full force of its repressive powers to deal with the strikers' leaders. Maclean, Gallacher, James Maxton and Muir were jailed, others were deported and the socialist paper, *The Worker*, was suppressed. However, this body blow to the CWC was only temporary and did not prove that either it or its socialist message was defeated because it was too politically advanced and hence out of tune with the sectional interests of defensive, albeit militant, trade unionism, as later events in Scotland, Ireland, Wales and England were to show.

Outside Scotland

'Red Clyde' was in the vanguard of the wartime workers' movement, but mass protests led by revolutionary socialists developed with as much force in other parts of the country. The election of shop stewards and the formation of shop stewards' committees were commonplace in most large factories which had been turned over to wartime production and in Sheffield a workers' committee under the leadership of J. T. Murphy was formed on the model of the CWC. Other industrial centres, among them Manchester, London and later Birmingham, also had workers' committees, but they did not last as long as their Sheffield and Clyde counterparts. In Sheffield, it was not dilution but the introduction of conscription in 1916 and the fear that it would be used as a means of removing industrial militants which prompted the formation of their workers' committee. The SWC attempted to involve women and unskilled workers from the start. Many local strikes in London (at the Woolwich Arsenal), on Tyneside, in Southampton, in the Midlands and elsewhere erupted throughout 1915 and 1916 in munitions factories, with craft workers, particularly engineers, at the forefront. It was not until May 1917 that this localised movement acquired a national character, although not yet an effective national leadership.

Two government decisions of especial concern to skilled workers provoked the May strikes. One was the plan to extend dilution to non-war work; the other was to abolish the Trade Card scheme, which exempted skilled craftsmen from military service. Beginning in Manchester, the strike spread rapidly throughout May to nearly 50 towns throughout Britain. An attempt had been made before the strike to convene a national committee of workers' committees, but this only got off the ground during the strike and hence cannot be said to have really led it. The government, typically, reacted by arresting the strike leaders, but revealed their concern about this mass militancy by appointing a Commission on Labour Unrest. One of the Commission's rec- ommendations was to capitalise on the craft sectionalism which had prompted the May strikes by offering a 12 per cent wage increase to skilled workers. The fact that this divisive tactic was met with a further upsurge of unrest, this time by unskilled and semi-skilled workers, also demanding wage rises, is an indication of a deepening awareness which was doubtless influenced by the revolutionary events in Ireland (the 1916 Easter Rising) and the first Russian Revolution in 1917. So although the May strikes had their origin in craft sectionalism and defensiveness, their outcome was to lay the basis for a nationally coordinated and ultimately broader and more political movement in 1918 and 1919. Without the previous political groundwork and subsequent leadership of the workers' committees such an outcome would not have been possible and the struggle would have exhausted itself in its own whirlwind spontaneity.

Women Workers and the Unofficial Movement

The Clyde workers' committee was reconstructed at the end of 1917. According to Gallacher, the first Russian Revolution 'was one of the most potent factors in the revival'. Significantly, its first action was to call a mass strike in support of the reinstatement of four sacked women workers at Beardmore's factory. The Sheffield workers' committee, having given active support to the non-craft workers' fight for the 12 per cent wage increase, was now clearly established as an all-grades committee. This was an important development since it ensured henceforth that the militant movement broadened from its original base among skilled workers. Furthermore the SWC, although a male-dominated organisation, outspokenly condemned not only craft sectionalism but also sexism. In its founding document written by Murphy, the SWC voiced criticism of the prevailing view whereby seven million women workers were 'tolerated with amused contempt as passengers for the war', and went on to explain that the cheapness of their labour was due to 'man's economic dominance over women which has existed for centuries', and now 'content to treat women as subjects instead of equals, men are ... faced with problems not to their liking'. These attitudes were mirrored elsewhere in the country, where despite the lack of workers' committees, the (by now almost universally recognised) shop stewards' committees sought closer co-operation with unions representing the unskilled, in particular, the Workers' Union, the most militant of them. This meant that for the first time women workers, the subject of so much exploitation and the object of so much suspicion, were drawn into the mainstream of the struggle. Female trade union membership increased by about 160 per cent during the war, but apart from the National Federation of Women Workers, the Workers' Union (WU) was the only union to make a serious commitment to organising women. By 1918 the WU employed 20 full-time women officials and had a female membership of over 80,000. This was more than any other general union and represented a quarter of the WU's own membership. There is little evidence, however, that the demands of women trade unionists, especially for equal pay, were ever placed high on any bargaining agenda during the war. Early on, in 1915, a conference called by the Women's War Workers Committee drew up a comprehensive list of demands, including the rights to training, trade union membership and pay parity. However, when in 1918 the first equal pay strike occurred, it was initiated, led and ultimately won by women. This was the strike of women tramway workers, which started in London before spreading to other towns in the South-East, over the offer of an unequal war bonus. The strike also spread to the London Underground. Mary Macarthur described it as 'a landmark for the women's movement and for trade unionism'.[7]

1918–19

All that was now required was a national leadership and a national focus. The former was achieved, despite an earlier attempt, when in January 1918 a national delegate conference of shop stewards was held in Leeds. This elected a National Administrative Council of the Shop Stewards' and Workers' Committee Movement (NAC). The government provided the national focus in the form of a renewed attempt, temporarily defeated in May, to conscript skilled men engaged in war production. The Military Service Bill, introduced for the purpose, could have proved divisive if the NAC had opposed it on the same grounds that skilled workers had

7   *National News*, 25 August 1918. Gertrude Tuckwell Collection 664d.

objected to it previously. After all, why was it less desirable to send skilled men to be slaughtered in a senseless war? Were their lives of more value than those of unskilled workers? This time, however, in the wake of the Bolshevik victory and Russia's withdrawal from the war, the NAC's opposition to the Military Service Bill took a more general anti-war stance. All further conscription was opposed and the NAC called on the government to follow the Russian lead and sue for peace. The full force of this now open attempt to unite the political and the industrial was not really effective until 1919. With the exception of the Clydeside May Day strikes, despite failed attempts in other parts of the country, there were no other anti-war or anti-conscription strikes in 1918. There are two reasons for this. One was the fact that conscription still remained, despite the NAC's attempts to broaden it, a sectional issue, opposition to which was of greater appeal to skilled workers. Second, that the government embarked on a far more thorough process of victimising militants than it had attempted in 1916. Nonetheless, the widespread political debates which were generated by the NAC's initiative laid the basis for the mass industrial and political action of the following year, even though the NAC, by 1919, was virtually moribund. Although it held two further conferences, one in 1920, the other in 1921, it formally dissolved in the following year.

The war ended in November 1918, but it did not bring peace on the home front. 1919 witnessed the broadest and most serious strike wave yet seen. Thirty-five million working days were lost in strike action – six times as many as in the previous year. This included strikes of those normally relied on to carry out the repressive functions of the state – the police and the armed forces. Miners, transport workers and printers joined those who had been taking action throughout the war. Their mood was influenced by the news of the workers' risings in Germany and Hungary and their strong support for the fledgling Soviet Russia. At the forefront was, once again, the Clyde workers' committee, which organised a mass strike in January 1919, accompanied by mass picketing, for the 40-hour week. Unlike the wartime strikes, this one was not defensive; rather, it was a political offensive against the power of capital. It was all the stronger for its well-established links with discharged soldiers and sailors. (Even before the war ended these latter were organised in the Federation of Discharged Soldiers and Seamen.) Women too were fully involved in the action and on the picket lines. The huge demonstration in George Square, Glasgow resulted in a battle with the forces of law and order, supported by young troops sent there by a panic-stricken government anxious to nip the Bolshevik spirit in the bud. Strike leaders were arrested and Glasgow fell under virtual military occupation. In Belfast too a huge strike wave paralysed the city. However, two fatal weaknesses were revealed in what otherwise appeared to be a revolutionary situation. The first was the lack of any coordinated national leadership, the absence of which enabled the government to pick off individual struggles one by one. The second weakness, linked to the first, was that the kind of leadership that did exist, for example on the Clyde, was not equal to the *political* challenge that the situation demanded. That is not to say that the CWC was not a highly political organisation, but its limitations were inherent in the fact that it remained a loose federation of workplace organisations, which while having a clear line on the daily struggles, had little in the way of a revolutionary perspective beyond a general support for socialist principles. This point was later expressed by Gallacher: 'We were carrying on a strike when we ought to have been making a revolution' (cited in *Revolt on the Clyde*).

The Communist Party

A turning point had been reached by revolutionary industrial militants in 1919. The peculiar British paradox, that of a mass movement without a political voice, and a tiny socialist (as opposed to labourist) movement without the masses, was by now glaringly obvious. Syndicalism had shown itself capable of confronting individual employers, but not able to sustain lasting advances in the face of the full repressive power of the state. The wartime industrial struggles had witnessed the emergence of a much closer unity between some of the hitherto aloof socialist organisations like the SLP and the BSP with the shop stewards, but the special conditions of war, during which the state was forced to make concessions for its own survival, blurred the distinction between industrial and political action. The theories of Marx and Lenin, as well as the practical lessons of the Russian and German revolutions, pointed to the necessity of a united revolutionary socialist party to lead the movement to a more permanent advance in the battle against the capitalist system as a whole. Events in Russia were followed with close interest, and when it became clear that British troops were being used alongside those of other capitalist countries against the revolution, a powerful solidarity movement emerged in the form of the Hands Off Russia Committee. Initiated by left-wing shop stewards, it even won the support of the Labour leadership. Its president, A. A. Purcell, was a member of the TUC's Parliamentary Committee, who must have sat uncomfortably next to such known revolutionaries as Tom Mann and Gallacher. Practical solidarity, following intensive agitation, was shown by East London dockworkers when they refused to load a munitions ship destined for Russia, the *Jolly George*. The threat that Britain might actually declare war against the Soviet Republic resulted in the formation of Councils of Action (over 350 were established in all parts of the country, largely based on trades councils), which pledged, with the support of the TUC and the Labour Party, to mobilise mass strikes should the threat prove real.

In this atmosphere, talk of communist unity became at once more urgent and more realistic. Attempts had been made to unite the disparate socialist parties and factions during the war on the initiative of the BSP, but it was not until after the war that any real headway was made. Earlier attempts (1917) at unity between the BSP and the ILP had failed due to the latter's rejection of marxism as the guiding theory for a new socialist party. It was apparent, therefore, that the minimum condition for participation in the postwar unity talks was an acceptance of marxist theory. Agreement on theory (and *in* theory) proved to be much easier than agreement on strategy and tactics. The talks in 1919 and 1920 revealed deep disagreements on two major questions – whether or not to affiliate to the Labour Party and whether or not to participate in local and parliamentary elections. The intervention, by letter, of Lenin in these debates certainly helped the less sectarian position to triumph, even though it failed to convince some of its supporters, like Sylvia Pankhurst of the Workers' Socialist Federation. By August 1920, the Communist Party of Great Britain had come into existence. It was, and for many years remained, tiny. Its influence, however, was immeasurably greater than the sum total of its membership. From the very beginning it had within its ranks the leading industrial militants who had led the massive pre-war strikes and who had formed the core of the Shop Stewards' Movement during the war. To these were added, either in 1920 or later, individuals and small groups who had either been 'converted' to marxism or induced to jettison pure syndicalism because of the war and the Russian Revolution. The South Wales Socialist Society, a descendant of the pre-war Miners' Reform Movement, and some of the Guild Socialists (like Robin Page Arnot, Ellen Wilkinson and Walter Holmes) fell into this latter category. A left-wing group within the ILP, including such individuals as Shapurji Saklatvala, R. Palme Dutt, Emile Burns and Helen Crawfurd, may be counted among the former.

It would be wrong to make any false claims about the significance of the formation of the Communist Party in 1920 given the stranglehold of the by now well-entrenched reformist and labourist traditions in Britain. Such traditions, nurtured and abetted by social imperialism, had deprived marxism of a mass following. Equally, however, it would be wrong to deny the importance of the Communist Party's existence. For at least 60 years it was the only significant marxist organisation in Britain providing a focus for the activities of the left, both politically and industrially. As such it was a force with which the ruling class and the right-wing Labour leadership had constantly to reckon.

Bibliography

Foster, J. 'Strike Action and Working Class Politics on Clydeside, 1914–1919', *International Review of Social History*, vol. XXXV (1990)

Gallacher, W. *Revolt on the Clyde* (Lawrence & Wishart, 1978)

Hinton, J. *The First Shop Stewards' Movement* (Allen & Unwin, 1973)

Klugmann, J. *History of the Communist Party of Great Britain*, vol. 1 (Lawrence & Wishart, 1969)

Murphy, J. T. *The Workers' Committee: An Outline of its Principles and Organisation* (Sheffield Workers' Committee, 1917)

Murphy, J. T. *New Horizons* (Bodley Head, 1941)

Rosenberg, C. *1919: Britain on the Brink of Revolution* (Bookmarks, 1987)

Rothstein, A. *British Foreign Policy and its Critics, 1830–1950* (Lawrence & Wishart, 1969)

Stewart, B. *Breaking the Fetters* (Lawrence & Wishart, 1967)

Winslow, B. *Sylvia Pankhurst: Sexual Politics and Political Activism* (UCL, 1996)

Part 3

Readjustment

10
ECONOMIC AND POLITICAL BACKGROUND, 1920–1951

The First World War and the temporary postwar boom had the inevitable effect of camouflaging the underlying chronic economic problems associated with Britain's loss of status as a prime manufacturing power. The inter-war years brought these difficulties, with their attendant social effects, to the surface once again, in a political climate that was far less stable nationally and internationally than it had been during the latter part of the nineteenth century.

This was a period of readjustment, economically and politically. The growing internationalisation of capital meant that Britain, as a debtor nation, could not fully control her own economic decisions. A new tension emerged between the interests of finance and industrial capital. Politically, an adjustment was necessary in the era of the mass franchise (universal after 1928) to accommodate a new, two-party system brought about by the decline of the Liberal Party and its replacement by Labour as the main opposition to the Conservatives. The international tensions caused by the rise of Fascism in the 1930s meant that national politics too was played out in the context of a world stage, which ultimately led to world conflagration in the form of the Second World War. The aftermath of the war presented an altered world balance, in which socialism, no longer confined to the Soviet Union, was seen by the capitalist world as the main enemy, both at home and abroad. The resultant Cold War was the backdrop against which the labour movement had to operate by the mid twentieth century and beyond.

The Economy

The Staple Industries

The decline in Britain's staple industries (noted in Chapter 5) was, after the war, an irreversible fact. The boost they had received under the impetus of the demand for munitions and uniforms during the war evaporated once the war was over. Coal, heavy engineering, shipbuilding, iron and steel, and textiles, the original foundations of Britain's industrial supremacy, but already challenged by foreign competitors after 1870, paid the price for failure to respond adequately to this earlier challenge, which was now compounded by the loss of export markets to old rivals and new ones in the form of Japan and the United States. Britain's return to the gold standard in 1925, with a currency that was overvalued, had a further detrimental effect on the competitive position of her exports in the world market. The inter-war period witnessed the inevitable results of this deep economic decline. It meant that although most industrialised countries suffered as a result of the world depression after 1921, Britain was in the worst possible position to recover. Even in comparison with Germany, the vanquished power which had lost all her colonies, some of her own industrial territory and much else besides, Britain's economy, with all the built-in advantages of her greatly expanded Empire (having been one of the main beneficiaries of the postwar share-out of the colonies of defeated nations), lagged sadly behind.

The continuing decline of the staple industries was in part responsible for the persistently high unemployment rates of the 1920s and 1930s. Despite the fact that new industries began to develop, they were located mainly in the Midlands and southern England, and did not compensate for, much less solve the problems of, the declining industries. A new phenomenon, that of the 'distressed areas', emerged as a characteristic feature of the inter-war years. Such areas, located in South Wales, the Central Belt of Scotland, Lancashire, Tyneside and West Yorkshire – the old industrial heartlands – remained impervious to faint-hearted attempts by successive governments to resolve their social problems. These were due, above all, to the absence of any concerted attempt by capital or the state to deal with the underlying economic causes of their plight. Unemployment in the distressed areas never fell below one million throughout the 1920s, but the 'Great Crash' at the end of the decade produced a prolonged slump in industry as a whole with even higher rates of unemployment in the 1930s. By 1932, 20 per cent of the employable population was out of work, and although the end of the year witnessed an economic recovery lasting for about five years, the staple industries only marginally benefited from it. Unemployment in the distressed areas remained at shockingly high levels of between 40 and 60 per cent and had even risen to 80 per cent in some of the worst blighted regions.

The End of Laissez-Faire

The war had seen, for the first time in the history of industrial capitalism in Britain, the abandonment of laissez-faire economics, as the state interfered in, regulated and commandeered those aspects of industrial production most vital to the war effort. Such controls were speedily relinquished after the war in the rush to resume traditional economic orthodoxy. But the experience of centralised state planning, even in the very modest form of wartime production, provided a vision of its future possibilities. It may have been that such planning, coming so late, could have done little to rescue the fortunes of Britain's declining industries, but it could have given a boost to the newer ones struggling to emerge. As it was, industries like electrical engineering, aircraft production, motor cars, man-made fibres, chemicals, glassmaking and others acquired a tenuous hold in the 1920s and only became really successful in the economic upturn after 1932. By this time, however, they had lost any potential they might have had for gaining a foothold in the export market. Thus, unlike the old staples, they contented themselves with meeting home demand. They thrived in this valuable, but more limited market, largely because they were protected from foreign competition due to the final and belated abandonment after roughly 100 years of the traditional British policy of free trade. The first protective tariff was introduced, without too much controversy, in 1932.

Although it stopped short of the kind of central planning that was advocated by socialists and which seemed to be so successful in the Soviet Union, governments in the inter-war years intervened in the economy to a far greater extent than hitherto. Apart from the introduction of protective tariffs, the state played an important role in encouraging new forms of industrial organisation which, by 1939, had transformed the structure of British business. In Britain, although some industrial giants had emerged before the war, the small firm, based on single or family ownership, retained a dogged existence. The growth of industrial concentration, the expansion of joint stock enterprises and the development of cartels and monopolies were commonplace elsewhere by 1918 but only took off in Britain thereafter. This process may have occurred, and did occur in the new industries, without government encouragement, as the example of Imperial Chemical Industries, the biggest of the giants, formed in 1927 by the merger of four smaller giants, showed. But the attitude of the government, which had always looked on cartels, monopolies and the like as unwanted forms of restrictive practice, undoubtedly changed to the extent that by the 1930s it was even prepared to pass legislation to enforce or encourage the process, particularly in the staple industries. The Coal Mines Act of 1930, which compelled the establishment of a cartel in that industry, and the 1935 Finance Act, which granted tax relief to successful monopolies, are examples of both aspects of the new policy. Related to these developments was the changing character of the ownership of British industry. The larger the firm the more capital required for its operation, hence rendering single individuals, no matter how rich, less likely to be able to supply it. Boards of directors representing major shareholders, among which could be counted banks or finance houses, replaced the old-style owner/managers. The now familiar fact of the separation of ownership and day-to-day control became established in the inter-war years. However, restrictive and monopolistic practices did almost nothing to revive the fortunes of the declining industries, even though they boosted the profits of the smaller number of employers who remained. They preferred to tinker with these new forms of organisation rather than address the central question of investment in new plant and machinery in order to modernise their undertakings.

The New Industries

As has been noted, the new industries, unlike the staples, were based on the domestic market. How was it that they succeeded in tapping home demand when unemployment was high and the economy, except for a few years in the 1930s, stagnated? The answer in part lies in the fact that for those who had work, disposable income rose due to the fall in the cost of living, accounted for chiefly by cheaper food imported from Britain's colonies. This meant that the surplus income was available to be spent on consumer goods, and this, coupled with a growth in population (due in the main to longer life expectancy), led to expanded domestic demand. Added to this was the considerable disposable income of the middle and upper classes, who, due to the decline of the servant population, had both the incentive and the spare cash to purchase the increasing array of consumer durables. It is also the case that, for the employed population, working hours were shorter and paid holidays more common (particularly for those in the new industries), giving rise to more leisure time which could be spent shopping (witness the massive growth of the chain and department stores) or relaxing by going to the cinema or listening to the radio. These forms of entertainment and others either took off or underwent a tremendous expansion in this period.

Most of the new industries were based in purpose-built factories using electricity as their source of motive power. Not dependent on coal supplies, and not needing to be near a port, because they were not export-oriented, they could locate themselves where they liked. Because they chose such unlikely places as Oxford, Luton, Bedford or the outskirts of London and Birmingham, these industries stimulated a boom in house building as workers flocked to them. However, the extent to which, despite government hopes, there was a wave of internal migration away from areas of high unemployment was greatly exaggerated. Such industries displayed other common characteristics. Early in their development they were almost always dominated by monopolies, duopolies or a small number of very large firms operating in a cartel. Their products thus became associated with such household names as Austin and Morris (cars), ICI (chemicals), Courtaulds (man-made fibres), Morphy Richards and Hoover (domestic appliances), GEC and AEI (electrical engineering), Marks & Spencer and Woolworths (chain stores), Unilever (food and much else besides). The list could go on. The factories established by such firms were very large and were based on the most advanced methods of mass production, utilising the technique of the assembly line and so-called 'scientific management'. This latter took the form of time-and-motion studies, the most common of which was the Bedaux system. The assembly line stimulated the demand for cheaper semi-skilled and unskilled labour, much of which was filled by women, whose job opportunities would have otherwise declined considerably after they were unceremoniously turned out of posts temporarily vacated by men during the First World War.

Unemployment

The inter-war period was thus one of contrasts. The poverty and despair of the depressed areas contrasted sharply with the hope and affluence promised by jobs and products of the mass consumption industries. It was as if two nations existed not just between workers and employers, but between workers who had a job, or the prospect of one, and those who were resigned to a life of almost permanent unemployment and doomed to the stigmatised pittance of a means-tested benefit. Not for them were the gleaming, tantalising products of the new industries displayed so temptingly in all the chain stores that mushroomed on every high street. Novels like Walter Greenwood's *Love on the Dole* captured such hopelessness and misery.

Unemployment in itself was nothing new, and indeed in comparison to figures with which we are familiar, the highest estimated total in September 1932 of 3,750,000 jobless is not all that startling. However, the sheer duration of the problem for almost the entire span of years between the two world wars and its resistance to upturns in the economic cycle endowed the unemployment of this period with an intrinsic character. It persisted even at a time when the building boom and the new industries were creating thousands of jobs. Some labour from the depressed areas migrated to fill the vacancies, competing with the indigenous workforce. This created a situation in which the high unemployment in the regions of declining industry was transported in diluted form to the growth areas. Thus even in the high-growth industries in a boom year like 1937, 17,000 car workers and 15,000 chemical workers were unemployed. Hence there was never a year between 1921 and 1939 when unemployment fell below one million. This is probably an underestimate, since then, as now, official figures hardly reflected the problem as they recorded only insured workers who registered as unemployed. This meant that any worker, like those in local government or agriculture, who were not part of the national insurance scheme (established in 1911 and dependent on both worker *and* employer to pay contributions), were automatically excluded from government unemployment statistics, as were a large number of married women, who would have been ineligible for benefit anyway. It was plain for all to see that this could not be passed off by the usual subjective dogma which held the jobless to be responsible for their plight – the problem was a structural one. Governments, although becoming more interventionist, did nothing to deal with the underlying causes of unemployment beyond attaching the name 'special areas' (1934) to its structural foundations. They also did next to nothing to remedy the social consequences, and a Labour government actually added insult to injury by cutting unemployment benefit by 10 per cent in 1931 during the most severe economic crisis.

Imperialism

The Versailles settlement divided German colonies between France and Britain. The British Empire was territorially at its largest in the inter-war years. This was accompanied by 'empire strengthening' strategies.[1] Cultural imperialism found new outlets in film and radio and it can be argued that, despite Britain's postwar economic difficulties, the inter-war years witnessed a truly hegemonic triumph of already well-entrenched imperial and racial ideology. The inter-war years saw the beginnings of greater labour movement interest in colonial issues, although this did not betoken a more enlightened attitude to race or a willingness to support the growing movement for colonial liberation. Government (including Labour government) interest in the colonies in this period was in the main motivated by two concerns: first, the fear that the Empire (now hugely expanded as a result of the First World War peace treaties) might be lost due to the rise of national liberation movements in many of the colonies; and second, the perceived threat of Bolshevism in the form of the Comintern, especially given the latter's involvement in the anti-imperialist struggle. The Comintern provided an alternative model of a form of internationalism which provoked fear and dread in the West, especially among the colonising powers. Such fears were not without foundation. In 1920 the second Comintern Congress conducted an in-depth discussion on the 'national and colonial question'. In the same year, under the auspices of the Comintern, the first congress of Peoples of the East was held. (The term 'East' was not used in its geographical sense; it was a generic term for non-white colonised people.) This was strongly anti-imperialist, concentrating particular invective towards British imperialism against which Gregory Zinoviev, a leading member of the Soviet Politburo, called the delegates to mount 'a holy war, above all against English imperialism'. In the late 1920s black anti-imperialists were welcomed in Moscow as students of the Communist University of the Toilers of the East. This attracted many existing and would-be leaders of national liberation movements.

The Economy in War and Peace, 1939–51

As during the 1914–18 war, the Second World War saw the government taking control or directing much of industry in the

1   Barbara Bush, *Imperialism, Race and Resistance* (1999).

interests of wartime production. The extent of the intervention was greater than before, but unlike then, the new Keynesian economic orthodoxy encouraged the state to maintain many of those controls once the war was over. Whereas in 1919 the influence of classical economics had encouraged the state to pull out, the inter-war years had, as we have seen, produced a contradiction between economic theory and economic practice. The state had become increasingly interventionist. By 1939, due to industrial concentration, it was relatively far easier for it to plan and deliver its wartime requirements. Once the war was over, having created a huge centralised economy, there was little objection, even among the Tories, to some degree of central control to remain in place so that the state could plan for its peacetime needs.

Women Workers

Although unemployment was high for almost the entire inter-war period, the proportion of women who worked actually increased slightly, from about 32 per cent in 1921 to 34 per cent in 1931. No census was conducted during the war, hence figures are unavailable for 1941, but as in the First World War women made a mass entry into social production during the war years and hence it is likely that the figure would have been unusually high. In 1951 it had returned to the norm, but did not decline nonetheless, standing at almost 35 per cent. Unemployment, as we have seen, hit the older staple industries most severely, and apart from textiles, these were the ones in which men predominated. The new industries were keen to use female labour on their modern assembly lines, which explains the fact that the South-East (the main locus of such industry) accounted for over a third of the total number of women employed. The second largest geographical region giving employment to women was the traditional one – the North-West, where women had been heavily involved in the manufacture of cotton and woollen cloth for almost a century and a half. The textile trade, as one of the staples, was also adversely affected by the decline in the export market, but its crisis was not as severe as that of the other older industries. Its decline was very slow in comparison and hence unemployment rates were not as high.

Despite the open recognition of the need for female labour in the new, high-profile industries, the same contradictory attitude to women workers remained as in Victorian times. An official (as in local and national government service) or ideological (elsewhere) marriage bar operated within the labour market to ensure that married women understood that their proper place was to attend to their *real* functions as wives and mothers. This line was reinforced by the cult of domesticity popularised by the huge growth of women's magazines in the 1920s and 1930s, the most popular of which, *Woman*, had a circulation of nearly one million by 1940.

Although the Second World War saw an all too brief respite for women in the traditional pattern of job segregation, the postwar scene witnessed its resurgence. By 1951 women were confined to six main occupational groups, and even though these were somewhat different from the pre-1914 pattern, they displayed the same characteristics in that such employment was defined by the kind of sex stereotyping which attempted to view it as a natural offshoot of women's domestic role and undervalued it accordingly. The decline in the textile trade and domestic service was more than amply compensated by the huge increase in demand for women clerks, typists and shop assistants. Of course, there is nothing intrinsically feminine about clerical or shop work. Indeed, in the nineteenth century such work was conventionally regarded as a male preserve. But the very process of feminising such labour fulfilled the vital economic function (for the employers) of cheapening it. Hence the very real fact of 'women's work' is also an ideological construct, founded on the huge economic gains to be made from the historical inequality of women's position within the labour force, reflecting their subservient role within the family.

Politics

For the labour movement this period is particularly significant in that it produced what might be regarded as the peak of all their aspirations – Labour governments. There were three of them. The first two (1924 and 1929–31) were both minority administrations. Only the third (1945–51) had a sufficient majority to act alone and accomplish anything. All three will be discussed more fully in later chapters.

The fact that Labour emerged as the main party of opposition should not cloud the fact that the Tories were still very strong and were effectively in office in one guise or another with or without Liberal (and Labour!) support (mainly as the National government) throughout most of the period. The First World War had divided the already weakened Liberal Party, with Lloyd George, having formed his own National Liberal Federation, still clinging to Tory support, and organisationally distinct from the mainstream Liberals led by Asquith. No fewer than seven general elections took place in the 17-year period between 1918 and 1935, with four of these having been held by 1924 (no elections were held between 1935 and 1945). Clearly, however strong the Tories were, this was a time of adjustment for them as they struggled to reassert themselves in the face of the mass franchise, considerable industrial unrest and a Labour Party which seemed poised to take advantage of the situation. The fact that the Conservative Party, in spite of in-fighting and leadership struggles, maintained its ascendancy until 1945 was helped by in-built advantages in its favour in the electoral system after 1918. Second votes for graduates and business owners helped the Tories, as did the redrawing of electoral boundaries, which gave them a solid bedrock of suburban seats to add to their rural vote. Irish Independence after 1921 removed around 80 anti-Tory seats in what was now the Republic of Ireland, while the Ulster Unionist MPs in the north accepted the Tory whip until 1972. To these Tory blessings can be added the weakness of the opposition, which never succeeded in challenging the ideological grip of individualism and property rights to protect which Conservatives, by their very name and nature, laid the surest claim.

Apart from the social consequences of poverty and unemployment, which forced their way occasionally onto an unsympathetic parliamentary arena and into the ongoing debates on the economy, politics until 1945 was dominated by foreign affairs, the course of which Britain no longer controlled. She reacted to rather than initiated world events, which were, of course, no less important for that reason. The 'threat' of the Soviet Union and the obsessive desire to isolate it took second place to the real menace of the alarming growth of Fascism in Italy and Germany, the territorial ambitions of which remained largely unchecked until it was too late. The Versailles settlement, drawn up by the victor powers at the end of the First World War, created an unstable balance of power in which the old Austro-Hungarian, Ottoman, Russian and German Empires had been dismembered in favour of a host of small and weak nation-states in central and eastern Europe. The League of Nations, established to maintain the peace in the new world order, proved to be unequal to the task and was in any case ill disposed to accomplish it since it too reflected the anti-Sovietism of its member states by refusing the Soviet Union the right to participate in its proceedings, even though Germany, which had been made to sign the 'war guilt clause', was admitted in 1925. International politics was overshadowed after the First World War by the might of the US, who although not a member of the league was the most powerful country to emerge after 1919. Britain, whether her rulers recognised it or not, was now a second-rate power, economically and politically. Even the lavish protuberance of her vast Empire could no longer hide this fact. Indeed, she was even forced to recognise changes in her autocratic relationship with the colonies under the pressure of the emergent movement for national liberation within them. The colonies that were dominated by white British settlers (Canada, Australia, New Zealand and South Africa) were granted Dominion status in 1931. The prolonged struggle for independence in Ireland had been crowned by the liberation from the British of all but Ulster. The mass movement in India and Egypt, following savage repression, resulted in some reforms, although not independence.

In Europe, Britain tamely tagged behind, although in full support of, American initiatives. These were largely focused on aiding the economic and military recovery of Germany, in defiance of the Versailles Treaty, in order to provide the US with a strong foothold in Europe while at the same time building a buffer against the presumed danger of Communist expansion. Hitler put paid to any idea that Germany would be a client state, but at the same time his own aspirations of world domination were openly publicised in his book, *Mein Kampf.* Together with the Italian leader Benito Mussolini they proceeded to put their expansionist aims into practice under the very noses of the major powers. In 1935 Italy invaded Abyssinia. In the same year, the Germans, by now well underway to reversing the Versailles settlement, seized back the Saarland and in 1936 reoccupied the Rhineland. These two prime industrial areas greatly aided not just Germany's economic recovery, but also her military potential. This latter proceeded by leaps and bounds, and in 1936 German rearmament was fully sanctioned by the powers. Sanction or no, it was clear from the German supply of military hardware to the Fascists in Spain during the Civil War (1936–39) that her arms industry was already very productive. It was quite evident that Germany was preparing for war, but provided Tory statesmen like Neville Chamberlain could be seduced into believing that any future war would be fought against the Soviet Union, they were more than happy to ride the international crises and tolerate Hitler's excesses. This meant turning a blind eye to the anti-Semitic and anti-democratic horrors of Nazi domestic policies. This was not too difficult since many leading British Tories shared views similar to Hitler's and Mussolini's, even if they expressed slight unease about some of their methods. In this sense the Tory policy of appeasing Hitler was not confined to Chamberlain and the aristocratic wire-pulling Cliveden Set (named after the country home of the Astor family, on whom the Set was focused). Although such views, culminating in the infamous Munich Agreement of 1938 with Hitler, have been roundly condemned since and the opposition to appeasement, supposedly led by Winston Churchill venerated as the real Tory orthodoxy, the fact is that hardly any Conservatives and not all that many Labour MPs had taken the fascist threat seriously at home (in its Mosleyite guise) and abroad since its inception. Indeed, of the two '-isms', most of them preferred, if forced to choose, Fascism to Communism.

When Britain was pushed finally and reluctantly to declare war on Germany in September 1939 her motive was not to rid the world of an evil creed, but to safeguard British interests. The more realistic anti-appeasers under Churchill (in coalition with Labour) proved better able to accomplish this more limited task when they ousted Chamberlain from office in May 1940 after the disastrous nine months of the 'phoney war', during which Britain did almost nothing. The main difference between those who sought in 1940 to combat Germany more vigorously and their pusillanimous predecessors was that the former had realised earlier that Hitler's plans were not simply to smash Bolshevism; nor, despite his Munich and other promises, were they confined to grabbing non-German territories like Poland and Czechoslovakia, much less to simply consolidating the German *Volk* in an expanded Reich. The Nazi policy of *Lebensraum* (literally, living space) required much more, including a colonial empire. The collapse of France, aided by her own fascist collaborators and the temporary Nazi–Soviet non-aggression pact of 1939–41, gave the Germans a free hand to pursue their plans for world domination and brought them ever closer to overrunning Britain. The entry of the Soviet Union into the war in 1941 took the pressure off the Western Front for a while as *Operation Barbarossa* (the German code-name for the elimination of the Soviet Union and its people) deflected the Nazi war machine.

Domestic politics during and after the war provided the Labour Party with its greatest ever opportunity. It played an essential role in Churchill's wartime Coalition government, and was the government between 1945 and 1951. How successfully it made use of this is the subject of Chapter 14.

Bibliography

British Labour Statistics. *Historical Abstracts 1886–1968* (Department of Employment, 1971)

Bush, B. *Imperialism, Race, and Resistance: Africa and Britain 1919–1945* (Routledge, 1999)

Constantine, S. *Unemployment in Britain between the Wars* (Longman, 1980)

Glucksmann, M. *Women Assemble: Women Workers in the New Industries in Inter-war Britain* (Routledge, 1990)

Greenwood, W. *Love on the Dole* (Penguin Books, 1972; first published 1933)

Halsey, A. H. (ed.). *Trends in British Society since 1900* (Macmillan, 1974)

Hannington, W. *The Problem of the Distressed Areas* (Gollancz, 1937)

Laybourn, K. *The Rise of Labour* (Edward Arnold, 1988)

Mowat, C. L. *Britain between the Wars 1918–1940* (University Paperbacks, 1968)

Pugh, M. *Women and the Women's Movement in Britain 1914–1959* (Macmillan, 1992)

Stevenson, J. *Social Conditions in Britain between the Wars* (Penguin Books, 1977)

11

LABOUR GOVERNMENTS AND UNEMPLOYMENT, 1920–1931

The economic problems of the 1920s and 1930s obviously had consequences for the labour movement, but these were by no means predictable. Mass unemployment helped to account for the fall in trade union membership from around 6½ million in 1920 to its lowest point in the inter-war years of 3¼ million in 1933. (Membership rose slowly but steadily thereafter.) But a decline in membership did not mean a decline in militancy. Strike action was almost as prevalent as hitherto and culminated in the biggest display of working-class strength yet seen – the General Strike of 1926.

The vibrancy of the movement cannot be measured simply by the number of days lost in strikes. Other indices include the existence and viability of a range of organisations capable of giving expression to working-class aspirations outside the workplace. Two such organisations were particularly significant in this period: one was the campaign, begun in the London borough of Poplar, to defend living standards in working-class areas by reducing the domestic rate (Poplarism); the other was the movement to organise and draw attention to the plight of the unemployed. In addition, in some areas, particularly in compact mining villages, trade unionism and community politics fused to produce a revolutionary outlook in such a singular fashion that such places earned the nickname 'little Moscows'. The fact that two (albeit minority) Labour governments took office in this period could also be said to be an indication of a more general political belligerency, but the experience of Labour in office only served to underline the continued need for extra-parliamentary organisation and showed once again the huge gap between leaders and led, or, more accurately, between left and right. The influence of the Communist Party in most of the mass campaigns in the inter-war period had the effect of politicising such protests, but at the same time sharpened the divisions between those who participated in them and the official leadership of the trade unions and the Labour Party. Divisions had always existed, but the fact that Labour became a party of government made it especially important for it to present its ultra-cautious and respectable face if it was not to incur the wrath of a state machine that saw the Soviet Union and hence Communism as its main enemy. The Labour leaders had managed to regroup after they had lost the popular initiative in the wake of the mass struggles during and immediately following the First World War. Given their continued commitment to reformist parliamentarianism, they were unlikely to learn the lessons the left was anxious to teach them. Rather, they attempted to tighten their grip on the movement and in doing so helped, alongside the more powerful vested interests of capital, to reduce the movements of protest, already struggling in a barren economic climate, to at best a minority current and at worst to the cries of despair of an almost defeated people.

The Labour Party

In 1918, the Labour Party, in belated recognition of its official existence, adopted a constitution and a programme. It also permitted individual members to join it as distinct from affiliated organisations. This did not mean, however, that it transformed itself into a mass campaigning party. Although it developed constituency organisations, these remained, as now, primarily vehicles to mobilise votes in local and national elections. However, in 1918 socialists could be forgiven for thinking that the party which they had fought to create had fulfilled their cherished dreams of becoming a mass socialist party. The new constitution adopted the famous socialist clause 4, which committed the party to secure for the workers by hand or by brain the full fruits of their industry and the most equitable distribution thereof that may be possible, upon the basis of the common ownership of the means of production and the best obtainable system of popular administration and control of each industry and service.

The other feature of the constitution was the introduction of a centralised method of electing the party's leadership at the annual conference on the basis of reserving seats for different categories of members. Five seats were allocated to local constituency organisations, four for women and the remaining 14 went to affiliated organisations. The fact that no distinction was made between political affiliates (like the ILP) and trade unions meant in practice that the latter now dominated the National Executive, resulting in a loss of influence of the socialist current. Thus the ILP, which had done so much to create the party, was now marginalised and the body it created lost the most active political guardian of its implied socialist conscience. The 1918 manifesto, 'Labour and the New Social Order', also heralded a distinctive and uncharacteristic break with Liberalism. It advocated nationalisation of some of the major industries and called for the 'scientific reorganisation' of the economy. But whilst the programme, drafted by Sidney Webb, was a radical departure, its essence expressed the Fabian desire to create a mixed economy rather than a socialist one. The fact that it and the constitution seemed so advanced is a reflection of and a tribute to the revolutionary spirit which had engulfed the labour movement worldwide in the course of and after the First World War. Socialists, particularly those in the ILP, may well have been pleased that the party even came this far, at least in theory, but their hopes were soon to be dashed when it came to the acid test of Labour politics practically applied to concrete issues.

The First Labour Government, 1924

The test came soon enough. The party increased its representation in the House of Commons in the general elections of 1922 and 1923 (taking 142 and 191 seats, respectively), by which time

Ramsay MacDonald had been re-elected leader – the choice of the left! No one, including MacDonald himself, expected that he would become prime minister in 1924. The Tories were in disarray over the issue which had historically divided them – tariff reform. Unable to unite his party and with no overall majority in parliament, their leader, Stanley Baldwin, dissolved it, leaving Labour as the next largest party free to form a government provided it obtained Liberal support. Such were the formal (and unfavourable) circumstances in which the minority Labour government of 1924 took office. Regardless of the wisdom or otherwise of accepting office on these terms, the fact is that Labour was so blinded by the lure of office that it unwittingly fell into a trap created for it by the other two parties. Tariff reform, whilst a problem for the Tories, was but a fig leaf to cover a more sinister manoeuvre. In a situation of high and rising unemployment, and with no policy to alleviate it, the Tories were genuinely concerned that it would only be a matter of time before a majority Labour government was elected. Such a government, if its 1918 manifesto was to be taken at face value, would pose a serious threat to the owners of wealth. Baldwin expressed this openly at a meeting of the Conservative Party after the 1923 election:

> It was on unemployment that the Labour Party relied on coming to power within two or three years. Their calculations were that the discontent in the country coupled with want of action on our part would have swept them into power and us out by 1926.[1]

Herbert Asquith agreed with him. For the Liberals, a Labour government 'with its claws cut' was infinitely better than one that was truly independent. As he put it: 'If a Labour government is ever to be tried in this country, as it will sooner or later, it could hardly be tried under safer conditions.'[2] This explains why the Liberals did not, as was in their power, help save the Tory government and instead threw in their lot for nine months to prop up, while it suited them, with this first Labour government.

1 Quoted in Allen Hutt, *The Post War History of the British Working Class* (1937).
2 Quoted in Ivor Bulmer-Thomas, *The Growth of the British Party System* (1965).

The establishment parties showed undue alarm at the prospects of Labour's radicalism, let alone its socialism. Although dependent on Liberal votes, this was not a coalition government and hence the fact that MacDonald went outside the ranks of his own party to find cabinet ministers was a matter of some concern to Labour's rank and file. He appointed Lord Haldane, a former Liberal minister, as Lord President and the posts of Lord Chancellor and First Lord of the Admiralty went to two Conservatives (Lord Parmoor and Lord Chelmsford, respectively). Such matters were decided at a secret meeting at the Webbs' house. The reason given by Philip Snowden (in his autobiography) for the choice of non-Labour cabinet ministers was quite simple:

> the most timid conservatives and the most frightened capitalists took heart from the presence in the cabinet of men like Lord Parmoor, Lord Chelmsford and Lord Haldane; they could hardly believe that these men would be the instruments for carrying out the socialist revolution.

Further evidence for the groundlessness of the fears of the establishment was to be found in the Labour government's attitude to the rising wave of strikes. It elevated its hostility to them almost to a point of principle. J. R. Clynes, the Lord Privy Seal, proclaimed that in its handling of strikes the government 'played the part of a national Government, and not a class Government, and I am certain that any Government, whatever it might be, could not in the circumstances have done more than we have done to safeguard the public interests'.[3]

Even moderate trade union leaders like Ernest Bevin of the TGWU complained of the threats emanating from the parliamentary leaders of the Labour Party during the dock strike. Such threats were made real during the strike of London's transport workers when the government went to the lengths of invoking the hated Emergency Powers Act, the force of which was not activated only because the strike was settled.

It is thus surprising, given the extent of the government's hostility to mass action, that the establishment went to the lengths

3   Quoted in Hutt, *The Post War History of the British Working Class*.

it did to discredit Labour. This came in the form of the infamous 'Zinoviev Letter', the publication of which was a classic example of establishment conspiracy and cost Labour, as intended, the 1924 general election. The government could have been toppled at any time. The issue which finally settled its demise was the Campbell case. J. R. Campbell, acting editor of the communist *Workers' Weekly*, published the famous 'Don't Strike' open letter to the army forces urging them not to act as strike-breakers. For this he was charged under the 1797 Incitement to Mutiny Act, but when the charge was dropped the government was held responsible and lost a vote of censure in the Commons. Three days before the ensuing general election, a letter purporting to come from the Communist International, signed by its president, Zinoviev, was leaked by the Foreign Office to the press and published in the staunchly Tory *Daily Mail*. In it the promise of 'Moscow gold' was made to finance armed insurrection in Britain, and although the letter was addressed to the Communist Party, the fact that it alluded to the draft treaties on trade and co-operation between Britain and the Soviet Union which had been negotiated by MacDonald's government, meant that a connection was supposedly made between the Labour Party and Communism. The fact that the letter was an obvious forgery and that anyone who was seriously concerned with the truth could not believe for one moment that MacDonald had any sympathies with Communism did nothing to prevent the 'red bogey' distorting reality and doing the sinister job for which it was intended. The Tories obtained a comfortable majority.

The Second Labour Government, 1929–31 – 'the Great Betrayal'

Although much had happened in the five years between the first and second Labour governments, the circumstances and the issues giving rise to the second were remarkably similar to the first. Once again the Tories' inability and unwillingness to deal with the sore of unemployment dominated the political scene, although this time the problem was compounded by a world-wide financial crisis which had a particularly sharp impact in Britain. The 1929 general election, the first in which all women over the age of 21 could vote, had produced great gains for Labour. The return of 287 Labour MPs made it the largest party in the Commons, although once again without an overall majority should the 260 Conservatives and 59 Liberal members combine against it. The fact that for two years they chose not to was partly because of the gulf between them on tariff reform, but also because they found it preferable to let Labour face the dilemma of having to take unpopular measures to deal with the economic crisis and thereby court the odium of its own electorate. Lloyd George said that he did not see why the Liberals should 'carry the ladder and hold it in its place for five years whilst the socialists are on the scaffold and doing all the building'.[4]

Although there was some discussion this time, following the experience of the previous minority administration, as to the wisdom of putting Labour again into a similarly unfavourable situation, the matter was quickly resolved in favour. Only the left Labour MP James Maxton proposed a serious alternative. He suggested getting the party to prepare a socialist legislative programme and obtaining a mandate to pursue it following a fresh election. The fact that this was hardly discussed is a reflection of the move to the right in TUC and Labour Party circles following the defeat of the General Strike. This was reflected too in the watered-down version of the 1918 programme, which appeared in 1927 under a new title, 'Labour and the Nation'. The left openly opposed it and offered their alternative in the form of the Cook–Maxton manifesto (named after its authors, A. J. Cook, the miners' leader, and Maxton, both leading ILP figures). The official manifesto made an appeal to the nation as opposed to class. Its tenor was similarly reflected in MacDonald's opening speech to the new House of Commons in which he wondered

> how far it is possible without in any way abandoning our party positions
> ... to consider ourselves more as a Council of State and less as arrayed
> regiments facing each other in battle ... so far as we are concerned, co-

4   Quoted in Bulmer-Thomas, *The Growth of the British Party System*.

operation will be welcomed ... so that by putting our ideas into a common pool we can bring out ... legislation and administration that will be of substantial benefit for the nation as a whole.[5]

On the main issue of the day, unemployment, Labour showed itself as reluctant as its predecessors to do anything constructive. Quite the reverse – it actually proposed to make the plight of the unemployed worse by cutting their already miserly benefit. Although not accepting in full the drastic 'remedy' of a 30 per cent cut in unemployment benefit proposed by the Royal Commission on Unemployment, the terms of reference of the May Committee set up by the government with the aid of the Liberals had an ominously similar objective. This was to recommend ways of 'effecting forthwith all practical and legitimate reductions in the national expenditure consistent with the efficiency of the services'.

Implicit in this was an acceptance of orthodox Treasury economics, which sought to place the burden of the financial crisis on those who could least afford it. It was not simply a question of rejecting socialist solutions – these had long been consigned to a never-never land. Labour was also about to reject alternative, more progressive capitalist solutions of the type advocated by the economist John Maynard Keynes, which were by now finding favour in TUC circles. The report of the May Committee thus precipitated a crisis within Labour circles, the outcome of which proved both unexpected and disastrous. The logic of the timidity of a minority government, dependent on Liberal support, assailed by the Tories and their friends in the newspaper world and above all caught in the web of its own ideological confusion, meant that when the crisis came Labour was incapable of doing anything other than that demanded of it by its political opponents. In this sense MacDonald and the eleven members of his cabinet who supported him in making the required cuts were only acting more consistently, albeit more treacherously, than the ten who did not. Faced with the unpalatable decision to make such cuts to the tune of £78 million, which in the light of the projected budget deficit were now demanded by Britain's foreign creditors if further

5   Quoted in C. L. Mowat, *Britain Between the Wars 1918–1940* (1955).

loans were to be forthcoming, the cabinet was split, not on the substantive issue, but on its severity. The May Committee and others backed the demand, which included a 10 per cent cut in unemployment benefit at a time (1931) when the numbers out of work were rising rapidly. The cabinet nonetheless did agree to a cut of £56 million, but this proved, as MacDonald was aware, to be too little for the other two parties. MacDonald thus went to the king to tender the government's resignation, but to the surprise even of his own cabinet supporters, he did not offer to resign himself. In a weird scenario, obviously prepared in advance, MacDonald suggested that he stay on as prime minister of a national government. In so doing he was consistent with the views he had announced in his speech to the Commons in 1929 – the national interest, second only to his personal ambition, came before class and party. The fact that his unusual offer was accepted with alacrity indicated prior planning. The Liberal Herbert Samuel advised George V on these lines:

> in view of the fact that the necessary economies would prove most unpalatable to the working class, it would be to the general interest if they could be imposed by a Labour government. The best solution would be if Mr. Ramsay MacDonald ... could propose the economies required. If he failed ... then the best alternative would be a National government composed of members of the three parties. It would be preferable that Mr. MacDonald should remain Prime Minister in such a National Government.[6]

Outside the Corridors of Power

Events in Westminster, while capable of adding to the burdens of the working class, were nevertheless remote from it even when Labour was in office. However, as Bevin observed during the dock strike of 1924, there was greater pressure for political conformity during a Labour government so as not to cause it any embarrassment. The pressure to conform was felt strongly in the trade unions given their organic connection with the Labour Party, and it led to the formation of organisations outside their

6   Quoted in Miliband, *Parliamentary Socialism.*

control in order both to escape the dead hand of officialdom and to encompass issues wider than the established labour movement was prepared to acknowledge. Prime among these was the vexed question of unemployment about which the official movement displayed at best perplexity and at worst unconcern.

The National Unemployed Workers' (Committee) Movement

The NUW(C)M, established in 1921 from the host of unemployed committees of ex-servicemen, sought, with varying degrees of success, to organise among the unemployed and to campaign for the next 25 years under the slogan of 'Work or Full Maintenance'. It was responsible for using daring and innovative methods of protest, including hunger marches, factory raids to protest against overtime working and mass demonstrations often aimed in particular at Poor Law Guardians who were still responsible for the administration of poor relief under the archaic provisions of the 1834 Poor Law Amendment Act (see Chapter 4). Women played a prominent role in the movement. Lillian Thring was the editor of the NUWM paper *Out of Work* and from the outset a place was reserved on the National Administrative Council for a women's organiser, held first by Thring and later, from 1929, by Maud Brown when a women's department was also established. (In 1929 the movement dropped the word 'Committee' from its title, and it was known more simply thereafter, as the NUWM.) Women's contingents were a regular feature of the hunger marches of the 1930s, especially when, following the introduction of the Means Test in 1931, whole families bore the direct burden of the unemployment of one or more of their members.

At its peak in 1933 the NUWM had upwards of 100,000 members, but in contrast there were periods in the 1920s when the movement seemed close to extinction. Its peaks and troughs not surprisingly roughly coincided with unemployment levels. The fact that its leadership was dominated by members of the Communist Party did not lessen its appeal, although this undoubtedly influenced the attitude of the TUC, which by 1928 was outspokenly hostile to it. Their hostility showed itself in two ways: the TUC either ignored the issue of unemployment altogether in the hope that it would simply go away, or when it resurfaced in the early 1930s with even greater force, made half-hearted attempts to set up rival organisations. Wal Hannington, the able full-time organiser of the NUWM, together with other leading communist activists like Harry McShane, Sid Elias and many others, managed to steer a relatively independent course for the movement through the troubled sectarian path of communist politics during the so-called 'third period' of the Communist International (1929–31) and beyond. The Comintern's temporary rejection of the strategy of the 'united front' of all working-class organisations in favour of the narrow 'class against class' outlook in which previous social democratic potential allies were now looked on as social fascists, did not have the devastating effect on the NUWM that it had on 'official' labour movement organisations. The NUWM was already unofficial and hence untainted, in Comintern speak, by the bourgeois outlook of such putative supporters, who anyway had decided earlier to hold the movement at arm's length. Although the politics of the movement's leaders was quite open, it was never the case that it was simply a front for the Communist Party. It achieved its support because it paid meticulous attention to both the general and individual problems of the unemployed. Its legal department assisted countless victims of the system to challenge the parsimonious jurisdiction of the Poor Law and later the Public Assistance Committees established in 1931.

Local Government, Poplarism and 'Little Moscows'

The extension of the franchise had an impact on local as well as national government. Labour steadily gained ground in local elections both for Poor Law Boards of Guardians and borough councils and in the capital for the London County Council. By 1919 Labour had a majority for the first time on the LCC to complement majorities won on eleven London councils in working-class areas. Outside London the Communist Party was so influential at local level in some areas that it shared power with Labour, extinguishing Liberalism for good as a force in local politics. The best known of these 'little Moscows', as they unpejoratively came to be known, were the mining villages of Mardy in the Rhonda Valley (South Wales) and Lumphinnans in West Fife (Scotland), along with the textile villages of the Vale of Leven in Dumbartonshire (Scotland)

At a local level Labour leaders had to be more responsive to local issues. Labour locally would have got nowhere if its leaders had adopted the same Olympian aloofness which characterised national politicians. Poverty and unemployment dominated the local as well as the national stage, with local responses clearly contrasting with the paucity of the national initiative. The imaginative and daring response in Poplar to such issues resulted in the imprisonment of the majority of its councillors and at the same time achieved such notoriety that it added a new noun to the English language – 'Poplarism'.

Essentially, the Labour councillors in Poplar, under the leadership of George Lansbury (editor of the *Daily Herald*), attempted to do all in their power to alleviate the problems of poverty and unemployment in the borough. This involved a variety of methods, including increasing the pay of council employees, in particular of women by paying them the same as men, creating more jobs and at the same time improving local roads and sewers through a big extension of public works and increasing the scale of outdoor relief to the poor. Controversial as all this was, the issue that brought the council into direct confrontation with the state was its decision, in February 1921, to use its local rates for its own purposes and to refuse to levy them for outside bodies like the LCC, the Metropolitan Police Authority and other London-wide organisations, which were financed from the coffers of all the London boroughs with little regard to their ability to pay. Poplar did not object in principle to paying something towards London-wide services, but questioned why the same principle did not operate in reverse. Rich boroughs could levy lower rates because they had no poor for whom to provide. Since the financial burden of poor relief rested with local councils, the poorer ones had been forced to increase their rates. The Poplar argument was simple – if the poor boroughs had to pay for London-wide services, then the richer ones should be forced to contribute to a pooled fund for the provision of local schemes to relieve poverty in those boroughs that could least afford to bear its rising cost. Hence arose the demand for the 'equalisation of the rates' and until this was conceded Poplar, at a council meeting in March 1921, voted (with one vote against) not to levy rates on behalf of central London bodies. This decision in itself helped the poor since it meant that rates were reduced, as were rents, since many paid rate and rent together. The wrath of the establishment was quick to descend – writs were served on 30 of the Poplar councillors, who despite the opposition of the London Labour Party orchestrated by its secretary, Herbert Morrison, stuck to their policy and were arrested and imprisoned in September 1921 amidst mass demonstrations in their support. Despite Morrison's backstage manoeuvres to reach a compromise with the government represented by Lloyd George and Sir Alfred Mond (chairman of ICI), the imprisoned councillors made it clear that no deal could be struck on their behalf unless they were involved in negotiations, which they insisted could only take place if they were freed and the principle of rate equalisation accepted. The fear of the Poplar action spreading to other supportive councils like Stepney and Bethnal Green induced the government to agree to the release of the prisoners, after six weeks' incarceration, and acceptance of their principal demand.

Poplar had won, at least for the time being. But instead of using this victory as a shining example of the best kind of Labour politics acting in the interests of the working class, Morrison capitulated to the inevitable propaganda of the Tories to discredit Poplarism as the antics of a 1920s-style 'looney left' bunch of irresponsible spendthrifts. He did all he could to disassociate the London Labour Party from Poplarism, as was shown clearly in a leaflet issued for the borough council elections which proclaimed in cold type: 'The London Labour Party does not associate itself with the demands for public assistance of a character which cannot be regarded as practicable in existing circumstances.'[7]

Such a calculation, based on the presumption that the politics of caution would bring Labour continued electoral success, proved disastrously wrong in the local elections in London in 1923. Labour lost control in five boroughs, including Morrison's base, Hackney. Whilst this was partly explained by the evaporation of the revolutionary mood which brought Labour success in 1919, the fact is that in Poplar, Labour defied the trend and increased its share of the vote. This, although Morrison and his allies would not acknowledge it, indicated the success of Lansbury's vision of municipal socialism, which was a far cry from the 'gas and water' Fabian variety. While he understood that socialism in one borough would not bring about the end of capitalism, he argued nonetheless that 'the workers must be given tangible proof that Labour administration means something different from capitalist administration, and in a nutshell this means diverting wealth from the wealthy ratepayers to the poor'.[8]

But although Poplar was able to withstand the opposition of its Labour critics in London, it was more difficult when such opposition was voiced by the Labour leadership at national level, especially when, as in 1924, Labour formed the government. Initially, Poplar had cause to place its hopes in the fact that the only left-winger in MacDonald's cabinet, John Wheatley, a supporter of Poplarism, was made Minister of Health and Local Government. But Wheatley was a lone voice, prevented from doing anything practical to assist the beleaguered council which was now embroiled in further controversy over its policy of paying a £4 minimum wage to its own employees. The Labour Party establishment joined the chorus of disapproval against this further Poplar 'crime', which was deemed profligate at a time when workers throughout the country were faced with savage wage cuts in the interests of economic efficiency. The hope that a Labour government would be sympathetic or even supportive was forlorn. Sensing the isolation of Poplar, the ensuing Tory

7   Quoted in Noreen Branson, *Poplarism, 1919–1925* (1979).
8   Quoted ibid.

government made clear its intention to take legal action and in 1925, to prevent this, the council climbed down. Poplar's submission was not cowardly. It marked a realistic recognition that one council acting alone, however well supported locally, could not fight the system indefinitely in conditions in which the movement was in retreat and the Labour leadership remained preoccupied with Labourism rather than socialism.

Bibliography

Branson, N. *Poplarism 1919–1925* (Lawrence & Wishart, 1979)

Bulmer-Thomas, I. *The Growth of the British Party System* (John Baker, 1965)

Croucher, R. *We Refuse to Starve in Silence: A History of the National Unemployed Workers Movement 1920–1946* (Lawrence & Wishart, 1987)

Hannington, W. *Unemployed Struggles 1919–1936* (Lawrence & Wishart, 1979; first published 1936)

Hutt, A. *The Post War History of the British Working Class* (Gollancz, 1937)

MacIntyre, S. *Little Moscows* (Croom Helm, 1980)

Miliband, R. *Parliamentary Socialism* (Allen & Unwin, 1961)

Mowat, C. L. *Britain Between the Wars 1918–1940* (Methuen, 1955).

Shinwell, E. *I've Lived Through it All* (Gollancz, 1973)

12

TRADE UNIONS, THE GENERAL STRIKE AND THE AFTERMATH

Despite the decline in trade union membership in the inter-war years (see Chapter 11), the continued militancy of its activists, which reached its climax in the General Strike of 1926, posed the greatest challenge in the twentieth century to the power of capitalism and by implication to the labourist ideology, which had always shrunk from such confrontation. 1926 marked a watershed. Trade union militancy was pushed to its ultimate limit in an unfavourable economic climate. It was faced with a powerful and well-prepared state machine, which seized with gusto the opportunity to deal a death blow to union defiance once and for all. The leadership of the trade union movement was also put to the test. As unwilling strike leaders in 1926, the TUC's concern had little to do with winning, and much more to do with ensuring that it prevented the unleashing of forces on both sides of the industrial divide over which it would have little control or influence. The aftermath of the strike proved to be disastrous for the trade union and labour movement, despite the fact that its leaders bent over backwards to accommodate themselves to a new situation in which both government and employers capitalised on their victory with barely concealed contempt for the power of labour, which they had been forced to tolerate hitherto.

The Trade Union Leadership

One aspect of syndicalist philosophy infiltrated official trade union circles, albeit for motives which were far removed from the revolutionary aims of its protagonists. The trend to union amalgamations proceeded apace after 1920. The impetus for this had been created during the war, during which centralised pay bargaining for discrete industrial groups had been accomplished by national federations of trade unions and employer organisations. A federation of engineering employers had been long established, thus it was no surprise that, albeit belatedly, the Amalgamated Society of Engineers joined with smaller craft unions in the industry to form the Amalgamated Engineering Union in 1920. Among unskilled and semi-skilled workers, amalgamations of unions of general labourers with those of dockers and carters produced the Transport and General Workers' Union in 1922. Under its first general secretary, Ernest Bevin, it was soon to become the largest union and exercised considerable influence within the Labour Party. The Gas Workers' Union was the satellite around which a number of smaller general unions, including the National Federation of Women Workers, clustered and produced in 1924 the National Union of General and Municipal Workers. Similar trends of amalgamations were evident among white-collar workers – in the Post Office (Union of Post Office Workers, 1920) and Civil Service (Civil Service Clerical Association, 1922). Another syndicalist principle used for pragmatic purposes was evident in the seemingly innocuous formation in 1921 of the General Council to replace the TUC's Parliamentary Committee. The new body had more extensive powers than the latter, but from the beginning it was clear that it was not going to be used to promote a coordinated onslaught on capital. Indeed, Bevin hoped that strikes would be fewer because of the power of this new organisation. Rather more modestly, while not treading on the toes of affiliates, the General Council hoped to promote better relations between them and to present an effective and hopefully united trade union front in its dealings with outside bodies.

Thus it was that a tighter and more centralised leadership, dominated by a small number of large unions, emerged from the mass struggles of the previous decade, and whilst this had the potential for promoting effective solidarity between groups of workers in struggle, it could also be used with great effect for precisely the opposite purpose. The fact that sectionalism rather than solidarity remained the hallmark of trade union and hence of TUC leaders (who always reflected change rather than initiated it) was paradoxically assisted by this greater centralisation. The development of national collective bargaining, which had stimulated union amalgamation and federation, betokened an industrial 'coming of age' of the trade union movement. It went together with official employer recognition of unions at workplace level alongside local bargaining procedures. The collective bargaining process even spread to industries in which trade unionism was not well developed. The system of joint industrial committees of employer and union representatives recommended in the 1917 Report of the Whitley Committee indicated the willingness of the government to encourage what they saw as a more orderly and centralised system of industrial relations. By 1921, 73 such Whitley Councils, as they came to be known, had been established and those which survived in the public and private sector (many of them in the public sector intact until the Thatcher years) concluded national pay and conditions agreements for their respective industries. Thus it was that the interests of government, employers and the trade union leaderships, all worried by the challenge to their authority during the war years, were served by snatching the initiative from the militants through the creation of these new centralised structures. The very militancy which had induced this development was now turned to the advantage of the leadership, which claimed credit for the concessions and in doing so both emasculated and incorporated its initial driving force – the shop stewards. Although the revolutionary organisation of shop stewards had collapsed, the postwar compromise between capital and labour could not ignore them. In most unions and collective agreements, stewards were given an officially recognised role far beyond their original one of dues collectors and recruiting agents. Nonetheless, workplace militancy continued in the years after the war and this forced a persistent tension between the potential of centralisation to achieve more effective class solidarity and the pressure to confine it within the bounds of traditional sectional interest. This tension reached its breaking point in 1926, the year of the General Strike.

The Miners

The decline of Britain's staple industries, as we have seen, was a prime cause of mass unemployment in the inter-war years. The position of the workers who remained employed in such industries was grim. They were faced with a concerted attempt by the employers to cut wages and increase productivity. Due to the fact that the coal mining industry accounted for a sixth of the male labour force and was the strongest and best organised in trade union terms, miners were at the centre of the employers' offensive and bore the main brunt of the postwar attack. A defeat for the miners would enable managerialist domination, which had taken such a knock in the war years, to be reasserted and open the way for a successful attack on other groups of workers. The mine owners also had another aim. During the war the state had assumed some measure of control over mining as an essential wartime industry. This had boosted the miners' demand for the nationalisation of the industry – a policy supported by the Sankey Committee (appointed by the government in 1920 to avert a threatened strike for a 30 per cent pay increase). Needless to say, the owners were vehemently opposed to any form of state intervention, let alone nationalisation. In the less revolutionary atmosphere of the 1920s Lloyd George dropped all pretence at concession and brought forward his plans to decontrol the mines. This coincided (probably not accidentally) with the owners' announcement of savage wage cuts to well below pre-1914 levels and an end to national wage agreements. The fact that employers in other industries were attempting similar tactics helps to account for the wave of support given by the labour movement to the miners when, as a result of their determined refusal to accept the demands of the mine owners, they were locked out. The Triple Alliance (formed in 1914 of mine, railway and transport unions) called a rail and transport strike, but due to the backstage manoeuvring of some of the union leaders, notably Frank Hodges and J. H. Thomas (secretaries of the Miners' Federation and the National Union of Railwaymen, respectively), the strike was called off at the eleventh hour. The

Daily Herald echoed the widely held view that this incident (unfortunately dubbed 'black Friday') 'was the heaviest defeat that has befallen the Labour movement within the memory of man'.[1] This perhaps exaggerated opinion was explicable in the light of the *Herald*'s earlier analysis that the attack on the miners represented 'a frontal attack on the whole working class by the capitalists and their Government'.[2] The miners were eventually starved into submission, leading, as predicted, to lockouts to enforce wage reductions on engineers, cotton operatives, builders, shipyard workers, seamen and others.

This appeared to mark the end of the trade union militants' forward offensive which had characterised industrial relations since 1910, leaving only the unemployed struggles to challenge the hegemony of the capitalist and labourist establishments. However, this defeat was by no means the dying gasp of a spent revolutionary creed as the renewed attack on the miners in 1925 was to show. By the time the mine owners, due to another slump in their badly run industry, demanded in 1925 yet another round of wage cuts and a lengthening of hours, they were faced with more formidable opposition from a regrouped coterie of militants who had, for the first time, gained leading positions in their own unions and on the TUC General Council.

The National Minority Movement

In that it encouraged workshop organisation and industrial unionism, the National Minority Movement shared similar aims with the syndicalist movements of rank-and-file militants which preceded it, but unlike them it fought to ensure that the aspirations of the membership of the unions in which it had influence was reflected in the election of a new type of leadership. The movement's founding statement, 'What the Minority Movement Stands For', was critical of the existing trade union leadership, which it condemned as 'a bureaucracy ... often under capitalist influence' and 'which frequently acts as a

1   Quoted in G. D. H. Cole, *The Common People* (1965).
2   Quoted in Hutt, A. *The Post War History of the British Working Class* (1937).

barrier to swift and conscious action on the part of the workers'. It listed as one of its activities 'contesting all trade union office elections with supporters of the Minority Movement of proved loyalty to the working class as candidates, and endeavouring to secure their return'. It thus built on the traditions of rank-and-file organisation, but did not erect 'rank-and-fileism' into a principle. Although the NMM was formed, in June 1924, under the auspices of the Comintern's Red International of Labour Unions (RILU) it was neither separatist nor sectarian. The RILU had already attracted support among militants, especially in the Miners' Federation, but also among engineers and transport workers. The NMM sought to unify the separate industrial groupings but stressed that

> It is **not** a separatist movement. It does **not** aim at bringing into being new and rival organisations to those already existing. On the contrary it actively opposes any attempts that are made to split the trade unions, and to establish brand new organisations.[3]

Whilst it would be wrong to make exaggerated claims about the success of the NMM, its influence was undoubtedly behind the election of a left trend in some trade unions, notably in the Miners' Federation, in which the militant A. J. Cook succeeded Hodges as secretary in 1923. Although Cook was not a member of the TUC General Council, by 1924 there was, for the first time, a left grouping on that body – A. B. Swales (Engineers), George Hicks (Bricklayers) and A. A. Purcell (Furnishing Trades). Amazingly, between 1923 and 1925 the general secretary of the TUC, Fred Bramley, was a left-wing socialist. Obviously the NMM can claim no credit for his appointment, but its effort in building a rank-and-file organisation was complemented by a man (Bramley) who was sympathetic in general terms to their aims as shown by the formation of a joint TUC–Soviet trade union committee. Of greater significance was the fact that when, in 1925, the next round of cuts in miners' pay was proposed and Baldwin warned that the return to the gold standard meant that

3   'What the Minority Movement Stands For' (n.d.).

all workers would have wage reductions, the General Council responded immediately to support them and planned, in the event of another miners' lockout, to call a strike of the Triple Alliance. This determined action, unlike that of 1921, took Baldwin by surprise and led to a climb-down, the reason for which, as he later told his biographer, G. M. Young, was because 'we were not ready'. On the day the strike was due to start, Friday, 11 July 1925, the government announced that it would grant a subsidy to the coal industry for nine months, obviating at least temporarily the necessity for wage cuts, while a Royal Commission conducted an inquiry. This victory, accomplished without strike action, was hailed in banner headlines in the *Daily Herald* as 'Red Friday', although as events were to show, Red Friday, significant as it was, was more of a truce than a victory.

The General Strike 1926

Although the government was caught unaware by the resolve of the TUC and the mass support for the miners in 1925, this did not indicate a lack of preparedness or willingness for a confrontation with militant trade unionism. Indeed, Red Friday galvanised the cabinet into taking the active preparations for conflict, which the hawkish Churchill had long advocated. The government established the Organisation for the Maintenance of Supplies (OMS) – a volunteer, 'private', strike-breaking body whose pretence at independence was belied by the fact that it received state funds for its operation and that its leadership was approved by the cabinet. By the time of the General Strike over 100,000 volunteers were ready, having been secretly trained by the OMS, to take over the running of essential services. At the same time the government made its own military-style preparations. Ten Civil Commissioners were appointed with their own staff and with full authority conferred on them by the Emergency Powers Act to run the ten regions into which Britain was to be divided. Thus all the arrangements for running the country were in place to be triggered in the event of a one-word signal from Whitehall: 'Action'.

In contrast, the TUC made no preparations whatsoever. They had made no plans to escalate the conflict after Red Friday; indeed, the fact that they had achieved a victory without direct action confirmed the right-wing labour leaders in their view that Baldwin's government was prepared to be reasonable. Beatrice Webb recorded in her diary that this view was shared by her husband, Sidney, who believed that 'the Conservative Government will go forward in our direction ... Public opinion will insist on the **middle** way ... it will be a collectivist middle way.'[4]

This was surprising considering the militant tone of the TUC Congress of 1925, but resolutions were one thing and decisive leadership quite another. In fact, although adopting resolutions to overthrow capitalism, condemning imperialism and supporting the extension of workshop organisation, all of which were socialist in content, the 1925 TUC Congress did not address itself to concrete strategy. Furthermore, the hand of the right wing was strengthened in the elections to the new General Council, which included again, after his brief spell as a cabinet minister in the Labour government of 1924, J. H. Thomas. Thomas had expressed himself as 'far from happy' about Red Friday 'because nothing is more dangerous to the future of this country than when employers of labour and the government are compelled to concede to force what they have refused to concede to reason'.[5]

He was to find a ready ally in the new TUC general secretary, Walter Citrine (acting until 1926). However inadequate, though, the general tone of this Congress stood in sharp contrast to the Labour Party conference of the same year. This was concerned primarily with an anti-communist crusade, resolving that Communist Party members should be barred from Labour Party membership and appealing to unions not to elect them as delegates. The government must have taken comfort from this since it exactly mirrored their own plans, in preparation for the coming conflict, to isolate the Communist 'ringleaders'. In October 1925 the government authorised a raid on 16 King Street, the Communist Party headquarters. Many documents were

4   Quoted in R. Miliband, *Parliamentary Socialism* (1961).
5   Quoted in Wal Hannington, *Unemployed Struggles, 1919–1936* (1978).

seized and twelve leading members of the party were arrested and imprisoned. The CPGB and the Minority Movement had consistently warned since Red Friday that the labour movement must prepare for the 'greatest struggle in the history of the working class' which would inevitably follow the termination of the mining subsidy. The party paper, *Workers' Weekly*, counted the weeks remaining in a box headed 'Warning'. The accuracy of their analysis was far too uncomfortable for the government.

That the warnings of Communists were not taken seriously by labour's leaders is only partly explained by their anti-Communism. The resolve of the government begs the question why they chose this moment to assert the full power of the state to crush the labour movement rather than resort to their more traditional strategy of divide and rule, especially when they knew that the dominant labourist position would do all in its power to avoid class confrontation. Although the mountain of evidence does not provide us with an easy answer, it is fairly clear that the Tory strategy was based on its understanding of the weakness rather than the strength of British capitalism in the inter-war years, which gave it much less room for manoeuvre and compromise than hitherto. Although trade unionism was much weaker in membership terms in the 1920s than it had been during and immediately before and after the war, the militant trend, led mostly by the Communists, was still powerful enough to block the restructuring of the British capitalism which, as we have seen, was to be accomplished at the expense of the workers in the staple industries. The defeat of this older and better organised section of the workforce was essential if a new climate of industrial relations was to be made to stick in the newer industries. A victory for the labour movement at the weakest point of capital formation – the coal industry – would have reverberations far wider than that industry, particularly when the weakness of British capital as a whole stood in sharp contrast to the development of socialism in the Soviet Russia – a point repeatedly made by the trade union militants. Hence the Tories chose in their propaganda to represent the fight of the miners and the widespread solidarity it attracted as a challenge not just to the coal owners but to civil society itself. Their own intelligence sources informed them that, given the effect of mass unemployment in sapping the strength of the trade unions, this was as good a time as any to deal the final blow and tame the movement once and for all.

The report of the Royal Commission (the Samuel Commission) was delivered in 1926. It recommended a reorganisation of the industry, but *not* its nationalisation. On the crucial question of wages, it rejected a continuation of the government subsidy and approved the wage reductions that the owners had tried to enforce the previous year. The gloves were off. The miners swiftly announced their intention to fight under the slogan 'Not a Penny off the Pay, Not a Second on the Day'. The owners posted the lockout notices and after fruitless attempts at negotiation between the government, the mine owners and the TUC, a special conference of trade union executives was convened on 1 May to approve plans for a 'national' strike in defence of the miners, which began on 3 May. The fact that the TUC presented the strike in terms of a routine industrial dispute displayed a ludicrous contrast to the government's insistence that it was a highly political event with potentially revolutionary significance. The strikers' newspaper, *The British Worker* (published by the TUC), was at great pains to argue that workers 'must not be misled by Mr. Baldwin's attempt to represent the present struggle as a political one'. The greater was the government scaremongering, the more the TUC sought to limit the scope of the dispute and to work for its speedy end no sooner had it begun. From the very beginning negotiations continued, at first secretly, between J. H. Thomas and Herbert Samuel, and then more openly. It resulted in the Samuel Memorandum – the so-called formula used to end the strike. This process was given a spurious legitimacy by the fact that the miners handed over their dispute to the TUC once the General Strike had been called. Had the government not adopted such a belligerent line, it is quite likely that the General Council would have fought shy of entering the conflict in the first place, but they were left with no choice after workers on the *Daily Mail* refused to print a leading article denouncing the strike under the banner headline

'For King and Country'. Baldwin chose to treat this as an act of war and the bluff of the TUC moderates was called.

It is only against the background of the TUC's reluctance to act, its readiness to negotiate at all times and its ideological unwillingness to recognise the political nature of the strike that the decision to call it off after nine days can be understood. However, it is less easy to understand why such a decision was made given the overwhelming support for the strike and its effectiveness, despite the carefully laid plans of the OMS. This success was due in large measure to the work of Trades Councils and Councils of Action up and down the country, which, because of their unique position as the local link between trade unionists and the community, were able to perform all manner of detailed work on picket lines and in soup kitchens and in producing general propaganda in the form of leaflets and meetings which brought the message of the strike to masses of ordinary people who might otherwise have remained uninterested or uninvolved. All such activities were accomplished in the teeth of police harassment and mass arrests, with the armed forces strategically positioned close to suspected 'trouble spots'. Paradoxical though it may seem, it was the very success of the mobilisation of the movement which frightened the TUC leadership and hastened their resolve to end the strike as quickly as possible. Rather than seeing such self-organisation as a great achievement, it was viewed by the TUC as a potential pole of rival authority in which Communists and other militants were playing a leading role. It was vital, therefore, that the TUC maintained its grip before it lost control of the mass movement, and this could only be done while it remained in charge of the situation. Thomas openly admitted this to the House of Commons:

> What I dreaded about this strike more than anything else was this: If by any chance it should have got out of the hands of those who would be able to exercise some control, every sane man knows what would have happened ... that fear was always in our minds ...we wanted ... even in this struggle to direct a disciplined army.[6]

6   Quoted in Hutt, *The Post War History of the British Working Class.*

Underlying this fear was the even greater one that loss of control would also mean an acknowledgement of the political dimension of the struggle, and now with the forces of the state ranged against them and spoiling for a fight this could lead to an overt class struggle for power – to revolution. (The *British Gazette*, the government's anti-strike paper, pointed this out on more than one occasion by characterising the strike as a challenge to parliament and asserting that if it was victorious, the General Council would become the rulers of the nation.) The TUC, aptly described by Kingsley Martin (later editor of the *New Statesman*) as 'a combatant in a war which had been forced upon it and which it feared to win', certainly was not ready for this. As for Labour's parliamentary leaders, it is doubtful as to what side some of them would have chosen.

Hence much to the surprise of the participants and to the shock of the miners the acceptance by the TUC of the Samuel Memorandum was used as the formula for a 'settlement'. In fact, the Memorandum settled absolutely nothing. It was merely a re-jigging of the proposals of the 1925 Royal Commission, with the difference that the Memorandum made vague the Commission's more explicit demands for wage reductions. No promises were exacted from the government on the continuation of the subsidy to the coal industry, the withdrawal of lockout notices or the resumption of negotiations. Nor was there any pledge to ensure that all the workers who had participated in the General Strike would not be victimised by their employers. This was nothing short of abject surrender on the part of the TUC. Despite the achievements of the left in building support for the strike even in areas like the more prosperous South where it seemed less likely, they were not strong enough to sustain it once the TUC had acted. The miners, on whose behalf the TUC had ostensibly been acting, rejected the 'settlement' entirely and were left, for six gruelling months, to fight on alone until they were starved back to work. During this time a breakaway right-wing association of miners in Nottinghamshire under the leadership of G. A. Spencer, a right-wing Labour MP who had opposed the strike, split away from the Miners' Federation, thus initiating the Spencer Union which remained outside the MFGB until 1937.

The Aftermath

In spite of the TUC's surrender, the General Strike was a remarkable achievement demonstrating the innate, and for its opponents frightening, strength of working-class solidarity. There is no denying the fact, however, that the wake of the strike witnessed a crushing defeat for the mass movement from which it took at least a decade to recover. Apart from the crushing blow to the miners there was widespread victimisation in many industries, especially in printing and the railways. Trade union funds had dropped by £4 million by the end of 1926 and union membership fell by over half a million in 1927 alone. Capitalising on its victory, government reaction was punitive. In 1927 it rushed through parliament the Trades Disputes Act by which general strikes and most sympathy strikes became illegal. The Act also outlawed the automatic political levy from members whose trade union was affiliated to the Labour Party, and instead introduced the requirement to 'contract in'. But as if this was not punishment enough, the embattled right-wing trade union leadership embarked on a 'new' course, the main aim of which was to punish the left, in particular the Communists, and to ensure that by co-operating with capitalism they would never again be faced with fighting battles which relied for their success on the uncertain outcome of mass mobilisation. Prompted by the TUC and following the example of the Labour Party, many unions now invoked bans and proscriptions against Communists holding office and showed open hostility to the Minority Movement. This followed a series of articles by Citrine attacking it. The persecution reached new depths in 1929 when the General Council published its 'Inquiry into Disruption', which alleged that disruptive activities in the trade union movement were the work of Communists under orders from Moscow.

Mondism

The new direction taken by the TUC was a rehash of old class collaborationist ideas in new packaging. The lesson it learned from the General Strike was simply that such class warfare was never to be repeated and that capitalism was here to stay. Citrine argued that 'trade unionism has reached the end of a defensive stage in its evolution' and that its new aim should be to

actively participate in a concerted effort to raise industry to its highest efficiency by developing the most scientific methods of production, eliminating waste and harmful restrictions, removing the causes of friction and unavoidable conflict.[7]

The TUC wrote to employers' organisations suggesting joint discussions along these lines. Alfred Mond and 21 other employers, mainly in the newer industries, responded favourably and hence in 1928 the Mond–Turner talks began (Ben Turner chaired the TUC General Council). A set of proposals were agreed which the TUC regarded as the foundation of the industrial relations of the future in contrast to the 'outdated', conflictual model of the militants. In return for trade union recognition and promises of no victimisation, joint conciliation boards would be established to head off industrial disputes. Conciliation was hardly new, but the proposal to create a National Industrial Council consisting of equal numbers of employers and trade unionists to engage in 'general consultations on the widest questions' was hailed as a wonderfully innovative departure. However, unlike similar efforts to reconcile both sides of the industrial divide in France and Germany after great postwar displays of workers' power, this British initiative was only moderately successful and even then only in the newer industries. The main employers' organisations representing the older industries overwhelmingly rejected the Mond–Turner proposals. These industries were all labour-intensive and, as we have seen, sought to maintain their profit by

---

7   Walter Citrine, *Manchester Guardian*, Industrial Relations Supplement, 30 November 1927.

reducing labour costs through sackings or wage cuts. The niceties of conciliation and consultation were lost on them. Whether the TUC liked it or not, the only way they could operate was through the 'old-fashioned' class war method and now that the TUC had decided to drop its 'defensive' stance, so much the better for the profits of these employers.

The fight against this decisive turn to the right was not as strong as might have been expected from the militant tradition against which it was directed. This was in part due to the psychology of defeat, but more importantly to the fact that the left, influenced by the Comintern's abandonment of the 'united front' strategy in 1929, entered its sectarian phase. The left adopted a bunker mentality, concentrating its attention on building rival organisations and strengthening the Communist Party, thereby, at a critical moment, leaving the right a free hand to impose its ideological domination over the movement as a whole. A powerful weapon in its ideological armoury was handed to the TUC in 1929 when it took editorial control of the *Daily Herald*.

Trade Unions and the Labour Party

Although the outcome of the second Labour government proved something of a shock to the trade unions, the policy of that government was in all essentials the political counterpart of Mondism. It would have been, given the closeness between the two wings of the movement, extremely difficult for Labour to have pursued the line it did had the TUC and its affiliates adopted a less collaborationist approach after the General Strike. The link between the two wings was also a physical one when from 1928 the Labour Party and the TUC shared the same headquarters (Transport House) as that of the largest union, the Transport and General Workers. Following the Labour debacle in the general election of 1931 the TUC General Council held the party together through a revamped National Joint Council linking the two organisations and on which the TUC now had as many members as the Labour National Executive and the parliamentary party combined.

The Effect on Women

The effect of the General Strike's defeat was, as we have seen, severe indeed for the labour movement as a whole, but for women workers and women trade unionists it was disastrous. The peak of women's trade union membership reached in 1920 (nearly 1½ million, 25 per cent of the total female workforce) had dropped to a mere half million by 1939, despite the fact that the percentage of women within the total workforce had risen. This bleak statistic cannot be accounted for by suggesting that women somehow became 'anti-union' in the inter-war years. Obviously, the decline in membership has to be placed in the context of the overall decline, but within this there were specific features which help to explain the factors affecting women. Chief among these were the attitudes of the unions themselves. In the general climate of unemployment, cost-cutting and reversion on the part of the unions to narrow and sectionalist attitudes, women workers were perceived as a threat. Their employment was rising (from 27 per cent of the total workforce in 1923 to 30 per cent in 1939) at the expense, or so it was thought, of that of men. This provoked two contradictory attitudes on the part of the male leaders, both of which were motivated by self-interest, rather than the interests of women themselves. On the one hand, many unions which organised in industries with a high percentage of women workers (e.g. USDAW, NUT, NALGO and the Post Office workers) sought to restrict the employment of women by calling for a strict application of the marriage bar, or the introduction of one. Almost all of them refused to campaign or shelved demands for equal pay and instead pursued wage claims which *increased* the differentials between men and women. Others, like the Union of Post Office Workers in 1935, went further and called for a halt to female employment altogether. In these ways many of the unions contributed massively to the problem that they thought they were addressing, namely the use of women as cheap labour in a time of recession and high unemployment.

On the other hand, the drop in trade union membership was a problem that might be redressed if only women could be persuaded to swell the declining ranks and boost the depleted coffers. Thus at the same time as pursuing negative policies on the employment of women, individual unions and the TUC were actively involved in recruitment campaigns. To its credit the TUC did at least recognise that women were less likely to be used as a source of cheap labour if they were unionised. It established, in 1925, its own Women's Conference and later, in 1930, a Women Workers' Group (later known as the Women's Advisory Committee) to assist the General Council to tackle the 'problem' of women. The Women's Committee was left to launch a series of recruitment campaigns which proposed, sensibly, to increase the involvement of women by establishing local women's committees. Such committees would themselves campaign around the issues of most concern to women workers and would, thereby, assist in recruitment. These attempts were greeted with solid indifference. In the wake of their failure, the General Council itself stepped in in 1937 and again in 1939 with its own remedy. It launched two campaigns, both based on the assumption that trade unionism would attract women if it appealed to them on the basis of such 'womanly' issues as personal health and beauty. Trade unionism, according to a special leaflet adorned with a radiant-looking female clad in a swimming costume, was the 'ticket' to health and beauty, presumably because it would ensure that improved wages secured by unions could be used to buy cosmetics and other adornments. Apart from the fact that such male-designed campaigns were grossly insulting to women's intelligence, they were an abject failure as the membership figures showed. Then, as now, women workers needed to be convinced of the tangible benefits of trade unions on the issues of most concern to them as workers rather than as putative beauty queens. Yet in the defeatist, defensive and sectional attitudes of the trade union leaderships of the inter-war period, precisely the opposite message was conveyed.

Bibliography

Cole, G. D. H. *The Common People, 1746–1946* (Routledge, 1965)

Farman, C. *The General Strike* (Rupert Hart-Davis, 1972)

Hannington, W. *Unemployed Struggles, 1919–1936* (Lawrence & Wishart, 1978)

Hutt, A. *The Post War History of the British Working Class* (Gollancz, 1937)

Klugmann, J. *History of the Communist Party of Great Britain*, vol. 2 (Lawrence & Wishart, 1969)

Miliband, R. *Parliamentary Socialism* (Allen & Unwin, 1961)

Skelley, J. (ed.). *The General Strike 1926* (Lawrence & Wishart, 1976)

13

THE LABOUR MOVEMENT, FASCISM AND ANTI-FASCISM, AND WAR

The collapse of the Labour government in 1931 created a political hiatus, temporarily filled by the TUC. The general election of that year, in which MacDonald and his supporters stood as National government candidates, had a disastrous effect on the parliamentary Labour Party, reducing it to just 46 MPs. Many of the big names who had forged the labourist consensus were swept up with or away on the tide of MacDonaldism. This left, for the first time, a distinctly socialist rump in parliament, almost half of whom were MPs sponsored by the Miners' Federation. Men with outspoken left-wing convictions like George Lansbury, Stafford Cripps and Clement Attlee now came to the fore as Labour's political leaders, and until 1934 were responsible for the production of some of the most radical policies that the Labour Party has known before or since.

The TUC's Political Influence

However, such men, although they held office in the years following the 1931 collapse, did not hold power and hence their effectiveness was limited. Real power was, as we have seen, in the hands of the TUC through the National Joint Council. Given the vehemently anti-left stance taken by the TUC and affiliated unions in the years following the General Strike, it welcomed with alacrity the opportunity to use its increased influence in the Labour Party for similar anti-left purposes. Thus it was that when for the first time the opportunity arose to build unity between the now apparently dominant labour left and the hitherto shunned extra-parliamentary movement, the TUC rose as a Colossus to champion the old-style labourist politics which had arguably been responsible for the mess the party was in now. The left was not strong enough to insist on the discussion and analysis of Labour's failings. It was far more convenient and certainly less embarrassing for those (i.e. the majority) who had gone along with the policies to blame the whole debacle on MacDonald. His somewhat meaningless punishment (considering he was prime minister of the National government) was, along with his supporters, expulsion from the Labour Party.

The undoubted influence of the left, as shown in Labour Party conference decisions between 1932 and 1934, amounted more to a triumph of words over deeds and as such represented a missed opportunity for those who sought to alter the fundamental course of the party away from labourism and towards socialism. This is not to minimise the achievements of those years in which a genuine commitment was made to put the party on a socialist course. 'For Socialism and Peace', the party programme adopted in 1934, outspokenly proclaimed 'that what the nation now requires is not merely social reform, but Socialism' and pledged a future Labour government to 'establish public ownership and control of the primary industries and services as a foundation step' with employees in them having 'an effective share in direction and control'. However, aside from conference decisions and policy statements, the force of the left's advance in practical terms was considerably weakened by the untimely and ill-judged decision in 1932 of the ILP to disaffiliate from the Labour Party. Its place as the socialist conscience of the party was inadequately filled by the newly formed Socialist League (1932) which, although presenting a much sharper ideological challenge to reformism than had the ILP, lacked the mass base that its predecessor had formerly achieved. Its membership never exceeded 3,000 and it was primarily London-based. The stranglehold of the TUC did not quash the popularity of socialist ideas in the Labour Party in the 1930s, but was sufficient to reduce their practical effectiveness and decisive enough to impose its dominance over two major policy areas, notably relations with the Communist Party and foreign affairs. As it turned out, these issues became decisively linked and prevented the party from playing as important a role as it might otherwise have done in the anti-fascist struggle at home and abroad because to do so would have meant working alongside the Communists.

Anti-Communism

By 1931 the Communist Party had jettisoned its sectarian 'class against class' line and sought to reconstruct alliances with the mainstream of the labour movement. The ground for unity was infertile even though the 1930s produced a rich crop of intellectual converts to marxism. Both the TUC and the Labour Party leaderships had already displayed hostility to Communism in the years following the General Strike before the Communist Party's sectarianism had provided them with a more legitimate excuse. In 1933 the CP formally proposed that the Labour Party join them in creating a 'united front' against Fascism and war. Not only was this met with a flat refusal from the Labour Party, but its National Joint Council issued a manifesto a few days later entitled 'Democracy and Dictatorship', which equated Communism and Fascism as twin evils to be opposed alike and from which the world could be saved only by asserting the supremacy of constitutional principles of which the Labour Party stood as a champion. The Labour left never succeeded in defeating this line, which persisted throughout the 1930s and led the Labour Party to reply to every proposal for joint action against Fascism with the repeated refrain that voting Labour was the only way forward. The fact that there was no general election after 1935 until the Second World War was over did not seem to persuade its proponents of the need to change the refrain. This TUC-inspired manifesto was followed in 1934 by the General Council's own circular in which unions were advised to exclude Communists from posts of responsibility and *instructed* Trades Councils, over which it had more direct jurisdiction, that they were obliged to operate such bans. Individual trade unions similarly caught the anti-communist disease with consequent effects on their attitudes to militants within their own ranks.

Trade Unionism

Trade union membership grew once again from 1933 when the worst effects of the depression were over. Although the tameness of the trade union leaders ensured that there were very few official strikes, this did not mean that the six years before the outbreak of war were marked by industrial harmony. The mutiny of the navy at Invergordon in 1931, while not signalling a more general rising, set the pattern for later, self-organised, rank-and-file disputes, which became the hallmark of militant activity in the 1930s. The Communist Party had been and remained in the forefront of the rank-and-file movement. The active and well-supported organisation of London bus workers, the bane of Bevin's TGWU, had its origins during the period of the party's sectarianism when it was attempting to form alternative 'red button' unions. Although the bus workers' rank-and-file movement remained an unofficial movement with Communists like Bert Papworth in the leadership, by 1932 its journal, *Busman's Punch*, stated unequivocally that 'Nothing could be more against the interests of Busmen at the present time than a breakaway from the TGWU, and nothing could suit the combine better.'[1]

In railways, engineering and mining, where similar forms of organisation to that of the bus workers had been initiated by Communists, great gains were made in expanding trade union membership often to hitherto unorganised areas like the aircraft industry. Despite the chronic weakness of trade unionism in the mining industry, militants managed to eliminate Spencerism (the company unions formed after the General Strike) by utilising the novel tactic of the stay-down strike. More could have been achieved had not the paranoid anti-Communism of the trade union leaders got in the way. The more successful were the militants the more determined was the leadership to smash them,

---

1   Quoted in Ken Fuller, *Radical Aristocrats* (1985).

even if this meant colluding with the employers against their own members. The starkest example of this was the TGWU's handling of the 1937 bus strike. The strength of the bus workers' organisation, which had its own status as a trade group with a seat on the union's executive, had succeeded in making the 1937 'Coronation' strike (a bus strike which coincided both with the Coronation of King George VI and Cup Final Day) official. However, Bevin ensured that the bus workers were left isolated and hence unable to win their demand for a seven-hour day. His purpose in facilitating the strike's defeat was to destroy the bus workers' rank-and-file movement. Bill Jones, one of the RFM leaders, later wrote that Bevin

> knew that we were going to be beaten and he worked that way ... he wasn't averse to the timing of the strike because he thought that the popular feeling [was] against us – being on strike while the Coronation was on – plus the fact that ... sewing up all the other sections would sink us.[2]

The aftermath provided Bevin with the long-awaited opportunity to dismantle the London bus workers' section and to expel its leaders, Papworth, Jones and others, from the union.

Anti-Fascism

The Labour Party's rejection of the call to form a United Front with others on the left meant that it was isolated from the increasingly broad-based movement in Britain which sought to expose the evils of Fascism internationally and to fight its home-grown variety in the form of Oswald Mosley's British Union of Fascists. Outside the Labour Party and TUC leaderships most progressive people did not equate Communism and Fascism and readily supported communist initiatives to combat it. Mosley tried first to tap what he thought were the latent fascist prejudices of the Tory-voting middle and upper classes. There were good grounds for this given the fairly widespread admiration for Mussolini and Hitler in such circles. However, the economic dislocation in Germany

2   Quoted in ibid.

and Italy which had pauperised the middle class in particular and made it a fertile fascist recruiting ground did not exist to such a degree in Britain where economic recovery after 1932 had ensured greater political stability. The Conservative Party, with its tough stand in defence of capital at home and its anti-soviet and later appeasement foreign policy, ensured that it remained a suitable vehicle for the expression of right-wing opinion. Anti-Fascists had managed to gain entry to the big BUF rally at Olympia in June 1934 to which thousands of influential people had been invited on a ticket-only basis, provoking awful violence from Mosley's black-shirted henchmen. This served to alarm and alienate respectable opinion and as a result induced Mosley to change his tactics. From 1935 onwards his overtly anti-Semitic propaganda was directed more specifically to the working class in an effort to encourage them to blame the Jews for their all too obvious economic hardship. This approach led the BUF to concentrate its activity in working-class areas and especially the East End of London, an area which accommodated 90 per cent of Britain's 330,000 Jewish population. (Jews accounted for a minuscule 0.8 per cent of the total population of Britain.) With police protection the BUF attempted to stage a number of marches and rallies, the most provocative and infamous being the attempt to march through the East End in October 1936. Anti-fascist groups led by the Communist Party prevented or stopped many of these marches, but in the case of the East End this was accomplished by barricades and pitched battles, particularly in Cable Street. Similar tactics were used by anti-Fascists in Bermondsey. Despite the broad unity achieved in mobilising thousands of anti-Fascists, the official Labour Party and trade union leadership took no part in, and indeed discouraged, such activities on the grounds that scenes of violence, which would of necessity be provoked by counter-demonstrations, would only serve to play into Mosley's hands. The official leadership of Anglo-Jewry, the Board of Deputies of British Jews, supported by the community's weekly paper the *Jewish Chronicle*, took a similar line. However, such caution did not reflect the views of the majority of Jews in the East End and elsewhere, who were subjected to frequent abuse and attack by fascist thugs. The Jewish Peoples Council against Fascism and Anti-Semitism was formed to offer determined resistance to the BUF. It worked closely with other organisations, especially the Communist Party, which counted many Jews among its London membership and reflected the progressive wing of Anglo-Jewry which had deep links with the labour movement through trade unions and Workers' Circles. Its first conference in 1936 showed that its appeal went beyond the many Jews who were socialists. Delegates attended from synagogues, Zionist groups, Jewish youth groups and ex-servicemen's organisations.

The tactics of the Communist Party, agreed after much internal debate, were twofold. First, the aim was to expose the fascist danger nationally and internationally and to ensure that it never gained a foothold in Britain by mobilising entire communities to fight it on the streets. This meant also fighting the police, who saw their role as protectors of the Fascists' right to conduct their propaganda openly. Second, the aim was, as Phil Piratin, one of the communist leaders in the East End and prominent in the anti-fascist struggle and later Communist MP for Mile End, put it, 'to cut the ground from under the fascists' feet'.[3] He and others argued that a distinction had to be made between the hard core of the BUF and the ordinary working-class people who were attracted to it. When the question was answered as to why such people were supporting Mosley, the party, having first dismissed such people as enemies, eventually came to the conclusion that

> there were certain latent anti-Semitic prejudices ... but above all these people, like most in East London, were living miserable, squalid lives. Their homes were slums, many were unemployed...therefore the Communist Party should help the people to improve their conditions of life, in the course of which we could show them who was really responsible ... and get them organised to fight against their real exploiters.[4]

This meant meticulous, slogging attention to local issues, especially the grievances of tenants against rack-renting landlords and slum conditions and slowly but surely building an effective

3   Phil Piratin, *Our Flag Stays Red* (1978).
4   Ibid..

tenants' organisation in Stepney in particular. The Stepney Tenants' Defence League actually employed three full-time paid organisers. It is impossible to assess the extent to which this kind of activity fulfilled the aim of winning away potential fascist sympathisers from the BUF. It is certain, though, that the prestige of the Communist Party was greatly enhanced. Piratin was elected to Stepney Council in 1937 and by 1945 there were twelve Communist councillors as well as a Communist MP – Piratin himself.

Spain

In 1936 Franco and his fascist collaborators, aided by arms and ammunition from Nazi Germany and fascist Italy, staged an insurrection against the elected Popular Front government of the Spanish Republic, unleashing a civil war which, by 1939, resulted in the military defeat of the elected government. It is perhaps hard to explain why the cause of Republican Spain attracted such widespread international support given that the fascist coups in Germany and Italy had passed without a similar scale of world-wide democratic mobilisation. Perhaps this is due in part to the fact that the victory of Fascism in those two countries had been achieved by the prior defeat of internal democratic opposition, and that such opposition had been rendered less effective in the case of Germany by the great hostility between the Communists and Social Democrats. Certainly by 1936 the real horror of Fascism, now well established in those two countries, was evident for all to see and the popular and broad-based opposition to it in Spain provided an opportunity for democrats of all political shades to show practical solidarity. Such work was now greatly assisted by the commitment of Communists to the strategy of the united front, a strategy which had come too late for the survival of democracy in Germany.

Whatever the reasons, a huge wave of support for the Spanish Republic quickly developed within weeks of the military assault upon it. This was unlike an ordinary solidarity movement, although those characteristics were also in evidence in Britain in the form of a National Joint Committee for Spanish Relief chaired by a Conservative MP, the Duchess of Atholl. This was supplemented by local Aid Spain committees, which mushroomed in almost every town. However, the uniqueness of the solidarity movement lay in the fact that it inspired men and women to actually go to Spain in the service of the Republic. From many countries, Britain included, volunteers were recruited (privately by Communists) to the International Brigade to fight alongside their Spanish comrades-in-arms, risking death and injury from the superior military strength of the Fascists. Two thousand British volunteers went, attached first to different units, but later forming the British Battalion under the command of Bill Alexander. Five hundred and twenty six of them were killed and many more were injured. Alexander's estimate of the total number of international volunteers is 42,000, of whom 20,000 were killed, reported missing or were totally disabled. In January 1937 the British government made it illegal to volunteer to fight in Spain, but this did not stop the process, it just made it more difficult. Although the British Battalion included Labour Party members, the official line of that organisation and of the TUC was strongly hostile to the volunteer movement and was even opposed, despite the broad political base of the Relief Committee, to giving any support at all to the Republican cause other than eventually agreeing, having first supported the government's non-intervention line, that Spain had the right to buy arms. Indeed Citrine (as TUC general secretary) even attempted to find a way of stopping unions from giving funds to the Dependants' Aid Committee. This attitude was doubtless influenced by the Tory press, which insisted on seeing the Republicans as crypto-Communists, and hence viewed a fascist victory as a timely defeat for a Moscow-backed communist revolution.

Apart from the Soviet Union, the countries affiliated to the League of Nations resolutely adopted a non-interventionist policy in Spain, although it was quite clear that Germany and Italy were breaching the League's covenant in their active support for the Fascists' leader, General Franco. The British government was the most stalwart in its refusal to aid Spain and hence colluded tacitly in Hitler's vision of a fascist victory in Spain as a dress rehearsal in the coming bid for world domination. Spain also provided a convenient opportunity to test the sophisticated weaponry to which so much of Germany's industrial production had been turned. In this sense, therefore, 'non-intervention' was plainly a euphemism for banning the supply of arms and volunteers to the Republican side, while doing nothing to prevent similar support for Franco.

The Approach to the Second World War

Popular awareness of and opposition to the fascist threat at home and abroad contrasted sharply with the benign approach of the government, which remained until 1939 far more committed to anti-Communism than to anti-Fascism. In practice this meant ditching Britain's responsibility as a member of the League of Nations (forerunner of the United Nations) to maintain peace through collective security by failing to take action when peace was threatened by Hitler's and Mussolini's aggressive and expansionist policies.

The TUC and Labour Party leadership accepted in broad principle the Foreign Office line. Anti-Sovietism was entirely consistent with their domestic anti-Communism. A statement agreed by both wings of the labour movement's leadership, 'War and Peace', published in 1934, rejected the policies of pacifism and the international general strike to prevent war and instead proclaimed the movement's duty 'unflinchingly to support our Government in all the risks and consequences of fulfilling its duty to take part in collective action against a peace breaker'. The only problem with this was that it was increasingly obvious that the government had no intention of pursuing such a policy and the Labour leaders were so preoccupied with the 'red scare' that they hardly noticed.

In the early 1930s, before the fascist threat to world peace had shown itself, the by then well-publicised horror of the 1914–18 war inspired mass support for the League of Nations as the only organisation likely to prevent a recurrence. The League of Nations

Union organised what came to be known as the peace ballot, which turned out to be the largest poll (apart from general elections) ever to be conducted in Britain. In all, 11,500,000 people voted in response to five quite detailed questions relating to international arms reduction, attitude to the League itself, the possibility of collective military security and/or economic sanctions and the banning of private arms sales. This was not simply a pacifist ballot but a clear statement of opinion on the way in which peace could be maintained. The overwhelming view was in favour of peace through collective security mediated by the League. The Tories were quick to seize upon the convincing message of the peace ballot which preceded the 1935 general election. Baldwin used it to jump on the bandwagon and declare support for the League and collective security. The hypocrisy of this was to be revealed weeks later when the Baldwin government signed the Anglo-German Naval Treaty by which the Nazis were given the go-ahead to build 35 per cent of the naval tonnage of the British Empire. By a strange quirk of fate the ballot results were announced in 1935, the year in which Italy invaded Abyssinia. It was soon discovered that the League was only as strong as its member states permitted it to be. Collective security was hardly put to the test other than in the form of pious phrases.

The United Front and the Popular Front

Apart from solidarity action with Spain, the years between 1936 and 1938 witnessed the emergence of a popular mass movement against Fascism and war the like of which had not been in evidence for almost a century. Clearly, this owed much to the decisions made at the Seventh Congress of the Comintern held in 1935. There Georgi Dimitrov, the Bulgarian communist who had attracted world-wide attention when he stood trial by the Nazis for allegedly starting the Reichstag fire, presented a report 'For the Unity of the Working Class Against Fascism'. This called for an end *in practice* to 'self-satisfied sectarianism ... which professes to know all and considers it superfluous to learn from the masses'. By implication this was a criticism of the fact that although Communists had officially renounced the 'class against class' doctrine three years previously the commitment to unity remained only a theoretical one. The victory of the Nazis injected a note of urgency into the debate. Dimitrov called for the building of united fronts in each country, but the distinction between this and the previous use of the term was that now such a front was not for the purpose of establishing socialism, but a 'mighty weapon which renders the working class capable not only of successful defence but also of successful counter-attack against fascism, the class enemy'. The section of the report that dealt with Great Britain illustrated the changed approach. Whereas hitherto the line would have been to campaign for a 'soviet' government 'as the only form of government capable of emancipating the workers from the yoke of capital', the most urgent task now was to defeat the National government and elect Labour, despite their poor record. Such a government would not carry out socialist measures, but at a minimum it must 'defend the most essential economic and political interests of the working class'. Other countries like France (1934) and later Spain had already attempted such a strategy and elected Popular Front governments. Critics, especially Trotsky and his followers, then and now thought that such a strategy amounted to the submerging of socialism in the interest of mass unity. To some extent they were correct, in the sense that because bourgeois democracy was perceived as preferable to Fascism, the advocates of united and popular fronts saw the necessity of defending the former. This did not transform them into bourgeois democrats, but rather because they were socialists it meant a realisation that whatever the limitations of bourgeois democracy it presented opportunities for socialist advance which would be totally nullified in conditions of fascist terror, the very existence of which was predicated on the annihilation of the labour movement. Harry Pollitt, general secretary of the CPGB, endorsed Dimitrov's line and took it a stage further. In his speech at the Seventh Congress he argued that the united front should be broadened in such a way 'that it can win to its support, not only organised workers, but every democrat and lover of peace, all sections of the petty bourgeoisie'.

This kind of thinking was readily translated into the broad movement to save Spain described earlier. It was evident in a great variety of other campaigns on international issues, some of which had unexpected dimensions. In 1936 the Olympic Games, much to the delight of the Nazis, were held in Berlin. The Socialist Workers' Sports International, which had been in existence and organising international competitions between teams of 'worker athletes' since 1913, decided to bring forward plans for a Peoples' Games and stage them in Barcelona in 1936 as an anti-fascist opposition to the official games. Four thousand athletes from most European countries thus gathered in Berlin, including 200 from Britain, some of whom withdrew from the Berlin Games in protest against Fascism. However, on the day the Peoples' Games were due to start Franco unleashed his attack on the Republic and the Civil War began. Although the athletes did not stay to fight, they celebrated the first fascist defeat in Barcelona by parading through the streets dressed in their blazers and waving their team banners in a gesture of anti-fascist solidarity.[5]

By 1937, apart from their large-scale involvement in the Spanish Civil War, Italy had conquered Abyssinia, while Germany, fully rearmed, had recovered the Saarland and remilitarised the Rhineland (both territories denied to her by the treaty of Versailles). A new note of urgency was now given to the opposition to appeasement policy of Neville Chamberlain, the new prime minister. Although the 1936 Labour Party conference gave a huge majority to the opposition of the national executive to the United Front, this did not end the issue. In 1937 the Socialist League agreed to launch a unity campaign together with the ILP and the Communist Party. A Unity Manifesto was issued, signed by leading members of all three organisations, calling for 'unity of all sections of the working class movement ... in the struggle against fascism, reaction and war and against the National Government'. Even though the manifesto called for the return of a Labour

---

5   Most of the information on the Barcelona Games was taken from an article by Matthew Sturgis, based on an interview with a member of the British team, Reg (later Lord) Underhill, in a special supplement on the 1992 Barcelona Olympics in the *Independent on Sunday*, 26 July 1992.

government as an integral part of this strategy, the response of the
leadership of the party was hostile in the extreme. Aware of the
preparations for this new venture, the NEC had already issued an
'Appeal for Party Loyalty'. It now not only vigorously denounced
the campaign, but expelled the Socialist League from the Labour
Party. Having anticipated this, the Socialist League dissolved itself,
leaving its former members free to involve themselves in the unity
campaign as individuals.

At a meeting of the Left Book Club in 1938,[6] the campaign went
a stage further rather more along the lines of what was already
known elsewhere as a Popular Front. Pollitt called for a people's
front 'of all peace and progressive forces with no prior condition',
although it did not preclude independent socialist activity being
undertaken at the same time. The theory behind such a strategy has
already been noted. Whereas the original pre-1935 conception of
the united front limited itself to a call for the unity of the working
class, the campaign now transcended class boundaries and party
divisions. It was addressed to all anti-Fascists regardless of party,
which would now include a section of the Conservative Party
led by Churchill which was increasingly critical of appeasement.
Whilst these Tories did not share the socialists' ideological hostility
to Fascism, they were, for their own reasons, openly opposed to
Hitler's plans for world domination and in favour of firm military
action to stop him. The Popular Front was therefore, apart from
being a means of a mass mobilisation of public opinion around
the simple and immediate slogan 'Chamberlain Must Go', also a
mechanism for splitting the Tories.

6   The Left Book Club was established in 1936, shortly before the outbreak of the
    Spanish Civil War, by the publisher Victor Gollancz in association with Harry
    Pollitt and John Strachey. It was closely associated with and provided imaginative
    propaganda for the campaign for united and popular fronts, and thereby with the
    Communist Party. For 2s 6d members received a Left Book of the Month. The
    books helped to educate readers about the horror of Fascism and war, but there
    was also a practical and mobilising side to LBC activity in the form of the Groups
    Department which employed full-time workers to organise left groups throughout
    the country – over 730 of them by the end of 1937. These not only discussed the
    monthly choice but raised money for Spain and other causes, and organised meet-
    ings, rallies and demonstrations. By March 1938 the LBC had around 58,000
    members and countless thousands, irrespective of political affiliation, attended or
    participated in Group activity.

Despite the opposition of small groups on the left influenced by Trotsky, who shrunk from any association for whatever purpose with 'the class enemy', the Popular Front campaign attracted mass support from all shades of opinion. Although it did not succeed in its desired effect of removing Chamberlain before he had effectively colluded with Hitler in the annexation of Austria (the *Anschluss*) and, by the infamous Munich Agreement, the occupation of the Sudetenland (part of Czechoslovakia), it had a powerful impact. Some 100 local Peoples' Front Committees were formed in 1938 and a Popular Front candidate, Vernon Bartlett, was returned at a by-election in Bridgwater in that year defeating the government candidate. Given the extent of support for the Popular Front campaign, which was clearly on the increase after the Munich fiasco, it is all the more surprising that the Labour Party leadership persisted in dogged and sectarian opposition to it. This resulted in 1939 in the NEC's decision to expel from membership of the Labour Party all those who continued to support the campaign. Stafford Cripps, Aneurin Bevan, Charles Trevelyan and others were among the victims. Cripps was a special target since he had defied the leadership by publishing, widely circulating and refusing to retract the Cripps Memorandum, which urged support for the principle of collective security and the union of all anti-government parties 'to act together and at once for the sake of peace and civilisation'.

The 'Phoney War'

The German invasion of Poland in 1939 finally forced Chamberlain's government to recognise the failure of appeasement policy and to declare war on Germany in September 1939. However, this declaration proved to be purely formal. Emboldened by the non-aggression pact struck with the Soviet Union in August, and confident that the British were unprepared for war, the German military machine struck. In a matter of months the German army overran eastern Europe including the Baltic States, had occupied Norway and Denmark in the north and in the west had occupied Belgium and Holland, and defeated France. Apart from the ignominious defeat and retreat from Dunkirk, from September 1939 until May 1940 Britain was hardly involved in the conflict which now engulfed all of continental Europe. Hence the term 'phoney war', used critically to describe the government's inaction, was an accurate description of its lack of involvement and lack of serious military preparation. Dunkirk had exposed, despite the bombast, Britain's military weakness. The LBC publication in 1940 of *Guilty Men*, written by a group of Labour MPs under the pseudonym 'Cato', was a savage indictment of appeasement and characterised the Dunkirk debacle as a defeat of 'flesh against steel'. The British army was, it said, 'doomed *before* they took the field'.

The pressure on the government to pursue a more active opposition to Hitler was maintained, although the popular front strategy suffered a setback as a result of the changed line of the Comintern which, by the end of September 1939, proclaimed that 'in this war blame falls on all the capitalist governments and primarily the ruling classes of the belligerent states'.[7] Having been at the forefront of the alliance to confront fascist aggression, the British Communist Party accordingly changed its line too. It was a dramatic and short-sighted reversal of policy which two leading members, including Pollitt, could not support. It was one thing to understand and view with some sympathy the difficult situation of the Soviet Union, which had been forced to abandon its frequent attempts to form an alliance with Britain and France against Hitler. The appeasement policies of both countries had precluded such a possibility, ultimately forcing the USSR to buy time to prepare itself for the coming struggle, which she might have to face alone. However, it was quite another matter for the Comintern, a month later and after European Communist Parties had already declared themselves in support of a war against Fascism, to hold that the needs of Soviet diplomacy should signal a change at the end of September that the war was a fight between rival imperialisms, and that Chamberlain and Churchill were as bad as Hitler and Mussolini. The pamphlet written by Pollitt, 'How to Win the

7   Quoted in R. Palme Dutt, *The Internationale* (1964).

War', issued shortly after war was declared, was withdrawn and owing to the fact that he stuck by the original party line, he resigned as general secretary and was replaced by Palme Dutt.

Labour's record during the period of the phoney war was not much better. Although the party rejected an invitation to be represented in Chamberlain's cabinet, it accepted the Tory call for an electoral truce and was deflected from a more strenuous criticism of governmental inaction by joining the furore occasioned by the Soviet invasion of Finland. The government, in contrast to its accustomed lethargy in dealing with Hitler, sent 50 bombers to help the Finns, and for a while it seemed that Britain and its allies had forgotten on whose side they were. The Germans decided the issue for them by the invasion of France and the Low Countries – an act which sealed the fate of Chamberlain, who was now unable to resist the Tory revolt which overthrew him in May 1940. Labour played little part in these developments, but reaped the reward of office in the new coalition government headed by Churchill.

Bibliography

Branson, N. and Heinemann, M. *Britain in the Nineteen Thirties* (Panther, 1973)

Cato. *Guilty Men* (Gollancz, 1940)

Fuller, K. *Radical Aristocrats: London Busworkers from the 1880s to the 1980s* (Lawrence & Wishart, 1985)

Fyrth, J. (ed.). *Britain, Fascism and the Popular Front* (Lawrence & Wishart, 1985)

Green, N. and Elliott, A. M. *Spain against Fascism 1936–9*, 'Our History' pamphlet no. 67 (n.d.)

Palme-Dutt, R. *The Internationale* (Lawrence & Wishart, 1964)

Piratin, P. *Our Flag Stays Red* (Lawrence & Wishart, 1978; first published 1948)

Pollitt, H. *Selected Articles & Speeches*, vol. 1 (Lawrence & Wishart, 1953)

Rosenberg, D. *Facing up to Anti-Semitism* (JCARP Publications, 1985)

14

WAR AND PEACE, 1940–1951

The roots of the first majority Labour government of 1945–51 were to be found during the Second World War when, from 1940, Labour participated as a full partner in Churchill's coalition government. During the war Labour leaders not only acquired invaluable experience of ministerial responsibility, after 20 years in the wilderness, but also helped to construct the collectivist practices of wartime that laid the foundations of the welfare state. Whatever the failings of the Labour Party in the 1930s, its domestic policy had advanced steadily along the lines of nationalisation and the redistribution of wealth, projecting the claims of the party as the natural successor in peacetime to the successful experiments at state control and 'equality of sacrifice' demanded by wartime conditions. In this regard the Second World War was unlike the First. The mass participation in the war effort and the popular radical spirit inspiring it were strong enough to exact its reward. This reward, whilst falling short of socialism, ensured a consensus to retain the state controls that had been grudgingly conceded during the First World War and were hastily dismantled after it.

Whereas the 1914–18 war was unpopular as a mismanaged fight between rival imperialisms, the war of 1939–45 was perceived differently. Whilst it undoubtedly retained the features of a capitalist power struggle, the mass mobilisation of opposition to the Axis Powers (Germany, Italy and Japan) was motivated by a higher ideal – the determination to rid the world of Fascism. Of course, not every participant in the struggle was a conscious anti-Fascist, but as news of the horrors perpetrated by Fascism and the heroic resistance movements of nations under its control gradually filtered through, so the war took on something of the character of a 'people's war'. The wartime alliance with the Soviet Union, whose decisive contribution to the defeat of Fascism was widely acknowledged, lessened for a while the anti-Sovietism and anti-Communism which had pervaded the inter-war years. In these conditions the postwar domestic policies of the Allied Powers were forced to pay regard to the needs of the masses to a greater extent than ever before. For Britain the political wartime consensus extended beyond state controls to social reform, enabling parliamentary Labourism in the form of the first majority Labour government to reach its 'finest hour'. The postwar Labour government represented the triumph and the limit of social change through the mechanism of reform within the framework of the capitalist system. The peaceful transition to a mixed economy and welfare state capitalism, the proud boast of Labour's leaders, could only have been accomplished under these special conditions of consensus, but as such even by the end of the 1940s it was threatened once capital and its Tory political voice had a chance to recover and realign itself under the aegis of the Cold War politics which dominated postwar international relations. As Labour was to find to its cost, its naive reliance on the parliamentary system and what it regarded as the neutral state machine were no substitute for the mass movement outside parliament to defend the reforms it championed.

The Labour Movement and the Second World War

Of the five members of Churchill's war cabinet formed in May 1940 two, Clement Attlee and Arthur Greenwood, were Labour MPs. Other Labour members held ministerial positions, the most important of whom in terms of labour relations was Ernest Bevin, Minister of Labour and National Service. Clearly Bevin's standing as leader of Britain's biggest trade union, the TGWU, was intended to deflect the kind of opposition to the control of labour which had been such a feature of the First World War. However, the measures introduced during the Second World War were similarly draconian. The Emergency Powers Act and Defence Regulations provided the government with all the power it needed to direct and control labour. Strikes and lockouts were banned under Order 1305, and the 1941 Essential Work (General Provisions) Order allowed for the dilution of labour and the direction of skilled workers to wherever they were most needed. Bevin established a Joint Consultative Committee of seven employers' representatives and seven trade unionists to advise on the conduct of the war effort on the home front. Hence labour was incorporated into the state machine more fully and apparently with a greater degree of acceptance than in 1914–18.

Until 1941 when the Soviet Union entered the war, Communists in Britain, having little commitment to the war effort, refused to be bound by the national unity consensus and in particular the ban on strike action. In fact, during the period of the 'phoney war' there was a general resentment of government attempts to control labour given that it was doing very little to mobilise for the war effort. The 'phoney war' cannot be held responsible for the Communist Party's continued opposition to the war. In a pamphlet published in 1940, after Chamberlain had been ousted, Pollitt proclaimed that 'it is time to organise against every encroachment on the living conditions and the rights of the worker'. He condemned Labour's coalition with the Tories as a device, reminiscent of ruling-class tactics during the First World War, 'to save capitalism and enable attacks to be made on the workers' and said very little about the war against Fascism. Given the party's record before 1939 and after 1941 on fighting Fascism, it is perhaps understandable that the collective communist conscience has chosen to regard this Comintern-inspired line as, at best, a woeful interruption. During the first few months of the war there were over 900 strikes, almost all of them very short, but illegal nonetheless. Despite the provisions of Order 1305 there were very few prosecutions until 1941 as Bevin, anxious to avoid the labour unrest of the First World War, sought to promote conciliation rather than conflict. The number of strikes increased each year until 1944, almost half of them in support of wage demands and the rest being defensive actions against deteriorations in workplace conditions. Coal and engineering were particularly affected. In fact, it was a strike in the Betteshanger colliery in Kent in 1942 which prompted the first mass prosecutions under Order 1305. Three officials of the Betteshanger branch were imprisoned and over 1,000 strikers were fined. Such repression and the general 'shoulders to the wheel' approach to industrial production in support of the war effort (strongly backed by the Communist Party after 1941) did not stop the strikes. In 1943 there were two major stoppages, one of 12,000 bus drivers and conductors, the other of dock workers in Liverpool and Birkenhead. Both were a considerable embarrassment to Bevin since they involved mainly TGWU members. 1944 marked the peak of wartime strike action with over 2,000 stoppages involving the loss of 3,714,000 days' production. This led to the imposition of Defence Regulation 1AA, supported by the TUC, which now made incitement to strike unlawful. Although not used, Regulation 1AA was in fact the most powerful anti-strike weapon possessed by any government since the 1799 Combination Acts and despite the fact that it aroused considerable opposition within the parliamentary Labour Party, it was, astonishingly, supported by the trade unions.

These figures of wartime strike activity surpass those of 1914–18 and yet similar conclusions cannot be drawn from them. Although backed by a growing Shop Stewards' Movement it is clear that unofficial action in this period did not have the kind of political inspiration that motivated the Workers' Committees of the First World War. This is partly due to the fact that the war itself, especially after the Soviet Union's entry, was a popular one. Similarly, the coalition government did much more than Lloyd George's administration to spread the burden of sacrifice (although it did not equalise it) through state controls and important measures of social reform. Such reforms included the provision of subsidised school meals and day nurseries, improved antenatal and infant welfare facilities, and the abolition in 1941 of the hated means test. Due to the sustained German bombing of urban areas (the blitz), the government also provided emergency housing. In 1943 the main provisions of the Beveridge Report, which laid the foundations of the welfare state, were accepted by the cabinet, although not acted upon until the war was over. Hence there was much less ground for sustained political opposition to the government than had been the case in 1914–18. The strikes that did take place thus had much more of a purely trade union character in defence of immediate interests and reflected the growing strength of organised labour. The fact that so many of them occurred in the mining industry was due in the main to the designation of coal mining as essential war work which entailed the direction of selected conscripts to work in the mines. These mining conscripts (the so-called 'Bevin boys') unsurprisingly were very unpopular among regular miners. Trade unions (TUC affiliates) increased their membership by about three million during the war – from roughly 4½ million in 1938 to around 7½ million in 1946 – and this was accompanied by the spread of recognition agreements to industries in which unions had only a toehold before the war. To some extent this extension of trade union rights was underwritten by the government, which, using the Essential Works Order, denied war contracts to firms that failed to conform to minimum standards demanded by the unions.

The Third Labour Government

No one was more surprised than the Labour leaders themselves at the scale of the Labour victory in the general election of 1945. Indeed, Attlee was so convinced of Churchill's popularity that he had initially wanted to fight the election as part of the wartime coalition. There appeared to be little on which the party leaders had disagreed during the war, although there was an ominous portent of the gap between the Labour leadership and backbench Labour MPs over the government's controversial handling of the situation in Greece. The Greek resistance, ELAS, having accomplished the miraculous defeat of the Nazi occupation forces in 1944, was set to establish its own government in which the Communist backbone of the resistance movement would have had a major part. The first signs of the anti-Communism that was to dominate postwar British foreign policy, but was temporarily put on the backburner in the interests of Allied unity during the war, now surfaced. The Allied troops which had belatedly assisted the Greek resistance now turned on their former friends and used force to crush ELAS in order to back those Greeks who had collaborated with the Nazis and in their interests forced the reintroduction of the monarchy and a right-wing government. (The fact that the Soviet Union gave no tangible aid to ELAS undoubtedly strengthened the hands of the Western allies.) The significance of this episode lies in the fact that it was an early indication that Labour, despite its domestic radicalism, intended to allow its foreign policy to be dictated by the traditional conservatism of the Foreign Office.

The size of the Labour majority in the 1945 election gave it a mandate for the first time to carry out its election manifesto, 'Let Us Face the Future'. Labour won 393 seats, the Tories 213, the Liberals were reduced to twelve seats and the Communist Party won two. This gave Labour an overall majority of 146, although the vagaries of Britain's 'first past the post' electoral system in fact gave Labour a minority (47.8 per cent) of the popular vote. The explanation of this victory lies as much in the political maturity and radicalism of British voters as in the undoubted popularity of Labour's programme, which caught the mood of an electorate which now wanted their wartime sacrifices to be rewarded by the creation of a fairer and more equitable society. Memories of the depression and the harshness of the many years of Conservative domination of the political scene were not forgotten in the heady peace celebrations. An appreciation of the role of Churchill as a wartime leader was not allowed to obscure the fact that before the war he had acted consistently against the interests of workers and trade unionists, the employed and the unemployed.

The undoubted radicalism of Labour's programme must also be set in the context of the postwar policies of the governments of the former Allied Powers. In Europe the Communists' role in the resistance movements was now reflected in their participation in, and in Eastern Europe their domination of, many peacetime administrations which pursued radical social change and redistribution of wealth. The New Deal policies of the Roosevelt government in the US, now continued by President Truman, were another indication of the pervasive popular radical climate immediately after 1945. Hence the British experience was not unique, although for Labour its ability to use the parliamentary system to achieve a better society was the ultimate test of its 45 years of existence. Their method thus showed continuity with the past, but the course they charted was far more decisive than previous Labour efforts. The sum total of the achievements of the 1945–51 Labour admin-istration are perhaps best appreciated now that they have been systematically dismantled by four successive Tory governments in the 1980s and 1990s. Labour proclaimed itself to be a socialist party 'and proud of it', but its 1945 programme did not promise socialism on the grounds that, desirable though socialism was, it 'cannot come overnight as the product of a weekend revolution' – a somewhat spurious argument given Labour's six years in office! 'Practical minded men and women' would understand this. Instead, the appeal was to undo the damage that 'hard faced men' had inflicted on the economy in the inter-war years, which had seen the 'concentration of too much economic power in the hands of too few men' ('Let Us Face the Future'). But although the analysis of the past was made in class terms, the vision of the future was one in which narrow class considerations melted into the 'national interest'. The programme was based on 'a genuine workmanlike plan conceived without regard to sectional vested interest'. It envisaged, through state planning, nationalisation, state welfare, improved housing and education, a more equitable system of taxation and price control to create a better society 'free from the horrors of unemployment and insecurity'. The proposals for nationalisation came as no surprise since they were based on policies developed with the aid of the Fabian Research Bureau in the 1930s. The only change in 1945 was that a plan to nationalise the land and the joint stock banks was now omitted.

Labour's Record in Office

In its essentials the Labour government fulfilled its election pledges, but did so inheriting the severe economic problems of the pre-war period with the added burden of the economic destabilisation of war. British exports in 1945 stood at a third of their already low 1939 level. The flurry of legislation covered three main areas:

nationalisation and economic planning; social welfare; and trade union law.

The immediate reward for trade union compliance in the war effort was one that could have been expected from a Labour government in any circumstances. The 1927 Trades Disputes Act (passed by a vindictive Tory government after the General Strike) was repealed in 1946. Welcome though this was, it marked no more than a return to the pre-1927 position, which still left the question of picketing and 'sympathy' strikes in some confusion.

Nationalisation and Planning

On the face of it, despite its watering down, Labour's programme of nationalisation was extensive and bold. Energy supplies, coal, gas and electricity were taken into state control in 1947. Similarly, the transport infrastructure, railways, most wharves and docks, London's buses and Underground system and later road haulage were nationalised. The major, but ailing iron and steel industry was nationalised in 1950, as was the Bank of England in 1946. Several smaller industries and services (including cables and telecommunications and parts of the hotel and catering trade) were also in state hands by 1951. By that year roughly 20 per cent of the national economy was controlled by the state and employed a workforce of over two million. However, in practice Labour's nationalisation programme, far from being a step on the road to socialism, was the means by which capitalism was strengthened. This was because only decaying and unprofitable sectors were taken into state control in order, as Herbert Morrison, the deputy prime minister, put it, to 'make possible the organisation of a more efficient industry' in the interests of the nation as a whole. The ailing industries comprised the industrial infrastructure and by relieving private capital of the responsibility of financing them, the government was in fact subsidising the private sector by providing it with cheaper and more efficient sources of power and transport. This, and the fact that astronomical sums in compensation payments were given to the former owners (£164,000,000 was paid in compensation to the mine owners alone), helps explain why there was so little opposition to nationalisation (except in the case of iron and steel) even from the Tories. The transition was made even smoother in that many of the former owners became leading figures on the boards of directors of their respective public corporation. Hence for the workforce of such industries there was very little of the change for which they had hoped from the nationalised industries. They had little say in their running, as this was left to government-appointed 'expert' managers and boards of directors. The fact that Labour's programme had paid so little attention to the mechanism of nationalisation permitted badly run private corporations to transform themselves into slightly better run but huge and remote public bureaucracies, tolerated in the short term, but inspiring little affection or support when they were later attacked.

Similar deficiencies can be seen in the mechanisms established to achieve the laudable aim of state planning and control. Much of this had already been set up during the war so it was simple enough to allow it to continue. The object was to promote a healthy economy by increasing Britain's gross domestic production and export potential. The means, via four civil service committees (manpower, materials, balance of payments and capital investment), fell far short of the aim, given the irreconcilable clash of interests between the profit motive of private capital and the so-called 'national interest' which Labour claimed to represent. This unacknowledged conflict was compounded by the fact that the very people appointed to police the planning mechanisms were themselves drawn from private industry. As one example among many, no fewer than 90 employees at Unilever occupied posts in the Ministry of Food. Although the government maintained a naive belief in the impartiality of such appointees, the ultimate failure of their endeavours is a personal and political reflection of the impossibility of harmonising public and private economic interests. Put simply the Labour experiment indicated that their concept of the 'national interest', while quite different from the Tory sham, was an illusory Fabian ideal and impossible to implement in a class-divided society. Labour's political opponents constantly appealed to the needs of the nation, but they made no secret of the fact that they identified this as synonymous with the needs of capital.

The fact that Labour, in both theory and practice, regarded itself as a neutral arbiter in promoting the economic and social well-being of the nation meant that, by default and in spite of their good intentions, their plan for a mixed economy slid into one of helping ailing British capitalism to cope better with its profound problems. The enthusiasm for change in the early years of the government gradually waned as Britain's economic problems proved more intractable. By 1947, the crisis year, it was clear that the middle course between socialism and capitalism, so earnestly championed by Labour's leaders in an effort to avoid Soviet-style state planning, was not working. As the problems mounted, even the limited attempts were ditched and political principle came to be sacrificed for more orthodox capitalist solutions. Labour, trapped by the logic of market forces, was forced to abandon even its weak attempts at control, which anyway had never extended to profits, exports or personal incomes. Within three years, Harold Wilson, at the Board of Trade, was ignominiously presiding over periodic 'bonfires' of licences and quotas. The clamour for decontrol of the economy became the rallying cry of private industry, backed by the Conservative Party and Tory press. Labour's economic plan, such as it was, was in tatters.

The extent of the reversal was to be seen in the 1948 and 1949 budgets which were based on the Chancellor of the Exchequer, Stafford Cripps' statement that 'the redistribution of wealth could go no further until new wealth had been created – and in the meantime there must be a ceiling on the social services'.[1] The impetus for retrenchment and a return to economic orthodoxy was also inspired by the government's reliance on US aid in the form of the Marshall Plan. The price to be paid for such aid was clearly stated by the Americans – Britain had to cut back on spending on welfare and had to decontrol the economy in order to make the entire European market more favourable for American exports. He who pays the piper calls the tune.

---

1   Quoted in D. Coates, *The Labour Party and the Struggle for Socialism* (1975).

The Welfare State

Labour's detractors often point to the fact that the main principles of the Beveridge Report were laid down before the Labour government's existence and were not opposed by the Tories then or subsequently (although whether the Tories would have actually implemented Beveridge in full is highly unlikely, as it was the fact that the report appeared during the war gave them an excuse for inaction). Indeed, the basic principle of using the resources of the state to provide and finance social need (collectivism) was pioneered by the Liberal Party under Gladstone in the nineteenth century and further developed by the reforming Liberal government of 1906 with universal schemes for national insurance and old age pensions. However, from the 1930s onwards Labour was the only party which made the extension of social benefits for all, from 'the cradle to the grave', a top campaigning priority and its achievement in government gave concrete expression to this via two major pieces of legislation in 1946 – the Social Security Act and the National Health Service Act. The former provided for sickness and unemployment benefit for all in need, provided they had paid the required national insurance contributions. The National Health Service aimed, according to the Act's preamble, 'to promote the establishment ... of a comprehensive health service designed to secure improvement in the physical and mental health of the people' and weathering the storm of protest from the doctors' organisation the British Medical Association, ensured that it would be free at the point of delivery.

Although Labour cannot claim the credit for the content of this legislation other than the fact that it had the political commitment to act on Beveridge's findings, its unique contribution was expressed in its insistence on the principle of universality. The Tories, whilst not attacking the legislation as such, advocated that it should be targeted at those *most* in need. This would have meant instituting a form of means test. Labour resolutely opposed this, not only because the means test with its association with the hard-faced parsimony of the 1930s was so hated, but also because it took the view that the welfare state would be a non-starter unless its benefits were genuinely open to all. This principle of universality remained the cornerstone of Labour's social policy for the next five decades and was not challenged until the 1990s by the Tories' sustained attack on the entire collectivist edifice. Apart from universality, Labour's policy at the time was criticised by the left, who wanted the health service to be nationalised and private medicine to be abolished. Aneurin Bevan, Minister of Health, instead pursued a course which attempted to placate the doctors' anger, which was chiefly fuelled by the fear that they might become salaried state employees. So, private medicine remained and the doctors were allowed to retain their semi-self-employed professional status by opting for a fees plus salary system or fees alone.

Women and the Welfare State

Aside from the health service, a huge deficiency of Labour's social insurance scheme, unremarked at the time, and hardly commented on by male historians since, was the effect it had on women. The benefit system was firmly based on the notion that the whole of civil society was organised into family units with a male breadwinner at the head of each. Married women, therefore, were not entitled to benefits on the assumption that, like children, they were dependants of the male head of household. Even if they opted to pay their own contributions, they would only receive reduced rate benefit on the spurious argument that their expenses were lower. Wittingly or not, Labour fell for the capitalist ideological construct of the family wage developed in the nineteenth century, which, as we have seen, bore no relation to women's reality at the time, and even less in the inter- and postwar period when the economy was just as dependent on the employment of female labour regardless of marital status. Such state myopia in relation to women had a practical motivation in that the welfare system was far cheaper to administer if its benefits were fully accorded to adult males only, but it was also based on a deep-seated supposition that the rightful place of women was in the home and that their entry into social production was secondary to their domestic responsibilities. The Beveridge Report was thoroughly impregnated by overtly sexist and indeed racist ideas on the 'place' of women and the role of motherhood.

> That attitude of the housewife to gainful employment outside the home should not be the same as that of the single woman. She has other duties ... Taken as a whole the Plan for Social Security puts a premium on marriage in place of penalising it ... In the next thirty years housewives as mothers have vital work to do in ensuring the adequate continuance of the British Race and of British ideals in the world.[2]

Such assumptions were given a further ideological boost in the postwar era by the 'scientific' findings of the psychologist John Bowlby, who popularised the theory of 'maternal deprivation'. He issued dire warnings about the harmful long-term effect on children and adolescents who received anything less than 100 per cent of their mothers' attention during their first five years of life. Apart from the impact that this had on female work patterns, the unchallenged acceptance of such views fed the truly reactionary Labour policy of closing the state day nurseries that had been opened to meet the needs of women workers during the war. This was a useful cost-cutting exercise, but there is no doubt that it was motivated by anti-feminist considerations. A joint circular issued by the Ministries of Health and of Education and sent to local authorities in 1945 expressed it thus:

> The proper place for a child under two is at home with his [sic] mother ... the right policy to pursue would be to positively discourage the mothers of children under two from going out to work.[3]

Hence despite the undoubted merits of the welfare state in general, its benefits for women left much to be desired, and indeed its family-centred orthodoxy did much to keep women locked into traditional subservience. In practice, the principle of universality was to apply only to the male half of Britain's population.

---

2   The Beveridge Report (1942), quoted in Elizabeth Wilson, *Women and the Welfare State* (1977).
3   Quoted in Sarah Boston, *Women Workers and the Trade Unions* (1987).

1947: The Turning Point

The Labour government cannot be blamed for the extraordinarily harsh winter of 1947 which exacerbated fuel shortages, nor can it be held responsible for the deep-seated economic problems which the war had temporarily masked or for the financial crisis of August 1947 – the gravest since 1931. However, it was responsible for the policies it adopted to deal with the crisis and it is on those grounds that it can be judged. The Chancellor of the Exchequer, Hugh Dalton (who dubbed 1947 the *annus horrendus*) and Cripps, his successor, embarked on a series of 'austerity' measures which effectively transformed Labour from a party of reforming zeal into one of retrenchment and economic orthodoxy. An attempt was made to reduce the balance of payments deficit by cutting back on imports. This affected imported foodstuffs especially and meant a cut in the already meagre rationing which continued after the war (the black market provided extra rations for those who could afford it). Spending on social services was cut drastically, and in 1948 the government introduced a wage freeze. Such policies presaged a growing convergence between austerity-minded Labour and the less hard-faced element within the Conservative Party. The term 'Butskellism' (an amalgam of the names of the reform-minded Tory R. A. Butler and Hugh Gaitskell, Labour's successor to Attlee), coined by *The Economist* in the 1950s, caught on as an expression of this trend.

Labour's manifesto for the 1950 general election, 'Let Us Win through Together', displayed the caution already evident in its post-1947 policies. Nationalisation was barely mentioned and the planning and control of industry was dropped altogether. Instead, under the sub-heading 'Encouragement for Enterprise', the manifesto stated that 'private enterprise must be set free from the stranglehold of restrictive monopolies'. Labour's somewhat pedestrian promise was to maintain full employment, raise domestic production and increase exports. The gains of the welfare state were proclaimed, the assumption being that they were complete in themselves, further improvements being unnecessary. Labour's pledges were so minimalist that by 1951 Morrison complained that the Chief Whip 'was having difficulty in finding enough legislative business to occupy the available Parliamentary time'.[4] The election campaign was lacklustre, a fact not reflected by the extraordinarily high turnout, which at 84 per cent was and remains a record. Although Labour's overall majority dwindled to five, its share of the popular vote remained high at 46 per cent, but since parliamentary votes count for more than popular votes, it was just a matter of time before a fresh election was held to give Labour a more workable majority. But by 1951 when the election was held, the tide had turned. Labour actually won more votes than the Tories, but the result of boundary changes gave the latter a slim majority and secured their position as the party of government for the next 13 years.

Labour's Foreign and Colonial Policy

Long-term judgements of the extent of Labour's radicalism in its domestic policy start from the assumption that in this sphere, initially at any rate, it was genuinely attempting something different. The same cannot be said of Labour's conduct of colonial, defence and foreign policy, which from the start was hardly distinguishable in essentials from that of the Conservatives. None of Labour's three election manifestos between 1945 and 1951 paid much attention to foreign affairs. On colonial issues the party had been silent for decades. Although some left-wing individual members, like Fenner Brockway, were active in support of the anti-colonial cause, the Labour Party itself had never taken a public anti-imperialist stance, despite the growth of independence movements in many British colonies. 1945–51 witnessed a high point in the struggle for colonial independence, particularly in the African continent, where the trade union movement, contrary to the prevailing Colonial Office orthodoxy, was vibrant and militant. There were general strikes in Nigeria in 1945 and in Kenya and Ghana in 1950, and many other industry-wide strikes in other colonial territories. However, the Labour Party took

4   Quoted in K. O. Morgan, *Labour in Power 1945–1951* (1985).

the traditional racist line[5] that Britain's African colonies were inhabited by 'backward peoples' of 'primitive culture', whose economic and political systems were so underdeveloped that they were 'not yet able to stand by themselves'. The conclusion drawn from this was that British rule had to be maintained 'as a trust for the native inhabitants'[6] until such time as the natives could be trained to govern themselves. This was, of course, little different from the classic nineteenth-century 'white man's burden' justification for the maintenance of empire. Now, as a government, Labour was forced to accept the fact that it ruled a vast colonial empire and the absence of an anti-imperialist policy inevitably implied its opposite. The Fabians filled the breach. In 1940 the Fabian Colonial Research Bureau was established. Its leading figures, Arthur Creech Jones (later Colonial Secretary) and Rita Hinden, argued against negative anti-imperialism and in favour of a 'positive' colonial policy. This was grist to the mill of Attlee, Bevin (Foreign Secretary) and Herbert Morrison (Lord President), who warmed as to the manor born as guardians of Britain's imperial role. Indeed, Bevin fully acknowledged the social imperialist argument as justification for Labour imperialism. In 1946 he proclaimed to an unshocked House of Commons:

> I am not prepared to sacrifice the British Empire [because] I know that if the British Empire fell ... it would mean that the standard of life of our constituents would fall considerably.[7]

On this argument it is possible to view the great achievements of the welfare state as the ultimate expression of the social imperialist ideal. The racist attitudes informing this were never far from the surface. Dalton referred to the colonies as 'pullulating poverty stricken, diseased nigger communities', but echoing the theme of the 'white man's burden' he did not advocate relinquishing them. In the case of South Africa, a prized part of the 'white' Commonwealth, Labour, perceiving its strategic and economic

5   As expressed in its 1943 pamphlet, *The Colonies.*
6   Ibid.
7   Quoted in Ron Ramdin, *The Making of the Black Working Class in Britain* (1987).

importance, was content to condone the vicious racism in the form of the apartheid system established by the Nationalist government under Daniel Malan after its election victory in 1948. The fact that Malan was an open supporter of the Nazis during the war did nothing to deflect Labour support. After the war, Labour adopted a policy of attempting to kill colonial independence with kindness. Labour's colonial policy during 1945–51 was primarily motivated by fear that grievances among colonial peoples could be 'exploited' by the Communists. Hence, whilst not motivated by anti-imperialist sentiment, Labour policy recognised that reform was necessary. One of the key features of the reform programme was to permit the development of non-militant trade unionism. This, together with labour legislation, was regarded as both vital in its own right, and also a measure of social control which, especially during the Cold War in the years following the establishment of the International Confederation of Free Trade Unions (ICFTU), together with the TUC, was regarded as a vital means of safeguarding British colonial investments, whether direct British rule survived or not.

The argument that the 'granting' of independence to the Indian subcontinent in 1947 indicates that Labour's colonial policy was progressive is not only specious but smacks of white supremacism. It fails to recognise the massive struggle of the Indian people over decades which, by 1947, threatened to erupt into open revolution. It was generally acknowledged, even by the Tories, that in these circumstances British rule was impossible to maintain and a 'damage limitation' exercise was the only feasible alternative. This took the form of exploiting ethnic and religious differences, which resulted in drawing artificial boundaries to create two states, India and Pakistan. In fact, this solution to ensure that British investments were safeguarded after independence provided the model for the neo-colonialist policies of the 1950s and beyond when Britain was forced to bow to the inevitable change in her traditional relationship with her colonies brought about by national liberation struggles within them. For the time being, however, Labour did everything possible to maintain the British Empire. In true social imperialist fashion, the super-exploitation of the colonies was used to offset the full cost of Britain's postwar reconstruction. Although the sterling area, which bound Britain, her Empire and Commonwealth in a system of imperial preference, was anathema to the economic interests of the US, who saw herself (as Britain had done in the nineteenth century) as the workshop of a free trade world, the US was nevertheless prepared to tolerate the British Empire for political reasons as it was seen as a useful bulwark against Communism.

In foreign affairs generally Britain still swaggered as a great world power, but in reality played second fiddle to the US, the new superpower standing as the protector of the entire 'free world' against communist encroachment. The Truman doctrine and Churchill's concept of the 'Iron Curtain' ushered in a new phase of anti-Communism in the form of the Cold War that followed the peace. The pursuance of Nazi war criminals took second place to the preoccupation with the new enemy, the Soviet Union. The somewhat ineffective opposition of the parliamentary 'Keep Left' group of Labour MPs, which advocated a vague 'socialist foreign policy', was no match for the determination of the Labour leadership to give active support to the Cold War line. Bevin, the Foreign Secretary, took every opportunity to stress that British foreign policy would not change under Labour. Britain's dependence on Marshall Aid provided a material reason for Labour support of the 'special relationship', with the US, while Labour's home-grown anti-Communism provided it with such ideological fervour that even the left, the Tribune Group and 'Keep Left' lamely succumbed, confining their criticism to mere detail rather than root-and-branch opposition to the general direction of foreign affairs.

Britain's defence policy was formed to meet the needs of her colonial and foreign policy. All three were bound by the timeless web of protecting the interests of capital, mediated now by pervasive anti-Communism and subservience to the US. An empire the size of Britain's demanded considerable military expenditure to police it, which explains why even in conditions of labour shortage her military establishment after the war accounted for 18.7 per cent of available manpower and military spending amounted to

18.8 per cent of national income. This was almost double the corresponding figure for the US. In total the Labour government spent more on defence than any other non-communist country and in 1946 Attlee earned the unenviable distinction of being the first British prime minister to introduce conscription in peacetime. Even more remarkable was the fact that in 1945, in conditions of absolute secrecy, hidden even from the cabinet, Attlee embarked on a programme of nuclear armament. In fact, it was not until 1952, when it was first tested, that Britain's possession of the ultimate and most deadly weapon of mass destruction, the nuclear bomb, became public knowledge.

The Labour Government and the Trade Unions

Two factors led to an almost supine compliance by the TUC with every whim of Labour policy during Labour's period in government. Of overriding importance was the very fact of the existence of a Labour government which, even when it pursued unpopular measures after 1947, drew the familiar 'don't rock the boat' response from the TUC. The trade union leaders compromised their independence in accepting Labour's wage freeze and anti-strike policies under its austerity programme in the belief that maintaining Labour in power was worth any sacrifice the working class was called on to make. The other factor inducing uncritical attitude was founded on the continuance of the anti-Communism the trade union leaders had already displayed before the war and now found little difficulty in sharing with the government. The rank-and-file opposition to the government's austerity programme after 1947, identified as the work of communist militants, was interpreted as an attack not only on the government, but also on the trade union leaders who tamely supported it, and hence fuelled their latent anti-Communism. A new wave of 'red baiting' was inaugurated with the publication by the General Council of two pamphlets, 'Defend Democracy' and 'The Tactics of Disruption'. Communists were labelled as 'abject and slavish agents of forces working incessantly to intensify social misery' and calls were made to ban them from holding office in trade unions and trades councils. Several trades councils were de-registered for failing to toe this line, but the only trade union which obeyed it to the hilt was the TGWU under its new general secretary, Arthur Deakin. Nine communist full-time officials were sacked from the T&G, including, yet again, Bert Papworth the bus workers' leader, who also lost his seat on the TUC General Council. The fact that other unions did not follow suit (with the exception of the National Union of General and Municipal Workers, whose rules already excluded Communists from holding office) is a reflection of the undoubted strength and influence of the Communist Party within individual unions and as leaders of the opposition to the wage freeze. In this sense the TUC's paranoia about communist influence was justified and they looked on helplessly as their own lack of leadership was thwarted by a succession of strikes in a variety of industries (railways, docks, engineering, mining), defying Order 1305, which remained in force until 1951. This, and the invocation of the Emergency Powers Act, marked the unprecedented use in peacetime of the legal and repressive apparatus of the state, all the more remarkable emanating as it did from a Labour government loyally supported by the TUC at every turn. Seven London dock workers were prosecuted under Order 1305 in 1951.

World diplomacy was not the only setting for the clash of rival ideologies. Anti-communist paranoia found a place as well within the international trade union movement, shattering the unity which had been achieved in 1945 when the World Federation of Trade Unions (WFTU) was established. The only national trade union centre which had held aloof from this body from its inception was the American Federation of Labor (AFL), although its then rival, the CIO (Congress of Industrial Organisations), did participate, along with delegations from 46 other countries. The British TUC hosted the founding conference in London and was enthusiastic about the meeting itself, although more cautious on the prospects for a permanent organisation. The dictates of US foreign policy and its Marshall Aid programme sought busily to divide East and West in every sphere of activity. The European Recovery Programme Trade Union Advisory Committee was the US mechanism for achieving the split in the WFTU, which remained as the last symbol of the unsectarian wartime alliance. The British TUC was a key and receptive pawn in this strategy, as was noted by the AFL leader, David Dubinsky: 'Once the British TUC frees itself from its paralysing ties with the World Federation the ERP Trade Union Advisory Committee will be able to go forward.'[8]

By 1949 his hopes were realised. Deakin, who was the WFTU president at the time, told the TUC in a remarkable about-face that the World Federation was 'nothing more than another platform and instrument for the furtherance of Soviet foreign policy' and led a walk-out to join the AFL in establishing a new anti-communist international, the International Confederation of Free Trade Unions, founded in London in December 1949.

Bibliography

Barnes, D. and Reid, E. 'A New Relationship: Trade Unions in the Second World War', in B. Pimlott and C. Cook (eds). *Trade Unions and British Politics* (Longman, 1991)

Boston, S. *Women Workers and the Trade Unions* (Lawrence & Wishart, 1987)

Coates, D. *The Labour Party and the Struggle for Socialism* (Cambridge University Press, 1975)

Cook, C. and Sked, A. *Post War Britain: A Political History* (Penguin Books, 1990)

Hutt, A. *British Trade Unionism: A Short History* (Lawrence & Wishart, 1941)

Labour Party. *Let Us Face the Future* (1945)

Morgan, K. O. *Labour in Power 1945–1951* (Oxford University Press, 1985)

Pollitt, H. *The War and the Labour Movement* (Communist Party of Great Britain, 1940)

Pritt, D. N. *The Labour Government* (Lawrence & Wishart, 1963)

Ramdin, R. *The Making of the Black Working Class in Britain* (Gower, 1987)

TUC General Council and Congress reports, 1945–51

Wilson, E. *Women and the Welfare State* (Tavistock Publications, 1977)

8   Quoted in Allen Hutt, *British Trade Unionism* (1941).

15

THE WORKERS THE LABOUR MOVEMENT FORGOT – WOMEN AND BLACK PEOPLE, 1926–1951

The experience of a majority Labour government in office represented the high point of parliamentary Labourism. The socialist experiment had never been tried and if it had it may well have been found wanting, but in a different way. Before the First World War its syndicalist variant had shown its limitations in its failure to comprehend the needs of women workers, and leading marxists like Hyndman had succumbed to the racist ideology inherent in their support for imperialism. Thereafter the left in general, trapped by the succession of capitalist crises at home and abroad, reacted defensively and never fully developed its socialist vision. Socialist theory based on an understanding of the inner workings of capitalism and imperialism was able to show the link between class exploitation and oppression, and hence displayed, in theoretical terms at least, the possibility of comprehending the specifics of the super-exploitation of women and black people mediated by the unspoken ideologies of racism and sexism. Practice, however, usually fell far short of theory.

Even during the most revolutionary phase of the history of the British labour movement (*c.* 1910–26), when so many values of the capitalist system were subjected to scrutiny, racism and imperialism remained comparatively unchallenged, including among the non-Hyndmanite marxists. One of the very few debates in the left press on the issue of racism appeared in *The Call*[1] early in 1917.

---

1 *The Call* was established in 1916. It was the fortnightly (later weekly) journal of the anti-war group within the British Socialist Party. When the pro-war Hyndmanites were defeated and left the party in 1916, *The Call* became the BSP's official journal.

This was precipitated by an article on 'Black Labour' by Tom Quelch[2] in which he supported the position of the Amalgamated Society of Carpenters and Joiners in their opposition to the Labour MP Arthur Henderson's proposal to introduce black labour into Britain for the purposes of erecting munitions factories. Apart from the predictable arguments that this would reduce wages for indigenous white building workers, Quelch proceeded to denounce the suggestion in crudely racist tones. What, he asks sarcastically, can be wrong with

> Fifty thousand jolly coons, looking picturesque in ill-fitting European clothes with scarlet bandanas round their heads, boyishly larking as they toil, shufflin' along in the approved fashion bringing with them the romance of the wilds coming to Britain?

One reason, he argued, for opposing black immigration was the effect it would have on women munitions workers, whose 'sex appetites are ... being starved' in the absence of their menfolk and who find it 'impossible to repress natural desires'. These women would be 'delivered into the arms of the vigorous Othellos of Africa'. But to crown his argument, Quelch also employed (spurious) anti-capitalist reasoning. Introducing black labour suited the purposes of the employers because 'race differences aid them in keeping the workers divided. A numerous black population would be of inestimable value to the employers as blacklegs and strike breakers. Ignorant blacks are cheap and unorganised.' The clearly stated basis for Quelch's assertions was the commonly held view that a race problem existed because 'there is a physiological difference between black and white'. So, was this the marxist view? According to G. Tchitcherine,[3] Quelch's line was not in accordance with that of the Second International. The International was, Tchitcherine pointed out, opposed to any restriction on the movement of labour, except that of indentured labour. He also took issue with Quelch's view that there was a physiological distinction between the races. The 'setting up of racial distinctions between workers' results in

---

2 *The Call*, 25 January 1917. Quelch, the son of the veteran SDF activist Harry Quelch, was a regular contributor to the paper.
3 *The Call*, 8 February 1917.

'the greatest hindrance to the universal development of labour solidarity' and plays into the hands of the capitalists. Quelch replied to this in the following issue of *The Call*[4] in terms more shocking (to us, but perhaps not then) than his original article. He did not deal with the policy of the Second International but confined himself to the white supremacist argument. Zulus and Basutos, he wrote, 'belong to a different evolutionary epoch' and thus 'their physical and mental characteristics are different from Europeans'. It would be better if they all stayed in their own countries – the races cannot mix.'

Within the Labourist tradition there was not even the theoretical base for addressing the issue of class exploitation, much less for understanding or acting on the deeply divisive ways in which capitalism has used the issues of sex and race to maintain its ascendancy.

The question as to whether a movement can be judged for what it failed to do is one that does not seem to trouble historians or commentators when their own particular hobby-horse is at stake. But there is a strange silence when we use the yardstick of the experiences of half the human race to weigh up the balance sheet. And when the balance sheet is the labour movement itself, the silence gives way to cries of teleological unfairness bordering on treachery. And yet women comprised half the population in Britain and a large (usually underestimated) part of its working population. Numerically the same cannot be said of black people, although it is often forgotten that a black population had been settled in Britain for a considerable period before the first major wave of migrants arrived (at the behest of the government) after the Second World War. However, taking the British Empire as a whole, black people far outnumbered their white rulers.

The Black Presence

Black scholars and historians have taught us much in recent years about the presence since Roman times (before the Anglo-Saxons

4   *The Call*, 13 February 1917.

arrived) of a black community in the British Isles. That such a fact has been hidden for so long is not attributable simply to the small size of the community; after all, women have accounted for around half the population and they too, until recently, have been similarly obscured by and from history. Reconstructing the role of black people within the labour movement is fraught with even more difficulties, but again, in common with women, their position has been and still is marked by their exclusion rather than their presence. The permeation of the ideology of white supremacism associated with Britain's imperial role and its (often unconscious) effect on the labour movement has already been discussed (see Chapters 5 and 7). After so many decades of the seepage of racist ideas, the conditions which fostered the possibilities for black leaders like William Cuffay and Robert Wedderburn to rise to prominence in the radical and Chartist movements had, by the twentieth century, been eclipsed. Despite the fact that the First World War had increased the black population living in Britain, particularly in the port cities of Cardiff and Liverpool, the black community was more isolated than ever. The incidence of race riots in Cardiff in 1919, with its repercussions in other cities, provides evidence of the deep racist attitudes of British workers, supported at the time by the labour movement. Demobilised sailors helped to swell the ranks of unemployed seamen in the declining shipping industry, and since this was one of the very few areas in which black people had found employment, the bitterness of white seamen was turned against the right to work of black Britons. The call to oust black seamen from their jobs in preference to their British (i.e. white) counterparts was supported by a TUC resolution in 1919 which supported the seamen's union campaign for preference to be given first to British white and then British black labour. This racist divisiveness quickly developed in the ensuing physical attacks on black families into a more generalised campaign to discredit the black presence by pointing out its moral undesirability and, to clinch the argument, its cost to the taxpayer. With the support of Labour, the government, in time-honoured fashion, blamed the 'alien' presence as the cause of the problem and passed two overtly racist laws, the Aliens Order of 1920 and, in 1925, the Special Restriction (Coloured Alien Seamen) Order. Both were concerned to restrict immigration, but the latter introduced a form of pass law specifically aimed at black seamen, irrespective of their nationality. Whether or not they held British passports they were required on demand to produce evidence of registration on pain of arrest, imprisonment or even deportation.

In this context E. D. Morel's outpourings seem hardly surprising. Morel was an ILP member and later Labour MP. In 1920 he wrote an article which was published by the left-leaning *Daily Herald* under the banner headline 'Black Scourge in Europe'.[5] In it he protested against the use by France of black troops in the parts of Germany they occupied after the First World War. It was the fact that black soldiers ('black savages' as he termed them) were being used which so incensed Morel. He asserted that 'primitive African barbarians are perpetuating an abominable outrage upon womanhood, upon the white races and upon civilization' because their unrestrained sexual appetites impelled them to rape white women and to spread syphilis. Although he claimed to have studied this issue in depth, Morel declared that he did not need specific reports to assert the validity of his charges because it was well known that 'the African race is the most developed sexually of any' and the black recruits to the French army come from 'tribes in a primitive state of development ... sexually they are unrestrained and unrestrainable'. Thus the *Daily Herald*, the leading socialist paper of the time and the only daily paper of the left, colluded with Morel's age-old racist stereotype of black men as oversexed rapists. Despite the disclaimer in a preface to the article that the *Daily Herald* was 'encouraging colour prejudice', its editorial backed Morel's view on the grounds that 'the manhood of these races' was 'not so advanced in the forms of civilization as ourselves' and warned that if such savages were to be used against Germans, 'why not against the workers here or elsewhere'?[6] The *Daily Herald* claimed a great scoop in being

5   *Daily Herald*, 10 April 1920.
6   *Daily Herald*, 10 April 1920.

the only newspaper to have had the courage to print 'the terrible facts' and proceeded to whip up a campaign to give voice to the 'wave of indignation'[7] which, it was claimed, had swept over England. Claude McKay, a Jamaican revolutionary poet who lived in London from 1919 to 1921, wrote a letter of protest to the *Herald*. It was rejected. He then sent it to Sylvia Pankhurst's paper, the *Workers' Dreadnought*,[8] which published it. McKay strenuously rejected the 'odious' claims made by Morel, which he regarded as an incitement to racial violence against the 'many members of my race, boycotted economically and socially, who have been dumped down on the English docks since the ending of the European War'. The *Herald*'s decision to print such inflammatory material was, according to McKay, 'not mitigated by your explanatory editorial'. In his autobiography[9] McKay explained that his motive in writing to Lansbury as the editor of the *Daily Herald* was to point out 'that it was the duty of his paper as a radical organ to enlighten its readers about the real reason why the English considered coloured troops undesirable in Europe, instead of appealing to illogical emotional prejudices'.[10] He went on to explain that these reasons were to be found in the fact that there was widespread strike action in the Rhineland and that the capitalists were using the race card in order to divert attention.

In view of such overt racial prejudice which fuelled the colour bar in the labour market, it is not surprising that black Britons suffered disproportionately from the generally prevalent high rates of unemployment in the inter-war years. In Cardiff, for example, it was estimated that roughly 80 per cent of black men were unemployed in 1934–35. The outbreak of the Second World War changed the employment situation for black people, although the underlying racism which confined their job opportunities and life chances in general remained unaltered. The labour shortage caused by conscription and the increased demand of wartime

7   *Daily Herald*, 12 April 1920.
8   *Daily Herald*, 24 April 1920.
9   Claude McKay, *A Long Way From Home* (1970).
10 Ibid., p. 75.

production eliminated domestic unemployment and led to a government-sponsored scheme for colonial immigration which provided a free passage to Britain and back. Some of the workers who came were, to the surprise of their white counterparts, highly skilled, thus overturning the traditional prejudices which ascribed underdevelopment to black people. Many, having had considerable labour movement experience in their own countries, joined trade unions here, although only two unions, the AEU and the electricians' union, the ETU, were welcoming. Additionally, around 8,000 West Indian soldiers in the British Army were stationed in the UK during the war, most of them working as flight engineers. After the war immigration was again officially encouraged owing to a continued labour shortage in Britain and high rates of unemployment in the colonies. The 492 Jamaicans who arrived at Tilbury in 1948 on board the *Empire Windrush* were greeted with a banner headline in the London *Evening Standard* which read 'Welcome Home'. This was followed by a steady trickle from the West Indies during the following decade, which by 1958 amounted to 125,000.

Black Resistance

Given the generally unwelcoming attitude of the labour movement to black people and the issue of racism in the post-1850 period, the black community relied on its own resources to tackle the problems which beset it. The self-organisation of black people has thus a long pedigree born of the hostility or indifference of white society. The organisations so formed had a dual function. They attempted to give some support to black Britons at the sharp end of racial prejudice and in addition were at the forefront of the anti-colonial struggle. This latter function could hardly be avoided, especially in the twentieth century when the legacy of the imperial exploitation of the black colonies in Asia, Africa and the West Indies forced fresh waves of black migrants to flee the hardships of their own countries and settle in Britain. It is beyond the scope of this book to look at the patterns of immigration to Britain. Not all who came were poor and many came to study

rather than in search of employment. The British colonialists had
done little to establish an all-through education system in most of
the countries that they dominated, though what they had set up
was thoroughly English in character. It was from those who came
to complete their education in Britain at the turn of the century
that the main (although not necessarily the first) intellectual
and practical challenges were launched at the insidious pseudo-
scientific racism peddled by white academics and intellectuals.
J. A. Thorne, a Barbadian doctor who had studied and qualified
in Britain, Celestine Edwards (a Dominican) and Henry Sylvester
Williams, among others, advocated and popularised the idea of
Pan-Africanism (pre-dating Marcus Garvey). For some this meant
finding a settled homeland for all those of African descent, for
others it meant campaigning to secure civil and political rights for
black people, but for all it meant inspiring a sense of pride in the
black race. This latter was no easy task given the predominant
white notion of black sub-humanism and the jingoistic expansion
of the European empires from the 1880s onwards. Williams was
the main force behind the establishment in 1897 (the year of
Queen Victoria's Diamond Jubilee) of the African Association,
one of the aims of which was 'to promote and protect the interests
of all subjects claiming African descent'. The first Pan-African
Conference was held in London in 1900 under the slogan 'Light
and Liberty'. It drew black delegates from around the world
and established the short-lived Pan African Association. The
conference attracted financial support from the Asian community
resident in Britain.

The main driving force behind Pan-Africanism in Britain,
Williams, attempted to set up branches of the Pan African
Association in Jamaica, Trinidad and the US. He was also involved
in Labour politics in Britain, becoming one of the first black men
to be elected in 1906 as a local councillor (for Marylebone). In
this he had the support of the most progressive trade union, the
Workers' Union. The other black pioneer in British municipal
politics was John Richard Archer. As a member of the Labour
Party he held office in Battersea variously as councillor, alderman,
mayor, election agent and leader of the council. As election agent he

skilfully piloted the successful candidature of Shapurji Saklatvala as the first black MP (and the first Communist) to be elected in Britain. Archer was also involved in Pan-Africanism, becoming in 1918 president of the African Progress Union formed in that year. This organisation, led by John Alcindor, was the largest of the black organisations active in the 1920s (the others being student bodies). In 1931, in the wake of the race riots in Cardiff and Liverpool, a Jamaican, Dr Harold Moody, founded the League of Coloured Peoples. Although this was a 'respectable' organisation of well-educated blacks, which acted as a kind of pressure group intervening on behalf of black people among whose moderate aims was 'to improve relations between the races', it contained within its ranks a variety of political views. In contrast to Moody himself, who was a committed Christian and definitely not a socialist, the League counted among its active members Ras Makonnen and George Padmore, both marxists and sometime members of the Communist Party, and Desmond Buckle, a communist activist. The marxist intellectual C. L. R. James also served on the League's executive for a while and contributed articles to its quarterly magazine, *The Keys*. These four, together with Jomo Kenyatta (later President of Kenya), provided the intellectual driving force behind Pan-Africanism in the 1930s and 1940s. Britain, the heart of the world's biggest colonial empire, was their base.

Socialism, and especially Communism, provided a point of contact between black activists and the British labour movement, especially in the anti-colonial struggles of the pre- and post-Second World War era, by which time communist or workers' parties affiliated to the Comintern had been established in almost every country in the world. Nonetheless, such contact was beset by differences in both theory and practice. These differences sometimes mirrored those within the socialist movement, revolving around the role of the Soviet Union, particularly during the Stalinist period, but there was an added dimension in the black movement because of differing trends within Pan-Africanism. Although there was no split or breech so characteristic of white left politics, there was nonetheless a difference in outlook between the two major black American Pan-Africanist leaders, the communist W. E. B. DuBois and Marcus Garvey. Put very simply and somewhat crudely, the former campaigned for the rights of black people to self-determination in the colonies linked to their full civil and economic rights in the white colonial heartlands, while the latter's position can best be summed up by the slogan of the Universal Negro Improvement Association (the organisation he founded for black people), 'Back to Africa'. Until 1928, the Comintern supported Garveyism and had paid detailed attention to the 'Negro question' as a key aspect of the anti-imperialist struggle. It saw the UNIA as integral to this. Within Britain, the as yet small black community was reinforced by a powerful stream of intellectuals and labour movement activists from the colonies, many of whom, like Krishna Menon (India), Kwame Nkrumah (Ghana) and Kenyatta, were later to become leaders in their own countries' post-independence. They played an important role in maintaining black consciousness through Pan-Africanism as well as fighting the anti-colonial battle against Britain.

Within Britain, the struggle of Indian immigrants found expression in what is arguably the oldest of the organisations of black workers with a continuous history; notably the Indian Workers' Association (Hindustani Mazdoor Sabha). This was established in Coventry in 1938 to support Indian independence However, the purpose and activity of the IWA changed in the 1950s partly because by then independence had been won, but more importantly because by then the Indian population in England had increased substantially with a wave of postwar immigration, from the Punjab in particular. Branches were formed in areas of Punjabi concentration – Southall (in London), Wolverhampton and Birmingham. When, in 1958, the individual IWAs came together (on Nehru's advice) to form the Indian Workers' Association (Great Britain), the national organisation adopted the following aims, to:

1. promote co-operation and unity with the trade union and labour movement in Great Britain;

2. fight against all forms of discrimination based on race, colour, creed or sex for equal human rights and social and economic opportunities;
3. promote the cause of friendship, peace and freedom of all countries;
4. keep its members and the people of Great Britain informed about political, economic and social developments in India;
5. undertake social, welfare and cultural activities.[11]

In this way the IWA firmly committed itself to the anti-racist struggle and the well-being of Indian workers in Britain, which it saw as being integrally linked to trade union organisation.

Apart from support given by some internationalist organisations like the Communist Party and assorted individuals on the left of the Labour Party, the predominantly white labour movement took little interest in the struggles of black workers and thereby turned its back on a fertile stream of ideas and experience. Such colour-blindness, was of course fuelled by the pervasive racist ideology which, if it did not lead to outright collusion with imperialism, at best led to a superior kind of paternalism, which sometimes showed pity for the poor downtrodden blacks in the colonies, and even occasionally in the 'mother country', but failed to recognise, let alone listen to, the highly articulate black voices which had raised questions and posed solutions long before the white liberals had even identified the problem. It was not only on the question of race that the labour movement failed to benefit from the years of work going on in the black community in Britain. No regard was paid to the fact that this small community also had within it trade union and labour movement activists of a very high calibre, some of whom had actually founded unions in their own country under conditions of illegality and who had considerable organising experience. Whilst black people maintained this commitment in Britain, joining unions even when they were not made particularly welcome, there was no similar effort on the part of most white activists to learn from their black brothers and sisters. Thus it was

11   www.connectinghistories.org.uk

that a kind of separate development between the two communities was unofficially institutionalised and survives to the detriment of the labour movement to the present day.

Women and the Labour Movement

The inter- and postwar period was bleak for women. The ideology of home and hearth fitted comfortably with the divisiveness caused by mass unemployment when women were frequently accused of taking men's jobs. Sexist ideas and practices had long been internalised into the labour movement, certainly at leadership level, but its presence was all the more marked after the General Strike for three reasons: first, the presence of women in the workforce was less hidden than it had been hitherto; second, female recruitment was consciously sought to stem declining union membership, which contrasted sharply with the third factor – the class collaborationist orientation of the trade union leadership, which in itself engendered an uncritical assumption of capitalist values as an antidote to the shared anti-communist paranoia. For women workers this meant that (as has been shown in Chapter 12) the unions and TUC gave with one hand and took with another.

For a while, the Second World War swung the pendulum in women's favour. The massive war effort entailed a correspondingly huge call on the labour of women, far greater than that in 1914–18. This was not peculiar to Britain. Throughout Europe and the US women's work was no longer seen as peripheral to social production, it was now at the very centre of it. This entailed a major, albeit temporary, shift in social attitudes, the practical expression of which was the provision of state measures like nurseries and free school meals to enable women to combine more easily their dual roles. Did the attitude of the trade unions change? In a purely pragmatic and opportunist sense it did, although even so not nearly as fully as might have been expected given the changed climate towards women. The TUC passed motions in 1940 calling for equal pay for women who took over men's jobs and for an end to the marriage bar. In 1942 the AEU at last opened its doors to women members and broke new ground the following year when it established a separate women's conference. Women's trade union membership more than doubled during the war years – it stood at 552,000 in 1939 and rose to 1,341,000 by 1945. But despite these advances, the warning signs were there. The TUC hardly mentioned women after 1940 on the assumption that their wartime position in the workforce was temporary and that after the war, if they worked at all, they would return to their traditional sphere as domestic servants. Indeed, in 1943 the TUC's Women's Advisory Committee drew up a memorandum outlining how they could be persuaded so to do. This pre-dated, and possibly even influenced, government thinking on the matter. In 1944 the Ministry of Labour issued a pamphlet which proclaimed that 'domestic service is a priority job'.

It is thus hardly surprising that gains women made during the war were so quickly jettisoned in peacetime. We know how swiftly the government moved to restore women's traditional role and the underlying assumptions behind it. Without a labour movement fighting to maintain such gains as nurseries and other wartime 'benefits', the Labour government's task of pushing women back was made infinitely easier. As the lapdog of the government it might be expected that the TUC would do all in its power to support everything that Labour did. But on the 'problem' of women it did not need much persuading since its attitudes were quite as reactionary on this as those of its political masters. This was clearly demonstrated by its policy on two issues in particular – equal pay and day nurseries.

Equal pay was hotly debated in the postwar period. In 1944 a Royal Commission established to enquire into the subject reported in 1946. It accepted equal pay in principle, but had advised against its implementation on the grounds that to do so would be inflationary. The TUC, mindful of its longstanding commitment to equal pay since 1888, but at the same time not wishing to 'embarrass' the Labour government, now advocated a compromise. In a pamphlet entitled 'Questions and Answers on Equal Pay' and published in 1948, it urged the government to implement equal pay in the public sector whilst accepting that it was a lost cause in the private sector. (Interestingly, one of the largest private sector unions, the AEU, did not share this view and boldly launched a campaign for pay equity in the engineering industry.) But even this compromise was meaningless, for in the same year, despite the urging of the Women's Committee, the General Council statement at the Margate conference declared that the introduction of equal pay

> would have to be considered in the light of the White Paper 'Statement on Personal Income, Costs and Prices' ... [and thus] it would be impractical for the TUC ... to extend its activities to include the holding of a series of large public meetings throughout the country.

Having thus decided against this minimalist effort it was but a short step the following year, 1949, at Bridlington for the General Council to ditch the issue altogether:

> In the light of ... the continuing need for counter-inflationary policies, the committee decided that a further approach by the TUC to the government on equal pay would be inappropriate at the present time.

If any progress at all was to be made on equal pay it would be up to individual unions to press for it – a somewhat forlorn hope at least until the 1950s when white-collar unions in the public sector, under pressure from their women members, engaged in an intensive campaign which resulted in 1955 in a government announcement that it would attempt to equalise pay in the public sector by 1961 in seven stages for some women workers (women manual workers, government typists and nurses were to be excluded). During the period of the Labour government, however, no progress was made and the gap between men's and women's earnings was, on average, 50 per cent.

A similarly depressing tale unfolded in relation to nursery schools. Their fate and the consequences for women were all the more grim since this was a cause which had apparently been won during the war and was lost thereafter. It was all the worse given that the reasons for closing the day nurseries were motivated as much by ideological as economic considerations and hence revealed once more, after an all too brief semi-respite, the deeply sexist seam running through all layers of British society, including its trade unions. The TUC offered no resistance to the government plan to cut the grant to local authority day nurseries; indeed, its report for 1947 presented to the 1948 Margate conference expressed its ideological approval. It prefaced its comments on day nurseries by 'welcoming the Minister of Labour's statement that mothers of young children should not be encouraged to go into industry' and went on to state:

> The General Council are therefore of the opinion that the case for Day Nurseries must be proved in each locality after an examination of all the circumstances, and that they should not press for a general extension of them.

Worse was to come. In a rare statement of its underlying philosophy, the 1948 Annual Report of the TUC contained the following gem of unenlightenment:

> There is little doubt in the minds of the General Council that the home is one of the most important spheres for a woman worker and that it would be doing a great injury to the life of the nation if women were persuaded or forced to neglect their domestic duties in order to enter industry particularly where there are young children to cater for.

The message for women was clear, but it was also contradictory in the light of the postwar labour shortage and the clear demand for female labour. How could the need for women's presence in social production be reconciled with its perceived ideological undesirability? The solution was the same as ever – to marginalise women workers in an attempt to hide the reality of their vital role in the labour force. This was accomplished in two ways – one traditional, the other new. Job segregation was the age-old lot of women. They were removed as far as possible from those areas of social production in which they could compete with men and consigned to jobs which could be more properly viewed as an offshoot of their feminine domestic responsibilities. The war had been but a temporary interruption to this pattern. The postwar period restored 'normality' (see Chapter 5). But where such total segregation proved impossible, the new device of part-time work was the solution, which presented itself as a neat way of ensuring that women fitted themselves into the ideological stereotype of wife and mother while at the same time avoiding any claim for additional state expenditure on such costly items as day nurseries. Such a construct fitted nicely with the ideological presuppositions about the role of the family enshrined in the state benefit system introduced after the war (see Chapter 14). So successful was the use of part-time work that it spread to almost all branches of female employment, and despite the lower wages offered was even welcomed by women workers, who saw it as the only way, in the absence of real practical help, to combine their dual roles.

Thus having colluded in the marginalisation of women workers with the added problem of their atypical employment pattern, the trade unions now viewed them as a weak link in organisational terms. It was far easier, in view of the notorious difficulties in organising part-time workers, to view women themselves as the problem, a problem that could be safely ignored in the postwar period of full employment and the welfare state, when it could be comfortably imagined that the family was secure in the care of its male breadwinner and that women who worked did so from choice to earn a bit of 'pin money'. Such was the ideology. Reality, as ever, was very different.

Bibliography

Lewis, R. *Marcus Garvey: Anti-Colonial Champion* (Karia Press, 1987)

Ramdin, R. *The Making of the Black Working Class in Britain* (Gower, 1987)

Rich, P. *Race and Empire in British Politics* (Cambridge University Press, 1990)

16

1951–1979 – CONSENSUS POLITICS?

It used to be thought that the 13 years of Conservative rule that succeeded the 1945–51 Labour government represented a continuation of Labour's policies. The term 'Butskellism' was used by *The Economist* to describe the perceived consensus of party politics in the 1950s and 1960s. In fact, the prevailing presumption, accepted until government records were released for research, has been that the consensus between the two parties lasted until the Thatcher government broke it in 1979.

Recent historical research,[1] however, has raised serious doubts about the validity of this view of postwar politics and in particular the notion that industrial relations ran a smooth course regardless of which party was in office. The consensus view gained greater credence when, after 1979, a more confrontational style of politics, spearheaded by the Tories, appeared to disrupt previous Conservative (and Labour) acceptance of the welfare state and the place of trade unions in a system of 'free' collective bargaining. Whilst it is true that the Thatcher years unleashed an unprecedented assault on trade union rights and a virulent attack on the 'nanny state', this did not mean that Tory and Labour politicians had benign attitudes to such policy issues before 1979 or that the parties were in full agreement based on their experience of coalition consensus derived from the Second World War.[2]

What is clear, however, is that the strength and influence of trade unions increased steadily throughout this period. Indeed, by 1979

---

1 H. Jones and M. Kandiah (eds). *The Myth of Consensus: New Views on British History 1945–64* (1996).
2 P. Addison, *The Road to 1945* (1975). Addison subsequently modified his view of the formative nature of the Second World War on postwar politics in the 1994 edition of *The Road to 1945*.

trade union membership was at an all-time high of 13 million members. Trade union strength, and in particular trade union militancy, worried both Conservative and Labour governments. The two parties shared a common aim of attempting to reduce union power at shop-floor level, and both parties, fixated as they were with reducing public spending, attempted to freeze or control public sector wage demands. The two parties, when in government, adopted slightly different methods to accomplish these twin aims, but a key strategy shared by both was a desire to detach the leaderships of trade unions from shop-floor militancy. One way of doing this was to establish various forms of tripartism – formal and informal meetings between representatives of government, employers and unions – often with the aim of securing agreement on prices and incomes policies in various forms. The desire to achieve such a policy, particularly with regard to incomes, dominated government strategic thinking for almost 20 years (1960–79). Another way of curbing trade union effectiveness was to impose legal restrictions on collective bargaining and union action. This route led to serious industrial confrontation during the late 1960s and 1970s and was eventually jettisoned until the Thatcher government successfully reintroduced legal restrictions on union activity. Before 1979 both parties attacked the public sector, most obviously, by seeking to contract it. Under Tory administrations Thomas Beeching and Alfred Robens slashed jobs and capacity on the railways and in coal mining, respectively. Labour did not reverse this policy.

Labour in and out of Office

The 13 years of Conservative rule (1951–64) witnessed four prime ministers: Winston Churchill, Anthony Eden, Harold Macmillan and Alec Douglas-Home (Edward Heath replaced Douglas-Home in 1965 in the first-ever Tory leadership election). During these years the Labour Party underwent its own leadership problems and policy differences. In 1955 Clement Attlee resigned as leader and was replaced by Hugh Gaitskell, the latter having won an election against two opponents who were to the left of him – Aneurin Bevan (the choice of the left) and the more centrist Herbert Morrison. It was widely expected that Morrison would succeed Attlee, but by 1955 Morrison was 75 years old. Gaitskell ushered in an ideological departure from the more traditional tenets of social democracy. This was expressed most cogently in Anthony Crosland's book *The Future of Socialism* published in 1956. It marked a major challenge to traditional socialist values, especially on the question of public ownership. Public ownership was deemed unnecessary on the grounds that, according to Crosland, capitalism was not endemically unstable. Thus, he argued, it was possible for governments to manage the level of demand and hence counter sharp swings of the business cycle. He did not condemn the profit motive; indeed, he said it was beneficial, opining that 'what is profitable is what the consumer finds useful'.[3] Crosland was thus happy to call himself a 'revisionist' – 'it was time to stop searching for fresh inspiration in the old orthodoxies and thumbing over the classic texts as though they could give oracular guidance for the future'. Such thinking undoubtedly gave Gaitskell the ideological impetus to attempt to revise clause 4 of the Labour Party constitution in the wake of the 1959 election defeat. He failed in this endeavour, although he was more successful in ensuring that the attack on public ownership contained in *Industry and Society* (1957) became accepted party policy. This 'quiet revolution'[4] was far more significant than the clause 4 debate or the to-ing and fro-ing on the nuclear issue: the attack on public ownership was an assault on a core tenet of Labour Party policy and in practical terms was never reversed. Such a revisionist triumph offset the failure to prevent the 1960 party conference from passing a resolution backing unilateral nuclear disarmament, despite the fact that the Gaitskellite multi-lateralists had won an unexpected ally in Bevan, hitherto the champion of the left. But the unilateralist victory was anyway short-lived – it was reversed the following year.

Nonetheless, the fact that the Gaitskellites had been defeated, albeit temporarily, in 1960, stirred the right wing to set up its

3 A. Crosland, *The Future of Socialism* (1956), p. 347.
4 S. Haseler, *The Gaitskellites* (1969).

own organisation within the party. This took the form of a group calling itself the Campaign for Democratic Socialism (CDS) and consisted of prominent members of the Parliamentary Labour Party, including Crosland, Robens and Patrick Gordon Walker, as well as others outside parliament, such as Bill Rodgers (general secretary of the Fabian Society). Rodgers later became chairman of the CDS. It published its own manifesto and aimed to set up a network of contacts throughout the constituencies and trade unions. It was immensely useful to Gaitskell since on detailed policy and general ideology (particularly its anti-Communism) the CDS's views were at one with the party leader's. Most of the shadow cabinet were CDS supporters or sympathisers. However, Gaitskell died in 1963 and was succeeded by Harold Wilson, after he defeated Jim Callaghan and George Brown in a three-corner leadership contest.

In 1964, when Labour at last, after 13 years, managed to win an election, it did so by the narrowest of margins (a majority of four and under very unfavourable circumstances. The incoming government inherited a deep economic crisis and a huge balance of payments deficit. The Labour Party described the situation thus:

> With a record – and almost incredible – deficit of over £750 million already incurred; with a rising flood of foreign goods; with the pound sterling imperilled; with prices soaring; with wages and salaries following hard behind – the nation in October, 1964, was plunging towards economic disaster and financial collapse.[5]

Wilson's response was to borrow massively from the International Monetary Fund and the Federal Reserve while at the same time attempting to introduce his own version of an incomes policy. At first this was voluntary, agreed with both the TUC and the employers, but within a year it was decided that compulsion was necessary. This was partly because the voluntary approach was unsuccessful owing to its failure to reduce the number of unofficial strikes, but also because the condition of further borrowing from foreign banks was based on effective control of workers' incomes.

---

5   Labour Party election manifesto 1966.

Hence in 1965 all wage claims were supposed to be referred to the Prices and Incomes Board.

At this stage, having secured the agreement of the TUC, the government was still pursuing the voluntary principle in respect of wage restraint policy. However, the surprise was that even when the government announced its intention to introduce compulsion by means of the 1966 Prices and Incomes Bill, the TUC General Council voted by a majority of 21 votes to 11 to accept the measure, which in effect meant abandoning one of the most cherished trade union principles: the right of free collective bargaining.

Given the government's tiny minority, Wilson called another election in April 1966. This time Labour was returned with a majority of 97, thus giving it the mandate it required for its National Plan, a key ingredient of which was pay restraint. Hence the Prices and Incomes Bill was reintroduced and became an Act. The aim was effective control of shop-floor wage bargaining in which shop stewards played a key role.

In 1965, as a response to cross-party concern about 'restrictive' practices, the closed shop and shop-floor militancy, the government had established the Royal Commission on Trade Unions and Employers' Associations, chaired by Lord Donovan (the Donovan Commission). Another reason for the appointment of the Commission was altogether more positive. It was to examine the issue of trade union immunities established by the 1906 Trades Disputes Act, but which now appeared to be called into question by case law, most notably *Rookes v. Barnard* (1964). The Commission reported three years later, but meanwhile and despite attempts to control collective bargaining through such devices as measured day work (strongly recommended by the Prices and Incomes Board), trade union militancy remained the Achilles' heel of the government's wages policy. This was exemplified sharply in 1966 by the seamen's strike, which attracted wide support from other unions, in particular the dockers, who refused to handle goods embargoed by merchant seamen. The government overreacted by declaring a state of emergency using the powers parliament had given itself in the 1914 Defence of the Realm Act. Wilson argued that the strike was 'endangering the security of the industry and the economic welfare of the nation'[6] and complained that it was led by a 'tightly knit group of politically motivated men'.[7] This was a reference to the Communist Party (CPGB) and its Industrial Committee, the secretary of which was Bert Ramelson. As we shall see, the CPGB had considerable influence within some unions and this included the National Union of Seamen. However, this influence manifested itself most sharply in the 1970s.

Trade Unionism

Trade union membership increased throughout the 1950s and generally workers' standards of living were maintained whilst the economy remained buoyant. This was the era in which Macmillan asserted in the apocryphal phrase that the country had 'never had it so good'. Until 1956, when Frank Cousins was elected as general secretary of the Transport and General Workers' Union (TGWU), the leadership of most major unions was of a right-wing disposition, and consequently virulently anti-communist. Trade union votes could be relied on to support Gaitskell and even extended to opposition to Wilson when he stood as party leader on the grounds that he (unlike Callaghan and Brown) was not a Gaitskellite. The TUC had already displayed its anti-communist credentials during the Attlee government when, in 1949, it published two pamphlets, *Defend Democracy* and *The Tactics of Disruption*. In 1955 it published a third diatribe entitled *The TUC and Communism*. In this the General Council asserted that while they did not proscribe opinion, they do 'condemn bad trade union practice and this is one of the crimes of which the Communist Party has been judged by our movement as guilty of instigating and directing'.[8] The pamphlet went on to argue that the Communist Party was not a party in the usual sense as it

6 news.bbc.co.uk/onthisday/hi/dates/stories/may/23/newsid_2504000/2504227.stm.
7 Quoted in Allen Hutt, *British Trade Unionism: A Short History* (1941), p. 230.
8 *The TUC and Communism* (1955), p. 3.

was controlled by Moscow. It claimed to expose the fact that CP factions operated in trade union branches and workplaces directed by the 'Industrial Committee at King Street'. The pamphlet blamed the rash of unofficial strikes on the Communist Party, which had 'tried unceasingly to impede the nation's economic recovery by opposing what they call the "speed-up" in industry and by fostering and fomenting unofficial disputes'.[9] Having watched 'every twist and turn of Communist tactics over a period of 35 years', the General Council concluded that the aim of the party was 'to infiltrate, subvert and capture the Movement to give it the economic power which it would use to undermine and destroy our democratic rights'.[10]

But despite the red scare warning of the TUC and many trade union leaderships this did not mean that activity at grass-roots level was extinguished as the number of unofficial strikes betokened, particularly in the engineering, dock, building, car and transport industries. According to the Ministry of Labour, 1957 witnessed the highest number of disputes since the war (although this was later exceeded in 1969 and 1970). In that year there were 2,859 disputes involving the loss of over 8,000 working days. (This latter figure had only once exceeded 3,000 lost working days since 1945).[11] However, both parties' determination to tackle the issue of strikes, and in particular unofficial strikes, were not fully met by the findings of the Donovan Commission. By the time the Commission reported in 1968, the leadership of another major union had passed to a left-winger. Hugh Scanlon succeeded Bill Carron as general secretary of the AEU. Now both the AEU and the TGWU opposed incomes policy and state intervention in collective bargaining. In this latter policy they were supported by Donovan. Although the Commission expressed grave concern about 'wage drift' and regarded the influence of shop stewards (in contrast to full-time officials) as detrimental to well-regulated workplace industrial relations, it nonetheless continued to espouse the principle of voluntarism.

9   Ibid., p. 5.
10 Ibid., p. 11.
11 Quoted in C. Wrigley, *British Trade Unions 1945–1995* (1997), p. 24.

Trade Union Rebellion and *In Place of Strife*

Voluntarism did not find favour with the Labour government. The Tories likewise were in favour of legal controls on trade unions, as was spelt out in their policy 'A Fair Deal at Work'. When in 1969 the Wilson government published its White Paper *In Place of Strife: A Policy for Industrial Relations* it effectively declared war on the trade union movement. It rejected one of the main findings of Donovan by introducing penal sanctions for unofficial strike action. There is some debate as to whether Barbara Castle, Secretary of State for Employment and Productivity, was the effective author of the White Paper or whether she was unduly influenced by anti-trade union civil servants.[12] Certainly, she was in no doubt as to the cause of the problem as she saw it:

> it was the absolute rash of unofficial and unconstitutional strikes. We called them unconstitutional because they were not, they were in breach of agreed procedures. They had not given proper notice. I mean workers ... [would] just down tools – like that. And they were about 1.8m of these unofficial strikes compared with some 600 of the official ones, the great big ones ... I and employers used to say we don't mind the major strikes as much as this chaos. Because if you know you're going to have a great showdown with a big union, you can prepare some defences. But, if suddenly, as happened at Girlings' Brakes Works, a dozen key men down tools, without warning, and walk out. They're helpless and so are the rest of the staff.[13]

She went on to say that the unions at national level were complicit in this rash of unofficial action:

> we suspect that in some unions, at any rate, they don't altogether mind these unofficial strikes. Because, you see, it means the workers are doing the job for them without any strike claim. So there's no run on the union funds ... – chaos was doing great harm to industry and Ted Heath, then

12 See R. Tyler, 'Victims of our History? Barbara Castle and *In Place of Strife*', *Contemporary British History*, vol. 20, no. 3 (2006), pp. 461–76.
13 Transcript of an interview with Barbara Castle made in 1999, http://www.unionhistory.info/timeline/timeline.php.

leader of the opposition, was ... making a meal of it ... enormous attacks on Labour for its weaknesses.[14]

Thus it was that the Labour Party embarked on a course which was almost certain to lead to collision with the trade unions, and in practice (and for other reasons) unleashed a wave of industrial militancy redolent of the 'great unrest' of 1910–14.

The Liaison Committee for the Defence of Trade Unions

Most histories of this period fail to mention, or at best make scant reference to, the main rank-and-file body within the trade union movement which led the opposition to the attempted legal strictures on trade union rights – the Liaison Committee for the Defence of Trade Unions (LCDTU). This is compounded (or possibly caused) by the almost complete neglect of the role of the Communist Party on the industrial scene in this period.[15] The same mistake was not made by contemporaries, especially the government and the TUC, who, as we have seen, recognised that the Communist Party exerted very great influence in this period. The LCDTU was formed in 1966 at a national conference whose main purpose was to oppose wage restraint. A second national conference in 1968 responded to *In Place of Strife* by calling for a day of strike action. This took place in February 1969 with widely varying estimates of participation and with no support at this stage from the two biggest unions, the TGWU and the Engineers. However, this was not the favoured strategy of the LCDTU; it did not see itself, nor did it wish to be seen, as an alternative TUC. Rather, its aim was to build up maximum pressure on the official movement from shop stewards, left-leaning district committees and executive committees so that the TUC itself was moved to oppose Labour government policy and to organise action against it. Thus it was that the next very well-attended LCDTU conference held in April 1969 urged the TUC to call a 24-hour national

14 Ibid.
15 A notable exception to this is J. McIlroy and A. Campbell, 'Organising the Militants: the Liaison Committee for the Defence of Trade Unions, 1966–1979', *BJIR*, vol. 37, no. 1 (March 1999).

strike. A strike did take place on 1 May, but it was not called or supported by the TUC, though it was supported by some trades, notably the dockers, printers and miners and in areas where the Communist Party was strong, for example the Midlands car industry, Sheffield and parts of Scotland. But it was by no means a general or a national strike. Nonetheless, the very fact that now two strikes had been called by an unofficial body undoubtedly had the effect of moving the TUC into taking some action. In June 1969 the General Council recalled Congress (the first special congress for 40 years) to debate a programme of action against government legislation. This was in effect a last-ditch attempt to get the government to change its mind by suggesting that in return for their dropping all legal sanctions against trade unions, the TUC would intervene to prevent inter-union and unofficial action. However, at this stage the government rejected the TUC's offer and seemed intent on going ahead with legislation, but at the last minute Wilson agreed to the compromise along the lines suggested. This was due to three main factors: clear disagreement had emerged within the parliamentary Labour Party; there was growing resistance among trade unionists and arising from this resistance and the warning from some of the more far-sighted leaders like Hugh Scanlon of the Engineers and Jack Jones of the Transport Workers that this opposition would burgeon into mass industrial action unless a compromise was reached. This appeared to be confirmed by the consequences arising from the change in leadership of the National Union of Mineworkers. In 1968 the NUM had elected a left-wing general secretary, Lawrence Daly. He fully supported the Yorkshire NUM's call for strike action in support of a 40-hour working week for surface workers. The strike rapidly spread to other coalfields and by November 1969, 125,000 miners were on strike.

Equal Pay

Parallel but almost unconnected with the industrial battles besetting Labour and Tory governments, the long fight for equal pay for women continued in the postwar period. The Labour

Party manifesto for the 1964 general election called for a Charter of Rights for all employees to include 'the right to equal pay for equal work'. Having neglected the issue since the first equal pay resolution was passed in 1888, the TUC Congress in September 1965 followed the Labour Party lead with a resolution reaffirming

> its support for the principles of equality of treatment and opportunity for women workers in industry, and calls upon the General Council to request the government to implement the promise of 'the right to equal pay for equal work' as set out in the Labour Party election manifesto.[16]

The Labour Party's election pledge may have been prompted by its desire to join the European Economic Community (EEC) so that it would be in compliance with the Treaty of Rome's clause requiring member states to adopt the principle of equal pay for women. However, the application was rejected and thus the Wilson government shelved the issue. Equal pay may have been forgotten for another decade or two were it not for the action of women trade unionists – this time in the private sector. In 1968 women sewing machinists at Ford's Dagenham factory went on strike over a re-grading demand. Clearly this was not a case of women doing the same work as the men, although their argument was that it required equal skill. This led to a number of other equal pay strikes and the formation by women trade unionists and others of the National Joint Action Campaign Committee for Women's Equal Rights (NJACCWER). A massive groundswell of protest against government and trade union inaction began to manifest itself. In 1968, against General Council advice, an amendment to a motion on equal pay was passed which called for TUC affiliates to support any union taking strike action for equal pay. The TUC even held a one-day conference on the issue in November 1968. Most unions by this time had declared forcefully in favour of equal pay and appeared to be keen to do something at long last for their women members. May 1969 saw a massive equal pay demonstration organised by NJACCWER. In order to

16   TUC Congress Report 1965.

forestall further unrest, Barbara Castle decided to introduce the Equal Pay Act of 1970. This permitted equal pay claims to be made from women in the public and private sectors if they were engaged in the same or broadly similar work. However, although the Act was passed in May 1970, it was not implemented until January 1976, thus allowing employers just over five years in which to make 'adjustments'. In effect, this meant that they had nearly six years to re-grade jobs in discriminatory ways, thus rendering them immune from the very limited scope of the Act.

The Conservative Government, 1970–74

The 1970 general election intervened before any kind of compromise agreement on industrial relations legislation was reached between the government and the TUC. The Tory election victory ensured that conciliation was not on the agenda and thus that confrontation was inevitable. The LCDTU again called for one-day stoppages, which the TUC countered by calling for demonstrations outside working hours.

Given that trade unions had shown a willingness to engage in political strikes while Labour was in office, it was obvious that such action would be redoubled if a Conservative government attempted to impose legal penalties on unions. The Conservative election manifesto of 1970 made it very clear that they fully intended to take up the fight where Labour had left it. Although they welcomed 'the TUC's willingness to take action through its own machinery against those who disrupt industrial peace by unconstitutional or unofficial action',[17] it went on to say that this was not enough to stem the rash of strike action, particularly unofficial strikes, which (according to the Tories) reached record levels in 1969. Thus they announced their intention to introduce a comprehensive Industrial Relations Bill in the first session of the new parliament, the aim of which was:

17 Conservative election manifesto 1970, www.psr.keele.ac.uk/area/uk/man/lab79. htm.

to strengthen the unions and their official leadership by providing some deterrent against irresponsible action by unofficial minorities. We seek to create conditions in which strikes become the means of last resort, not of first resort, as they now so often are.[18]

The bill, which was introduced in January 1971, was much more draconian than *In Place of Strife*. It proposed to 'lay down what is lawful and what isn't lawful in the conduct of industrial disputes'.[19] Any dispute which endangered the 'national interest' would have to be agreed by secret ballot, and a 'cooling-off period' of not less than 60 days would be imposed. It outlawed the closed shop and sympathy strikes. It sought to achieve in one fell swoop what the Tories under Margaret Thatcher and John Major enacted by degrees a decade later with eight shorter and specific Acts between 1980 and 1993. Thatcher and Major clearly learned the lesson from the scale of opposition to the 1971 Act; they sought to achieve the same ends but by different means.

Once again the LCDTU called for the TUC to organise mass stoppages – a demand which fell on deaf ears until March 1971 when the first major union, the AUEW, decided to back the strike call. Once the bill became law in August 1971, the main focus of the LCDTU policy was on non-compliance with the Industrial Relations Act. This meant refusing to abide by the clauses requiring registration of trade unions and non-recognition of decisions made by the new National Industrial Relations Court (NIRC). But the growing resolve of the trade union movement to defy the Industrial Relations Act was expressed at last by a motion carried at the TUC Congress in September 1971, which called for the expulsion from the TUC of any union which registered under the terms of the Act. Matters came to a head when the first fines totalling £55,000 were imposed. The union charged was the TGWU arising from the dispute of the London and Liverpool dockers against a container firm. Containerisation threatened dockers' livelihoods both because container ships with their roll-on roll-off cargo did not require traditional dock labour, and because container

18 Ibid.
19 Ibid.

ports were established outside the Port Authority areas in which dockers' wages and conditions were subject to regulation. Despite the fact that the TGWU attended the NIRC, on the advice of the TUC and in clear defiance of its own policy, the London dockers continued their action. This led to the arrest and imprisonment in July 1972 of five leading shop stewards from Tilbury docks – Bernie Steer, Vic Turner, Tony Merrick, Cornelius Clancy and Derek Watkins (subsequently known as the Pentonville Five). The government seriously misjudged the mood of the movement. The LCDTU demanded a general strike and mass demonstrations were organised. The general strike demand gained increasing resonance to the extent that the TUC was finally prepared to endorse it. The threat of a general strike and mass demonstrations to free the Pentonville Five forced the government to climb down by using the archaic expedient of the Official Solicitor to authorise the release of the five dockers from Pentonville prison. They were then carried shoulder high down the Pentonville Road with the lead banner exhorting the huge demonstration: 'Arise Ye Workers'. In practical terms the result of this victory was that other unions now defied the Act, most notably the AUEW during the Con-Mech dispute. The legislation may have been on the statute book, but such was the organised hostility to it that government was fearful of using it.

However, opposition to the Act was not the only problem facing the Heath government. A series of industrial disputes involving 'work-ins' and strikes threatened the government's stability. Inspired by the occupation of the shipyards by the workers of Upper Clyde Shipbuilders, many other 'work-ins' (a tactic to avoid redundancy) were organised, for example by print workers at Briant Colour Printers, by steelworkers at the River Don works in Sheffield, at Plesseys in Scotland at Meridien motor cycle works and many, many more. In addition, building workers and miners staged national strike action. Probably the most significant challenge to the government came with the victory of the miners in 1972 as a result of their first national strike since 1926. Not only did the strike break the government's incomes policy, but, like the dockers' dispute, it also drove a coach and horses through the Industrial Relations Act. The mass militancy of the miners, combined with the solidarity action shown to them by other workers, particularly in action around power stations – Saltley being the most famous example – was interpreted by anti-trade union forces as 'a victory for violence'[20] and brought about Thatcher's resolve to introduce a raft of legislation to curb the perceived power of the unions.

But although the Wilberforce Inquiry (established to resolve the dispute) recommended that the miners' pay claim be met on the grounds that they constituted a 'special case', the conflict was not over. The miners defied the Heath government's attempt to impose a pay norm on them in line with their incomes policy. This led to an overtime ban, followed by another strike in 1974. The government's response was to impose a three-day week ostensibly to save coal stocks and to raise the same question that Baldwin had posed during the 1926 General Strike: who rules Britain, the government or the trade unions? This was the central issue on which Heath decided to go to the country in February 1974 (a second general election was held in October of the same year). In the first of the two elections, the Conservative manifesto warned of 'the danger from within' brought about by 'a small number of militant extremists [who] can so manipulate and abuse the monopoly power of their unions as to cause incalculable damage to the country and to the fabric of our society itself'.[21]

The Fruits of Militancy and the Labour Government, 1974–79

Labour won both 1974 elections with a pledge to repeal the 1971 Industrial Relations Act and restore free collective bargaining. Clearly, the new government had learnt its lessons from the failure of *In Place of Strife* and the even greater ignominy of Heath's 1971 Act. The inescapable conclusion was that the

20 For an excellent refutation of this common interpretation of the strike, see J. Phillips, 'The 1972 Miners' Strike: Popular Agency and Industrial Politics in Britain', *Contemporary British History*, vol. 20, no. 2 (June 2006), pp. 187–204.
21 Conservative election manifesto, February 1974, www.psr.keele.ac.uk/area/uk/uktable.htm.

trade union movement in the late 1960s and early 1970s was a force to be reckoned with, and although the Communist Party had an undoubted influence among the activists through such organisations as the LCDTU, it would be indulging in conspiratorial fantasy akin to Tory propaganda to write off this 'forward march' as the work of a few dangerous, politically motivated militants. Despite the growing problem of unemployment (which stood at 500,000 when Labour took office in February 1974 and had risen to 1½ million in 1979), trade union membership continued to rise, as did the class combativeness of key sections of the trade union movement. The TUC leadership was easily satisfied with the conciliatory attitude of the Labour government and was thus willing to enter into an agreement with it, commonly known as the 'Social Contract'. This formed the basis of Labour's election manifesto of October 1974 from which the following extract is taken:

> At the heart of this manifesto and our programme to save the nation lies the Social Contract between the Labour Government and the trade unions, an idea derided by our enemies, but certain to become widely accepted by those who genuinely believe in government by consent – that is, in the democratic process itself as opposed to the authoritarian and bureaucratic system of wage control imposed by the Heath government and removed by Labour. The Social Contract is no mere paper agreement approved by politicians and trade unions. It is not concerned solely or even primarily with wages. It covers the whole range of national policies. It is the agreed basis upon which the Labour Party and the trade unions define their common purpose.[22]

Although the agreement was described by the activists and forces on the left of the movement as a 'con trick' – an expedient to stem the tide of militancy and bind workers into an acceptance of 'the system' – it is easy to understand the seductive power of the Social Contract.[23] Unlike that offered by New Labour in the 1990s, this one offered much and delivered a series of genuine

22   Labour election manifesto, October 1974, www.psr.keele.ac.uk/area/uk/uktable. htm.
23   This contradictory, superficial allure was expressed in the title of a Communist Party pamphlet by Bert Ramelson, *Social Contract: Cure-all or Con-trick?*

reforms, including in 1974 the Health and Safety at Work Act and the Trade Union and Labour Relations Act, and in 1975 the Sex Discrimination Act (and the Equal Opportunities Commission). In addition, as one historian of the period has arguably overstated, cabinet ministers in the 1974–79 government were 'willing to defend union rights publicly, on a scale and with a regularity that has no recent parallel in British political history'.[24] Whilst this was true of the first twelve months of the new government as it sought to undo the damage inflicted by the Tories, good relations with the trade union movement did not survive. The government repealed the 1971 Industrial Relations Act and replaced it with the Trade Union and Labour Relations Act. This was amended in 1976 to broaden the protection for trade disputes and to remove some of the barriers the Tories had introduced in relation to the closed shop. Despite this, loopholes in the law remained as the Grunwick dispute (1976–78) at a photo processing plant clearly showed. The Employment Protection Act (EPA) of 1975 was a highly significant piece of legislation in that for the first time it gave statutory rights to shop stewards and union representatives and awarded them time off for trade union activity and training. (The Health and Safety at Work Act did the same for safety representatives.) This ushered in a massive expansion of trade union education conducted by the TUC and affiliated unions, which survives to this day. The EPA also accorded statutory power to the new Advisory Conciliation and Arbitration Service and established the Employment Appeals Tribunal. In addition, the Act established rights to maternity pay and a guaranteed right for women to return to their job after maternity leave.

Certainly this was a very promising beginning, but it foundered on the issue of government economic policy and specifically its incomes policy. The attempt to control incomes first by voluntary and later by statutory means ultimately proved a major barrier to the unions' jealously guarded right to free collective bargaining, especially in the public sector, over which government policy had more control. Initially, there was no statutory wage control. TUC leaders advocated voluntary wage restraint as a quid pro

24   D. Coates, *Labour in Power* (1980), p. 58.

quo, in the spirit of the Social Contract, for the government's social reforms, however, this did not satisfy Labour's desire for counter-inflationary measures. Critics of the government were equally critical of the TUC for entering into such an historically unprecedented agreement 'to collaborate with the government and the employers to cut real wages, and to police the implementation of the cuts'.[25] Similarly critics on the left argued that the Social Contract did not represent a genuine quid pro quo arrangement since in return for agreeing to a £6 maximum pay increase, the government had agreed to acts of elementary justice which were Labour Party conference policy pre-dating the Social Contract. It was clear by 1975 that the government favoured a statutory incomes policy, predicated on the orthodox Treasury notion that high wages are a main cause of inflation. This thinking was emblazoned in very bold type on the back page of a widely distributed government pamphlet which quoted Wilson as saying: 'One man's [sic] pay rise is not only another man's price rise: it might also cost him his job – or his neighbour's job.'[26] Contemporary critics of the government[27] argued that almost from the outset the government went as far as to reject a traditional social democratic Keynesian model[28] as the price to be paid for EEC membership[29] and loans from the International Monetary Fund and Central Bank. Stuart Holland opined that 'Labour since 1974 has managed British capitalism in a manner which would have been inconceivable for British Conservatism of either the Heath or Thatcher variety'.[30] Whilst there was general

25   B. Ramelson, *Bury the Social Contract* (1977), p. 2.
26   *Attack on Inflation: A Policy for Survival – A Guide to the Government's Programme* (1976), a 'popular' guide to the White Paper *Attack on Inflation* (1975).
27   See, for example, the collection of essays in K. Coates (ed.). *What Went Wrong?* (1979).
28   A fact fully acknowledged by the Chancellor of the Exchequer, Denis Healey, in his autobiography *The Time of My Life* (1990), p. 378.
29   The view that the EEC referendum marked a decisive turning point in Labour government policy and practice is also held by later writers, e.g. H. Kerr, 'Labour's Social Policy 1974–79', *Critical Social Policy*, vol. 1, no. 5 (1981); D. Coates, 'Labour Governments: Old Constraints and New Parameters', *New Left Review*, vol. 1, no. 219 (September–October 1996).
30   Ibid.

acknowledgement that inflation was a very serious problem, there was growing opposition to the increasingly monetarist turn in Labour's economic policy as a means of dealing with the deepening economic crisis. The left advocated an alternative economic strategy, which gradually won widespread acceptance within many unions and constituency Labour parties. This strategy argued for a range of demands, including import controls, reduced expenditure on armaments, withdrawal from the EEC, increased public expenditure, greater state investment in British industry, a shorter working week, redistribution of wealth and a return to free collective bargaining. By 1976 the government, with the agreement of the TUC, sought to impose a 4.5 per cent wage ceiling. However, given that prices were rising (as was unemployment), there was increasing opposition to wage control and 1977 witnessed a growth in strike activity – usually unofficial, except for the eight-week national firefighters' strike for a 30 per cent wage increase. Clearly, the government had no intention of conceding to this demand, although it should be noted that its parsimony did not extend to the highest paid, as the Boyle Committee's recommendations indicated. Given the scale of the opposition on the ground, the TUC no longer felt able to enter into a third round of pay policy. This, as Healey acknowledged, created great problems for the government, which in hindsight he felt was handled badly and led to the defeat of Labour in the 1979 election. In 1978 the government unilaterally introduced a pay norm of 5 per cent. Of this Healey wrote:

> It was typical of the hubris which can overcome a successful government towards the end of its term. If we had agreed on a formula such as 'single figures' we would probably have achieved an earnings increase much smaller than we got; and we would certainly have been able to avoid the 'winter of discontent'.[31]

Recognising the continuing strength and power of the shop stewards, Healey went on to say that pay policy was doomed anyway because:

31 Healey, *The Time of My Life*, p. 398.

> In Britain it is difficult to operate a pay policy even with the co-operation of the union leaders. For the real power lies not in the union headquarters but with the local shop stewards, who tend to see a rational incomes policy as robbing them of their functions.[32]

The TUC did not (and still does not) exert power over its affiliates. While Healey lamented these (for him) uncomfortable truths, it is nonetheless testimony to the continuing influence of the Shop Stewards' Movement that it was able to mount a challenge to the orthodoxy which sought to blame workers for the ills of capitalism. It is in this context that the strike wave of 1978–79, pejoratively dubbed the 'winter of discontent' by Larry Lamb, editor of the *Sun*, must be seen.

Inspired by the nine-week Ford strike, which resulted in a 17 per cent pay settlement, other workers took industrial action to redress the fall in real wages over the past five years. Public sector manual workers, arguably the hardest hit, joined the action in great numbers. By 1979 the number of working days lost was greater than during the three-day week imposed by the Heath administration. Predicting the possible outcome of a general election *before* the strike wave of 1978–79, Ramelson argued in 1977:

> The real question … is whether a Labour Government will be held responsible by the electorate for bringing about mass unemployment, drastic cuts in living standards…as well as drastically reduced social services … [and that this has] increased the chances of the return of a Tory government.[33]

The Tories capitalised on the industrial unrest and, together with their supporters in the mass media, contributed to the still widely accepted myth of over-mighty trade unionists holding the country to ransom. This was the justification for their long-held desire to introduce anti-union legislation, a promise they made in their 1979 manifesto. They proposed three immediate changes. The first was to limit the right to picket to the workers' own place of work; thus making solidarity (or 'secondary') action illegal.

32   Healey, *The Time of My Life*, p. 399.
33   Ramelson, *Bury the Social Contract*, pp. 17–18.

Second, the Tories promised to deal a blow to the 'objectionable weapon' of the closed shop by banning it altogether in the Civil Service and ensuring that elsewhere it could be sustained only if an overwhelming majority of the workers involved voted for it by secret ballot. Third, under the innocuous heading of 'wider participation', the Tories promised to introduce and fund secret postal ballots for union elections and other issues in order to counteract their assertion that 'too often trade unions are dominated by a handful of extremists who do not reflect the common-sense views of most union members'.[34] Strangely, at a time of mass militancy, the Tories won the election: they carried out their promises as outlined in the 1979 manifesto – the consequences for the trade union movement were and remain devastating.

Bibliography

Addison, P. *The Road to 1945* (Cape, 1994)

Coates, D. *Labour in Power* (Longman, 1980)

Coates, K. (ed.). *What Went Wrong?* (Spokesman, 1979)

Crosland, A. *The Future of Socialism* (Cape, 1956)

Haseler, S. *The Gaitskellites* (European Research Forum, 1969)

Healey, D. *The Time of My Life* (Norton, 1990)

Hutt, A. *British Trade Unionism: A Short History* (Lawrence & Wishart, 1941)

Jones, H. and Kandiah, M. (eds). *The Myth of Consensus: New Views on British History 1945–64* (Macmillan, 1996)

Wrigley, C. *British Trade Unions 1945–1995* (Cambridge University Press, 1997)

---

34 Conservative election manifesto, 1979, www.psr.keele.ac.uk/area/uk/man/lab79. htm.

IN CONCLUSION

The story of a movement, still alive and kicking, can hardly be concluded, even though some would have us believe that today, in the twenty-first century, the labour movement is a spent force and that its history is no more relevant than that of the lost tribes of ancient Judea.

Although this survey stops in 1979, the decades since then have witnessed great changes as the structure of the working class has continued to alter to reflect the new technology of the microchip, the privatisation of the public sector and the (mis)fortunes of the British economy, which has sunk permanently into the doldrums of deindustrialisation. The basic industries, on which Britain's industrial pre-eminence was based, have now become extinct, despite the heroic battle in the 1980s to retain an already decimated coal industry. But a working class still exists and so does the labour movement. The evidence is before our eyes in the daily battle between capital and labour, which continues to be waged in altered forms and circumstances despite the current legal restrictions to emasculate it. The fact that we are in an era of declining trade union membership and high unemployment, during which we have witnessed more defeats than victories, should not lead us to question the movement's viability any more than in the nineteenth century when its trade union wing was pitifully small or in the late 1920s and early 1930s when defeat and decline were also the order of the day. The history of the labour movement has always been a halting and problematic one.

This is not the place to examine the labour movement's current form and prospects, nor is it appropriate to wax lyrical about its 'glorious past' or, alternatively, to be cynically downcast about its lost opportunities. The past is there and cannot be altered. It can only be studied, discussed and, hopefully, better understood.

So, what can be concluded from the first 200 years? The most obvious point is that the labour movement has an uncanny ability to rebuild and renew itself, with the consequence that its detractors, keen as they always are to write the movement's premature obituary, continue to be wrong-footed. Working-class organisations do not proceed in a linear onward and upward fashion; they are always marked by peaks and troughs in activity, effectiveness and membership. These ups and downs are not always crudely determined by economic circumstances but have a great deal to do with the prevailing level of political class consciousness. The fact that this elusive construct escapes causal explanation does not invalidate its existence. At key moments its presence determines the defiant rather than the defensive aspect of the movement when it consciously seeks to break the ideological yoke chaining it to capitalist society, its norms, practices and values. The development of the British labour movement throughout its history is a product of the tension between rival ideologies – between the vision of harmonious accommodation within the capitalist system and the vision of a different system altogether. Variously, the ideologies inspiring these visions and the practices which they motivated could be called, in their pure and most polarised forms, left or right, radical or reactionary, socialist or capitalist, revolutionary or reformist. Rarely are the complex battles which shape a movement played out in their starkest forms, but nonetheless the underlying tension is there. In Britain, the infinite capacity of the first industrial nation to accommodate dissent led ultimately to a dominant labourist consensus which, while offering at times the possibility of hope and change, accepted the parameters of the existing social order and sought to defend its interests within it. On the other hand, those whose consciousness of class led them to challenge consensus and collaboration bequeathed to us the legacy of defiance, and this legacy, because of its hostility to and rejection of the settled values of capitalist society, began to encompass, albeit in halting measure, the wider cause of the struggle to end oppression as an integral part of the fight to eradicate class exploitation.

But this is all very general and theoretical. No one would deny a left and a right trend within the labour movement today and likewise it would not take a genius to notice that the forces of the traditional left are in disarray. Defiance is in short measure and a defensive form of labourism reigns supreme. Explanations are far harder than observations. Why political class consciousness (socialist consciousness) emerges more strongly at certain times defies any clear-cut explanation. It is far easier to explain the existence of class collaboration and the fact that the forces of the left even at the time of their greatest strength were never powerful enough to shift the reformist labourist consensus. The struggle between the rival ideologies within the labour movement is one of the themes of this book. The fact that the reformist consensus in its various forms dominated from the 1850s onwards has, I hope, been explained. The great unanswered question remains particularly relevant for the class-conscious activists of today – namely, under what circumstances and by what means can the consensus be broken in order to end class exploitation once and for all? Throughout these 200 years support for such a project has assumed a much greater significance than those who today ridicule the socialist cause would have us believe. Splits and divisions often marred the effectiveness of the cause, but the reason why it had more of a mass appeal in the 1880s and not the 1870s, or in the 1940s and not the 1950s, for example, cannot be explained solely by analysing internal weaknesses. This begs the question, the answer to which, if we knew it, would have yielded a magic formula which, if applied, could have led us to a socialist paradise long ago.

Perhaps a clue revealed in this book is the one that prompted its writing in the first place. For socialism to have a genuine and lasting mass appeal its vision must address the needs of the entire working class and must practise the politics generated by its theories – those of democratic collective involvement. This means consciously extending its appeal, as some of the early socialists attempted, to *all* workers and in particular those most vulnerable to super-exploitation because of their race or gender. This entails an understanding that working-class unity is not just a desirable dream but is an essential project and that its achievement is only possible if differences born of life experiences of centuries of disunity founded on oppression are recognised and respected. It also means that forms of organisation must not only reflect those differences but must actively seek to overcome them.

Such a perspective has proved to be far harder to accept in Britain where the political objectives of the labour movement, after 1850, were sacrificed to a defensive and somewhat narrow trade union movement founded on the experiences of the skilled and better-off section of male workers. The unions formed in the mid-Victorian period, which laid the basis for what exists now, pre-dated the formation of the political wing of the movement and became its servant. In other words, initially at least, politics followed economics. But in creating its political wing, the accumulated sectional interests of the trade unions founded a Labour Party whose eventual strength and importance as a party able to form the government of Britain turned tail and ultimately mastered its creators. If this political creation had held to the socialist vision that from time to time emerged within it, this history might have had a different conclusion. But the fact that this was not to be cannot be ascribed to a capitalist conspiracy in which the trade unions can be seen as the organs of pure class struggle whose interests were sacrificed to the power-hungry ambitions of a collection of besuited white men who either forgot or consciously ignored the movement's origins. Rather, as this book has attempted to show, no single branch of the movement was the repository of political correctness and that the resulting mish-mash was the product of the interplay between often conflicting forces mediated in the last instance by the seductive ideological, political and economic power of capital. Even to pose the question as to whether things might have been different is profoundly unhistorical. The fact is that it wasn't and the real test of historical understanding is better posed by asking another question: faced with options in any given situation, why was it that one particular course was followed rather than another? Real choice was and still is quite rare, or at any rate very limited, circumscribed as it always was by the unequal balance of power between capital and labour, but if we deny absolutely the possibility of choice, then we deny too the possibility of change and must therefore conclude that the labour movement's course and development were predestined. Clearly, events like the 1926 General Strike and the experience of the third Labour government show that within the welter of debate, a conscious decision was made to pursue one line rather than another, and at such moments the consequences of such decisions displayed continuities with one kind of ideological tradition and that such decisions had far-reaching repercussions for the future.

The defensive labourist tradition which usually prevailed was itself forced to change and adapt under pressure from its opponents. At its best this tradition delivered a powerful solidarity of predominantly male workers to defend hard-won gains against the encroachments of capital – the sentiment of fraternity or brotherhood expresses its essence in both language and fact. The defiant, radical and socialist tradition glimpsed in its theory and practice something wider – comradeship. Comrades are brothers and sisters in struggle, black and white. Comradeship builds on fraternity but transcends it. The use of such terms as comrade or brother is at one level simply linguistic, and would thus seem to have more resonance today given our greater consciousness of the sexist connotations of language. There was little reflection on such semantic implications for the greater part of the period covered in this book. At a deeper level, however, the fact that such terms were used at all did indicate, consciously or unconsciously, a distinction between the defensive and the defiant traditions within the labour movement, and there is little doubt, as this book has tried to show, that the latter tradition was less afraid to include within it the 'outsiders' within the working class – women and black people. The distinction was not rigid, merely indicative of a trend or tradition. However, it is for the labour movement activists of today, the products and the inheritors of the dual traditions, to interpret this their history as they will, and fashion the future as they must.

INDEX

Compiled by Sue Carlton